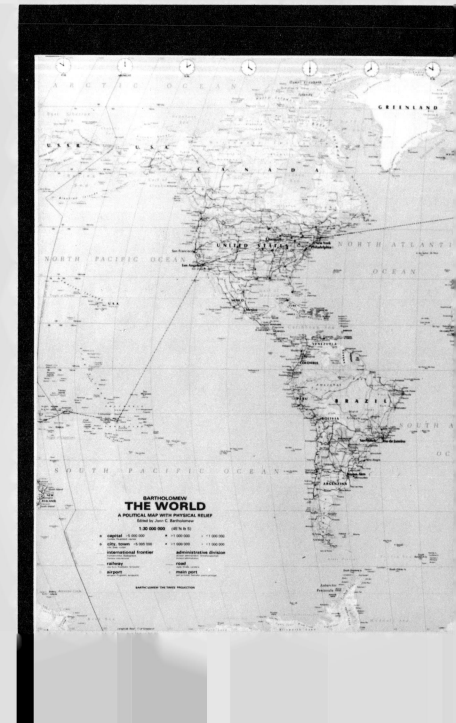

BARTHOLOMEW
THE WORLD
A POLITICAL MAP WITH PHYSICAL RELIEF
Edited by John C. Bartholomew

1:30 000 000   (45°N & S)

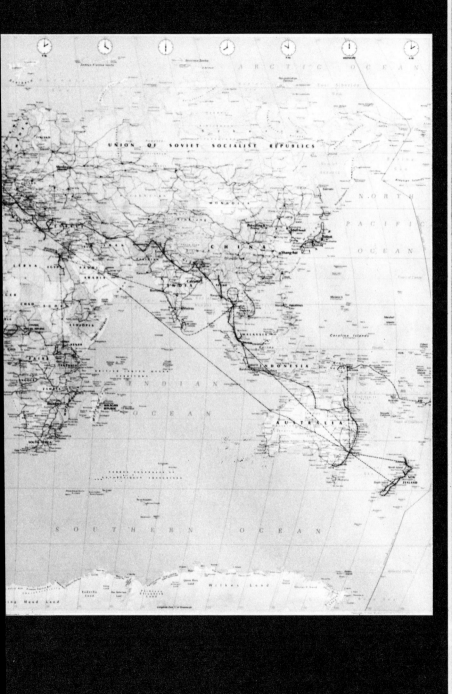

Wanderlust

OVERLAND THROUGH ASIA AND AFRICA

DAN SPITZER

PHOTOGRAPHS BY
MARZI SCHORIN

RICHARD MAREK PUBLISHERS
NEW YORK

DS10
S65

Library of Congress Cataloging in Publication Data

Spitzer, Dan.
    Wanderlust : overland through Asia and Africa.

    1. Asia—Description and travel—1951—
2. Africa—Description and travel—1951–1976.
3. Spitzer, Dan. I. Title.
DS10.S65   915'.04'42   78-27894
ISBN 0-399-90036-5

To Marzi, who shared every adventurous mile.

Wanderlust

Contents

Introduction

How many of us, weary of the daily routine, dream of tearing away to explore lands and cultures truly different? Exotic Asia, indomitable African jungles, paradise isles of the South Pacific! We have all traveled there via books, films, and television. But to actually go?

Like most people, I assumed travel outside the Western world to be expensive and perhaps a bit hazardous. An avid armchair explorer since boyhood, I delighted in ravishing collections of *National Geographic*. Conjuring up images of towering Himalayas, spear-wielding Stone Age tribesmen, or ferocious creatures of the wilds, I would imagine myself there. But being neither rich nor particularly brave, the idea that I would spend two years traveling virtually twice around the world, basically overland, seemed preposterous. Looking back now, it strikes me that the most difficult undertaking of this odyssey lay in making the decision to go.

How does one become a world traveler? In my case, a burning desire to see with my own eyes those places and peoples so different from the Western world was realized through a peculiar twist of fate.

At the end of a one-year teaching contract at a small college in Vermont, I found myself unemployed. The job market glutted in my field, I was faced with the dilemma of what a PhD in Latin American Studies is qualified to do besides teach.

Fortunately, Marzi Schorin, the woman with whom I have lived for ten years, shared a lure of the road. A public-health nutritionist, Marzi had been employed by the United Nations in Jamaica and seriously considered working in third-world countries. Her knowledge of nutrition would prove invaluable on the overland route, getting us through some rough stretches in good health.

Long before my employment difficulties, we had discussed leaving the country. Politically active during the sixties at Berkeley and the University of Michigan, we had watched petty ideological squabbles destroy the New Left. Feeling near asphyxiated by the apathy of the seventies, we sought an alternative.

Our naive plan called for touring Europe, discovering a congenial place to settle, and doing some writing on political and social themes. With romantic visions of Hemingway and Miller in mind, we sought societies in which attitudes and values differed from our own. But Europe proved disillusioning.

Landing at the onset of summer, we found the continent jammed with American and European tourists; foreigners frequently appeared to outnumber locals. Some restaurants even printed their menus in English, German, or Swedish rather than the mother tongue.

This tourist influx, coupled with postwar industrialization, had produced such cultural similarity that often the only visible national differences were language and cuisine. We strayed further and further from the beaten path, hoping to find people who still retained a significant measure of their cultural heritage. But no place was left unscathed by external influence. Even where tourism and industrialization had little penetrated, television and radio had contributed to a cultural homogeneity.

It was easy to meet young Europeans in trains and pensions. Many were critical of U.S. politics, materialism, etc. Fine—there was unquestionably substance to their critique. But something rang false, and soon we understood.

Our continental companions were aping the very values they condemned. Interest in their own rich past was negligible, lost in a world defined by slick cinema and imported television. Despite the standardized uniform of blue jeans, there existed not the celebrated "international youth culture," but merely a carbon copy of the "Pepsi generation." European youth sought to be American in everything but name.

We met few fellow travelers who were particularly stimulating. Their primary concerns seemed to be smoking dope and getting laid in another language. Rushing from hostel to museum in country after country, they made certain to take in everything, seeing nothing.

Was the whole world a pitiful parody of America? Sitting dejectedly at a café on a supposedly "unspoiled" Greek isle overrun with foreigners, we contemplated our next move. With inflation biting at our budget even in southern Europe, we briefly considered returning home.

Then, across a communal table, we overheard a ruddy Englishman inform his companion that with an international student ID, one could fly from Athens to Istanbul for a mere fifteen dollars.

"Turkey?"

Marzi and I looked at each other.

It was in Istanbul, beneath the silhouette of mosque and minaret, that we were initially captivated by the East. Appetites for adventure whet, we cautiously crept a bit further afield, unlocking with utter fascination the timeless traditions of rural Turkey. We were hooked! Wanderlust surged through our bloodstream. The world was ours for the seeing!

Irreversibly set in motion, we embarked upon an Oriental expedition, crossing the blazing sands of Afghanistan, trekking the high Himalayas, penetrating the tangled rain forests of Southeast Asia. Returning to the West, we took a brief respite from our ramblings. But before long, as the comforts of familiar surroundings began to pale, a thirst for lands unknown spirited us on to the sultry west coast of Africa. From Ghana, we traversed that great continent overland, slicing through the rugged jungle homelands of the Bambuti pygmy in the equatorial heart of the former Congo, and pursuing big game on a photographic safari in the teeming wildlife reserves of Tanzania. Playing a dangerous hunch, we proceeded to the fear-crazed Uganda of Idi Amin. There we parlayed that regime's endemic corruption into a remarkable black-market air ticket, enabling us to return to the States via Egypt, Southeast Asia, New Guinea, and the South Pacific.

How could we, hardly an affluent couple, afford to spend two years circling the globe? Without professional or familial responsibilities, we had the time. As for cost, our expenses were minimal, far less than we would have spent in the States. All our transport, food, and lodging amounted to less than three thousand dollars per year! We usually found clean accommodations in Asia for roughly a dollar per night. In Africa we slept either in our tent, with Peace Corps, or at mission stations.

Even on our budget we ate well, for the Orient offered a myriad choice of cuisine, as delicious as it was inexpensive. For less than half a dollar we dined on sizzling shish kebab in Islamic Asia, fiery curries on the Indian subcontinent, and savory rice-based recipes in Southeast Asia. Occasionally we would "splurge," feasting on lobster or chateaubriand for the princely sum of two dollars. As there were few restaurants in the African bush, we cooked most of our own food on a one-burner gasoline stove.

In the Orient trains and buses were usually quite comfortable and always extremely cheap. On the other hand, getting around in Africa, where public transport was rougher (or nonexistent), proved a challenging experience in itself.

Most of our journeys took us through regions where a vast majority of inhabitants are still tied to the soil. "Overlanding" gave us an infinitely better handle on the people, their traditions, and the terrain than we could have possibly grasped via air travel. By taking public vehicles, we were able to meet a cross section of citizenry and gain insight into their national customs and political circumstance.

Overlanding, moreover, created a "camaraderie of the road"

among fellow Western travelers that provided both an important source of further education as well as a mobile community. Riding the same transport and lodging in budget hotels, travelers shared a plethora of novel experiences and much invaluable advice. The common bond born of overland travel led to friendships of an international scope.

What kept us going for two years? Extraordinary first-hand encounters amid cultures hundreds of years old. Continual immersion in an educational process far more meaningful than those long years spent cloistered behind university walls. The exhilaration that came with being free to move as we chose, unfettered by time constraints or professional obligations. The realization of how little money or possessions were needed to travel 'round the world—overland.

We would pitch a tent in the depths of Congolese jungles to a booming of not-so-distant drums, thrill to the roar of lions outside our campfires in the splendidly untamed Serengeti, and tingle with the drama of Balinese sword dancing. And as each day we were bombarded with the challenge of the unexpected, our thirst for adventure expanded.

But the journey was not entirely exotic. Marzi and I confronted hardships and obstacles en route which strained our tolerance, patience, and perseverance. The travels exploded myths and punctured preconceived notions, profoundly altering our perspectives. We emerged changed individuals, cynical of simplistic international prescriptions for social reform aimed indiscriminately at radically diverse societies. At the same time, we became appreciative of those unique ways of life so fundamentally at odds with development in a Western sense.

In order to share our journey with you, I have attempted to write an account not merely evocative, but also provocative. To lend the depth of social commentary and critique, I have deliberately eschewed the conventional "travel book" format. For while we were exposed to much that was ingratiating, we also discovered a good deal that was disturbing—at times shocking. Some of the conclusions drawn will be controversial, though, I hope, also thought-provoking and entertaining. I simultaneously wish to convey the sense of humor, pathos, challenge, and excitement that only overlanding can provide.

This book is dedicated to fellow overlanders whose need to know, spirit of adventure, and disdain for a humdrum existence propels them from the creature comforts of home to taste the ecstasy of the unknown.

Book One
ASIA

TURKEY

Gateway to the Orient

Rumors of sexual harassment and rip-offs troubled me as Marzi and I flew into Istanbul. This apprehension, mingled with the excitement of expectation, caused my heart to beat wildly. My imagination worked overtime, conjuring up storybook images ranging from Islamic splendor to barbarism.

Alas, as our airport bus entered the city, the montage recalled a typical European metropolis. Modern high-rise buildings lined boulevards choking with traffic. Lurid billboards exalted American TV imports. The familiar stench of factories and automobile exhaust was all-pervasive.

But wait a minute! As we crossed over the Bosporus and into the "old city," the cars were replaced by fez-crowned men in baggy trousers drawing merchandise-laden wagons through narrow passageways. A bizarre, pungent aroma assaulted us. And echoing around the city's seven hills, the wail of a muezzin's call to prayer sent shivers of promised adventure up our spines.

Indeed Instanbul proved unique in every way. Although the city straddles two continents, the historic tentacles of neither Europe nor Asia, tugging culturally in opposite directions, have managed to fully possess it. Today Istanbul remains a curious hybrid—a realm whose mysterious allure would serve as a catalyst, catapulting us upon a journey to the East.

The Sultanahmet, or "old city," throbs with Oriental intrigue. Here rest historic Istanbul's great mosques and the treasures of Islamic empire. Here too, overlanders seek their quarters amid the ancient shrines and bustling bazaars.

In the East there are but two classes of accommodations: the characterless $30–$50-a-night establishments and simple $1–$2 travelers' retreats. Although some budget inns were truly the incarnation of an Oriental version of *The Pit and the Pendulum,* we usually managed to find lodging that was reasonably clean and, therefore, perfectly adequate.

In general, the rooms we frequented in Asia were cubbyholes barely spacious enough to house the basic bed and chair. A light flickered dimly from a single naked bulb swinging overhead on a decomposing cord. On rare occasions an antiquated sink protruded from thin, peeling walls. But the stained porcelain provided little cause for rejoicing, as invariably, rusty taps on full, nothing would be emitted other than an exhausted gurgle or groan.

Now and then we enjoyed the dubious luxury of huge whirling fans which dangled from the ceiling, resembling gargantuan flying insects. Their speed was impossible to satisfactorily regulate; we were usually left with a choice of HI, guaranteed to induce pneumonia, or LO, a lethargy slower than death. Some fans were attached so tenuously that I feared the blade would break loose at any second and shear us in half.

But if decently kept, even the most spartan of rooms served their function. They were for sleeping, period. After all, we had not come to Asia merely to while our time away in a hotel.

It is beyond me why anyone would spend a king's ransom in Hiltons or Inter-Continentals merely for a place to sleep. These establishments aim for a sterile "consistency of standards" so that lodgers might feel at home whether in Pakistan or Pittsburgh. We noted that the luxuriously appointed lounges had all the conviviality of a Miami resort, with little interaction among guests.

How striking was the difference at budget hostelries! In the evening a "campfire" atmosphere prevailed, and the travelers would relate their daily encounters in lands where the unusual is the norm. The lobbies served as entertainment, social, and informational watering holes. I came to relish those nightly confabs with fellow overlanders, for the participants were not merely spinning yarns but recounting adventures they had actually lived.

The only really distressing feature of some Oriental inns was the state of their communal toilets. A considerable disparity with the Western notion of sanitation exists through much of the world. Well-scrubbed restrooms do not rate high priority. A few overflowed with excrement.

Asian toilets are merely holes with a foot imprint strategically placed on either side. To the uninitiated, the watchword of such facilities is standing room only—or should I say, squatters' rights. After a period of acclimation, I actually came to prefer the Oriental style, as no contact was necessary with a dirty seat.

It was always essential to stock up on toilet paper in major urban centers. Since most of the world uses their left hand to wipe themselves, we soon understood why it was impolite to point or eat with one's left. To gesture at someone with the left hand is the Oriental counterpart of "giving the finger." In the old days, under Islamic law, a convicted thief had his right hand severed. This guaranteed starvation, for no one would let him near the communal food bowl.

We spent several days exploring the many wondrous sights of the Sultanahmet: the masterpieces of the Topkapi and Aya Sofya, the architectural genius of great-domed, minaret-flanked mosques. In Europe I felt an enormous dichotomy between the artistic legacies and the contemporary society. We would jump from a museum reflecting the distinctive custom and craft of an epoch far removed to a push-button modern world. In contrast, the unique social order mirrored in Istanbul's antiquities seemed in keeping with life in today's Sultanahmet.

19

Here the drama of life is played out on the streets. Merchants' cubicles line twisting cobbled corridors exuding a raw essence of exotic odors, including some repugnant smells we would eventually learn to tune out. Past the kiosks streamed an endless parade of peddlers with pushcarts, overwrought porters, scurrying tea vendors balancing minuscule cups on shiny silver trays, and shoeshine boys snapping their cloths.

At that exquisite temple of the Ottoman Empire, Suleymaniye Mosque, we observed the Islamic services which are still held there regularly. Before entering, we were asked to remove our shoes, wash our feet, and a scarf was issued to cover Marzi's head, Inside, streaked by the opaque light of ornate stained glass, the faithful knelt, giving praise to Allah as Turks have for centuries.

Upon leaving the ancient temple, I was jolted with the realization that we had not yet returned to the twentieth century. A dozen men wearing leather pack saddles on their backs staggered from a warehouse. These human beasts of burden were transporting heavy merchandise to local shops. One even bore the weight of a refrigerator. Time and again in the course of our travels, we found that human labor, because it was so cheap and abundant, would prevail over the mechanization of Western society.

During our stay in the Sultanahmet Marzi and I were constantly confronted with sights extraordinaire. As we walked toward the Grand Bazaar, we were transfixed by the image of an immense furry creature ambling in our direction. Although held secure by a strap and chain, the beast was decidedly too large to be a domestic household pet. Finally we gasped, "A bear!"

The creature's master, a short dark gypsy sporting a 1940s blue serge suit jacket and loose-fitting cotton trousers, exuberantly returned our greeting.

"You have backache? Bear sit on pain—guarantee quick fix. Only ten lira."

"Perhaps some other time," I replied.

"That's O.K., my friends, now we dance for you."

The gypsy sang a rhythmic melody and extended a tambourine to a grudgingly outstretched paw. The bear reared up on his hind legs, swaying heavily to his master's hypnotic chant and punctuated each refrain with a shake of the tambourine.

Their performance over, we bade good-bye to the ever-smiling gypsy and his hairy companion. Asking no money, the Turk proclaimed his pleasure in meeting us, fervently expressing the hope that we would enjoy his country. Until now, the strangeness of my surroundings had conveyed a nameless foreboding. The gypsy's straightforward cordiality made me realize how foolish I was, for nearly everyone had been so spontaneously friendly.

Sometimes too friendly! "Feel City," as Marzi euphemistically refers to Istanbul's Grand Bazaar, is the world's largest covered market. In its teeming passageways, she received anonymous pinches aplenty. "At least they don't discriminate," I remarked, attempting to console her after a grizzled old man lasciviously stroked my bottom.

Pawings aside, we were mesmerized by the din of screaming touts, haggling shoppers, clanging metalsmiths, braying donkeys, and the soon-to-become familiar "baksheeshing" of beggars. The sheer animation of the bazaar swept us along through its colorful labyrinth of stalls. Vociferous merchants hawked the Orient's finest leather work, skillfully embroidered apparel, jewelry, pottery, and metalware. These could be had for a song, provided one was willing to barter.

As we drew near their kiosks, merchants would cry out, "Special for you, my friend, student prices! Come into my shop, come in!"

It was in the Grand Bazaar that we were intially exposed to the art of bargaining. For the next two years we would haggle vehemently for everything from tunics to toilet paper. Barter was often quite pleasant. Merchants would invite us to sit down for tea and we would discuss their country, its culture, and local politics. Occasionally, we grew weary of dickering for outright necessities. But upon returning to the West, I felt rather helpless in being unable to exert some bargaining leverage over items with exorbitant set prices.

In the Spice Bazaar, an amulet hanging from a vendor's neck caught my eye. It was inscribed with the Star of David. Upon inquiry, the merchant acknowledged being a Jew from a small

Hebraic community on the outskirts of the city. He noted that relations between his people and their Moslem neighbors had been good for the past decade, with the exception of the last Arab-Israeli war had which roused some verbal abuse.

"My community has resided in Turkey for centuries, sometimes in the face of severe oppression. I personally get along with the Turks; many are my friends." Then he sighed, adding wistfully, "Every so often my friends tend to forget themselves. . . . But name-calling is nothing, I can live with it. Turkey is my home."

Istanbul evenings found us sitting around the gardened café of our hotel, where overlanders returning from India gathered. Their tales of exotic adventure encouraged us to go further. But this notion was strongly tempered by one woman's dissenting voice.

"So many bloody hassles. . . . I'm tired of smelling shit every-where, having my boobs grabbed, paying off bureaucrats, staying in flea-traps, running sick to stinking toilets every two minutes. Sure it was an experience, one I'll never repeat."

There was no strong rebuttal; all overlanders could relate to at least some of these grievances. The woman's complaint, while not fully discouraging us, nevertheless raised some nagging doubts. Would the headaches and hazards of overlanding outweigh the benefits?

Although we were becoming accustomed to the ubiquitous odors, we had not yet adjusted to the marked lack of hygiene. This kindled our greatest fear—sickness. As for sexual abuse, Marzi had already been exposed to "The Helping Hand" in Istanbul, a city where Western females are hardly a phenomenon. Would she face insuffer-able difficulties in the more orthodox Islamic societies to the East?

These reservations in mind, we decided to first explore some of the Turkish countryside instead of taking the grueling four-day train direct to Tehran. This would provide a test case: if ensuing hard-ships proved insufferable, we could easily return to Europe.

Roaming this mammoth country for the next month, we were struck by the convivial warmth of the Turkish people as well as in-credible, though little-known, sights like the Goreme Valley and Pamukkale Hot Springs. Our gravest apprehensions were soon laid to rest, discomforts accepted as part of "the experience."

The real Turkey lay outside Istanbul. Getting about the countryside proved no problem on plush, late-model Mercedes buses. At fares oriented toward what the locals could afford, even long-distance rides were exceedingly cheap, averaging about one dollar for every five hours on the road. To counter desert heat, purified water was stored in a cooler and sold for a penny a bottle. A steward walked down the aisle at frequent intervals, pouring fragrant perfume into passengers' hands; this service was wisely provided after all toilet stops, thus eliminating undesirable odors within the coach.

Turkish transport, however, was not without its unpleasantries. Some Turks, unaccustomed to the motion of travel, ran to rear windows when ready to retch. Since the back door could become rather congested with these miserable souls, we learned to reserve seats toward the front. But there was nothing we could do about the passengers who carried lambs or goats which in turn harbored fleas. These ravenous microscopic monsters, always one jump ahead of your slapping hand, could make even the shortest journey interminable. The dancing fleas' movements seemed remarkably well coordinated with the redundant Turkish music played full-blast over the loud speaker. What first sounded exotic became repetitious ad nauseum.

Crossing rural Turkey by bus, we gazed upon a bleak landscape of barren, rocky brown hills and bone-dry plains. Outside the coach, the sun was blinding; the slightest air movement kicked up choking clots of dust, congealing the tongue, constricting the gullet. Yet, amazingly, even in the midst of this seemingly uninhabitable terrain, there were scattered signs of human existence.

Incredulous, we would spy an isolated farm, a peasant woman sifting grain, a lonely shepherd tending his flock. In irregular, irrigated fields subsistence cultivators employed primitive, donkey-powered threshers for harvesting wheat. Any questions we had about the source of cooking and heating fuel on these treeless plains were soon answered by the mountains of dried camel or donkey dung which towered over each peasant's diminutive dwelling. These hardy Turks could teach us a thing or two about conservation of energy.

It was incredible to discover peasants scratching out a livelihood from such a hostile environment. On the parched central plains of

Anatolia, the key to survival for better than a century has been the cultivation of opium. But calamity struck the region when the Nixon administration, threatening curtailment of economic aid, persuaded the Turkish government to outlaw the harvesting of the poppy. Struggling farmers, with neither the money nor the know-how to shift to another cash crop, were ruined. Many peasants were reduced to begging. Starvation was rampant.

As much as we sympathized with the plight of the Anatolian peasant, the tragedy of heroin addiction in the States was not lost upon us. But later in Laos we were shocked to witness the CIA assist in the export of opium from Southeast Asia. The sincerity of President Nixon's "War on Drugs" was called into question.

Turkish hospitality could be downright overwhelming. Overnighting in small towns visited by few tourists, we were almost always invited home by locals for a meal. Our congenial hosts plied us with kebabs, borek, and baklava till bursting. We soon discovered that Turks become insulted if you refuse their offer of more food and simply will not take "no" for an answer. What an inopportune time for our stomachs to be introduced to the higher bacterial count frequently accompanying Eastern food preparation!

How often did I hear "Just one more fig!" Fresh Turkish figs may be succulent, but they are nothing short of disastrous when one has the runs (as we chronically did those first few weeks). So, not wishing to appear impolite, we would—groan—suicidally force ourselves to eat "just one more fig."

Outside Istanbul, Marzi's dark complexion and straight black hair served to minimize sexual hassles, for rural folk often took her for a "Europeanized" Turk. As a measure of both self-protection and cultural sensitivity, she always wore long-sleeved blouses and ankle-length skirts. While this made her uncomfortable in the hundred-degree-plus heat, she noted that it was not nearly so draining as the dress of most Turkish women.

Rural females, geared to a lifetime of labor, still do the bulk of the farming in Turkey. We observed them working the fields, swathed in several thick layers designed to hide any semblance of form. Some even wore woolen boots to the knee.

Kemal Ataturk, Turkey's brilliant progressive leader, banned the outward trappings of subordination: the veil and the harem. Looking to the West, he concluded that a nation's capacity for modernization could be measured by the freedom of its women. In the course of our journeys, we too would find this often an appropriate yardstick.

But Turkey's great socio-economic revolution more or less died with Ataturk some fifty years ago. Suffering under the rule of ineffectual politicians and military leaders, the country never has realized its economic potential. Correspondingly, for a majority of women, the rigid life style of a repressive Islamic order still holds sway. That sacred center of Turkish life, the mosque, segregated to this day by sex—men up front, females relegated to the rear—symbolically reflected for us the lowly status of Turkish women.

After roving about the countryside for some time, we discovered the perfect spot to unwind. Pamukkale, which translates as "Cotton Fortress," is well named. This dazzling hot-springs area is composed of peppermint-striped alabaster cliffs out of which thermal waters percolate. Over the years, the springs have gradually layered the malleable bluffs with a series of picturesque limestone ledges. Climbing these, we languished under an undulating series of womb-temperature waterfalls which gushed from the springs, skipping joyously some three hundred feet down the colorfully configured cliffs.

On the way up, we refreshed ourselves by sinking into warm mineral pools, washing away the desert dust which clung to every pore. We watched the sun's rays play upon the translucent terraces, bathing their charcoal, pink, and chalky hues in an ever-changing kaleidoscopic feast for the eyes. Returning to the summit in the cool evening, we were entranced by the surreal transfiguration of some oddly chiseled limestone into immense glossy molars which shone grotesquely in the moonlight.

We might have remained here forever, had we not heard of a place even more remarkable.

South of Ankara, amid cruel Cappadocian wastes, rests that bizarre world of Turkish troglodytes, the Goreme Valley. The eerily eroded, vividly tinted volcanic spires suggest extraterrestrial sand castles. I felt myself thrust within a lunar landscape awash with technicolor. Running my eyes up from the floor of the valley, I detected rough-hewn doors and windows which imbued the huge cones with a comical face. In the seventh century Christians seeking refuge from Moslem marauders carved their homes and churches into these protective volcanic formations. The Goreme's soils were so soft that shepherd's staffs served as shovels.

Peering into one such chasm, I was startled to discover life astir in that lunarlike crater. A family of five troglodytes forgave my intrusion and invited me in for tea. Like other poor peasants of the Goreme, they chose to reside in the centuries-old caves of their ancestors rather than waste any of their precious subsistence plots for dwelling space. Such "houses" provide natural insulation: cool in summer, warm in winter. I found them roomier inside than the standard peasant abode. But Goreme's cave dwellers must live with the perils of erosion, which can tragically crumble walls without warning.

Entering a "kebabci" in the tiny hamlet of Urgup, bordering the valley, we noticed that the tables had been set with grimy dishes. I called this to the attention of the waiter, who whipped out an even filthier cloth, giving each plate a smart, quick wiping. After spraying the table in a paroxysm of sneezing, he smiled toothlessly, gesturing us to sit down. There was no other restaurant open at the time, so we stayed. One's standards of cleanliness become radically altered in the Orient.

About to finish our meal, we were joined by a rotund man in a bright red fez. He had been drinking quite a bit of "raki" and was in high spirits.

"Which better, Turkey or Greece?" he slurred combatively, twisting his bushy mustache.

It was not necessary to be diplomatic. I replied honestly that Turkey was infinitely more interesting and its people friendlier—less out to put the squeeze on foreigners.

Hearing this, he pounded the table in ecstasy and ordered the waiter to bring us a bottle of one of Goreme's excellent local wines.

"You visited underground cities?"

Undaunted by our perplexed expression, the Turk, who happened to be a dolmus (taxi) driver, exclaimed, "You must see! Come, I take you there baksheesh."

Curious, we accepted his invitation. Since he drove his battered old Plymouth with typical Turkish motoring machismo, it was lucky there were few other vehicles on the isolated dirt track.

In the third world, the right of way belongs to "whoever gets there first." As overlanders taking public transport, we would learn to laugh off the inevitable close shave, staring death in the face. While we surely traveled with some of the world's most maniacal drivers, the alternative was transport by air—where we would see little, meet no one, experience nothing.

Several miles beyond the Goreme, the dolmus screeched up the unmarked side street of a sedate settlement. Hewn here into solid rock were the portals of a once-thriving subterranean world, whose genuine history might have sprung from the pages of the weirdest science fiction. Kaymakli was a city built eight stories underground as protection against the onslaught of second-century invaders. Archeologists estimated that, at one point, Kaymakli housed fifteen to twenty thousand inhabitants!

How did these "mole people" live? To decipher the secrets of their sepulchral city, we descended deep into the bowels of the earth. Fearful of becoming forever lost in the dark maze of passageways, we stuck close to our intrepid dolmus driver who ungainfully wielded a torch in one hand while swigging raki with the other. His belch made me jump as it shattered the tomblike silence, reverberating up and down all eight stories. Either inhabited Kaymakli was a nerve-splitting cauldron of noise or its thousands of residents communicated in a continually repressed hush.

Staggering in his raki stupor, our guide was nonetheless well informed. His torch illuminated a network of odd-sized catacombs, and as we ducked our heads to enter a tiny chamber, our leader declared, "Family live here." Apparently each nuclear unit had some modicum of privacy. We next toured larger vestibules, said to have flourished once as workshops and livestock stables. Indeed this city was self-contained, the first underground mall.

The most massive of the inner sanctums were the kitchens. Although ingenious ventilation shafts ran from the basement to camouflaged outlets above ground, preservation of oxygen was still essential in such crowded confines. Kaymakli's cookfires were necessarily limited to a single kitchen for each level. "Imagine the amount of food preparation per pantry! What modern diettian could administer this?" Marzi wondered.

Kaymakli's single entrance made the city extremely easy to defend. But should it have been impossible to exit above ground, a nine-kilometer tunnel ran from the bottom story to another heavily populated underground metropolis, Derinkuyu.

These ancient cities raised a host of questions which may never be answered with certainty. Did the inhabitants spend most of their lives underground? If so, what impact had such closed and cramped quarters on their psyches? And of what terrifying invaders were the inhabitants so frightened that they felt obliged to burrow under the earth? The foreboding darkness and cold, dank air made me shudder on that last thought, and it felt so good to emerge to the warming rays of the sun.

I was grateful that this extraordinary subterranean world lacked the screaming commerciality of the better-known and more accessible sites. But one enterprising Turk hopes to change all this and put the underground cities on the tourist map. On rocks overlooking the entrance to Kaymakli he has painted a bright red arrow and in big, bold letters: "DISCOTEK."

After the marvels of Goreme and Pamukkale and the kindness we received from the not at all "Terrible Turks," we easily reached a decision. On to India!

First we had to get our Persian and Afghan visas in Ankara. While we waited for the bus, a vacationing engineer and his wife offered us a ride in their fintailed 1956 De Soto. (It appears that a goodly number of the gargantuan American gas guzzlers of that era have been reincarnated in Turkey.)

On the surface, the young couple epitomized the extreme materialism we were to see in the third-world nouveau riche. The husband chattered on endlessly about the sports car he hoped to purchase. His caked-in-cosmetics wife bombarded Marzi with details of the latest "in" look for Ankaran sophisticates, Yet surprisingly, they also shared a love for the simple and unspoiled.

"If you are in no hurry," they cordially offered, "we would like to show you a very special place a bit out of the way."

Swallowing dust on a bumpy back road, we eventually reached its end, a sheer cliffside. The Turk parked the car, and we embarked upon a footpath descending into a virtually unknown Shangri-La called the Ihlara Valley. For twenty minutes we cautiously wended our way down the slender trail threading the steep precipice. At its base, we crossed a swaying footbridge spanning a beautifully clear river whose waters surged swiftly through a fertile wooded dell. In caverns honeycombing the canyon's walls lived peasants whose ancestors had resided in this isolated vale for centuries.

No tourist influence here, the people of Ihlara lived a self-contained existence providing full subsistence through flocks of sheep and vegetable gardens. No exhaust fumes or rumbling of traffic, the only vehicle the donkey cart, the solitude of silence broached solely by the rushing flow of that life-giving river.

A sixteen-year-old Ihlarian, Mehmet, introduced himself and inquired where we were from. Hearing that the engineer lived in Ankara, Mehmet asked if it were true that the city had buildings as high as the surrounding cliffs, shops where machines made the air cool, dramas which could be seen over black boxes?

"I am saving enough for bus fare—someday I will work there," asserted the youth.

In response, the engineer graciously proposed, "You are welcome to come along with us and see for yourself. I know a construction foreman who can find you some lodging and a job. Of course," he added paternalistically, "you must be willing to work harder than you do in the fields."

The young farmer was beside himself with joy.

Later, we weaved through the snarled traffic of Ankara, a featureless metropolis constructed under the aegis of Ataturk, who saw his dream of building Turkey a "Western" capital fulfilled. I was completely turned off by the city's noise, smog, sterility, and crowded anonymity. Marzi echoed my thoughts, whispering how keenly appreciative she was now of the tranquil existence at Ihlara. Then I looked over at the young peasant. Gazing at the skyscrapers and glittering lights, he radiated the excitement of discovery. For Mehmet, Ankara was progress personified.

The couple put us up for the night. How proud they were of their modern apartment, especially the tiled bathroom with its Western sit-down toilet—certified hallmark of "civilized affluence." In their zeal to make us feel at home, they took us to an American-style restaurant and treated us to hamburgers and potato salad. Afterward, our hosts sought to suitably entertain us by snapping Turkish-dubbed "Mission Impossible" on their TV.

What a marked contrast between the life style of this upper-middle-class couple and that of their rural countrymen. But a common denominator lay in their friendliness and genuine interest in us. Nowhere in Europe had we been so deluged with hospitality and goodwill.

It therefore came as a rude shock to feel the drastic change in atmosphere in the town of Erzurum. The people were extremely pushy, sullen, and hostile. Despite her conservative attire, Marzi was harassed unmercifully. We had not seen this side of Turkey before. Situated near the border, Erzurum's culture had much in common with neighboring Iran. Little did we realize that this sexual aggressiveness and overall nastiness were merely an ominous precursor of misadventures to follow in Persia.

IRAN

Lust in the Dust

At the Persian frontier we endured an exasperating wait for our passports to be stamped. The immigration captain, ignoring our documents, languorously gossiped with his colleagues until quitting time. Then at a speed one would have thought impossible for him, he dashed for the door, pinching Marzi en route. His replacement sauntered in and leisurely immersed himself in a mountain of paperwork. Finally he picked up our passports and within two minutes we were on our way. Three hours' wait for a lousy stamp!

We soon learned that, when dealing with non-Western authorities, it was unwise to schedule anything to follow. In the States and Europe, bureaucratic delays might by measured by the minute, in Asia by the hour or the day, in Africa by the day or even the week.

Third-world countries are still largely agrarian and the legacy of time gauged more by the season than the clock is evident. A few travelers glorify this, labeling it "human" as opposed to "business" time. Most others view these frustrating procrastinations as the selfish power trips of petty officialdom. Yet, no matter which interpretation one prefers, an overlander has little choice but to gear way down and alter his tempo; the sole alternatives are madness or ulcers.

This snail's pace, coupled with preposterous reams of bureaucratic red tape, turned efficiency into a foreign notion. Observation of locals would teach us that a small gratuity handed to the right party could usually expedite matters and dissolve seemingly impenetrable formalities.

Through the blisteringly hot, arid desert extending from the border to Tehran, we passed numerous bands of nomads and their camel caravans. Such migrants have followed unmapped routes for centuries, knowing exactly where to find that most precious commodity, water. Indeed, when it came to securing liquid refreshment, the passengers of our deluxe coach proved not nearly so adept as the nomads.

One reason for having chosen this particular bus company was its advertised promise of free soft drinks. By midday, the sun beat down so fiercely that we felt grilled from the inside out. Never had the notion of chilled Coke sounded so appealing. Although we rarely drank it in the States, Coke was often the only safe cold beverage available outside the West. (We knew some travelers who scrupulously avoided amebic tap water, yet drank soft drinks with ice.)

Drained of bodily fluid, we repeatedly asked for our drinks, only to hear the steward reply, "Shortly, my friend, shortly." Finally, the bus pulled up at a café managed, of course, by the transport company. Here, thirsty passengers guzzled overpriced tea or Coke till bloated. Back on board, the cunning steward readily tendered the contents of his cooler, with few takers.

Amid desert flats, the horizon appears infinite. Shortly after dawn, a faint outline of skyscrapers materialized in the distance. As the barren plains gave way to a clutter of buildings we knew we had reached the Persian capital, Tehran. This sprawling, sweltering metropolis, so out of place in its sandy surroundings, provided some of the most vexing difficulties on our entire journey.

In less than three decades Tehran has mushroomed from a sleepy desert hamlet of twenty-five thousand into a nouveau-riche mega-lopolis of four million. The quantum leap from caravan center to conglomerate capital for the world's second richest oil reserves has taken its toll on a beleaguered citizenry. Barely one generation removed from the countryside, most Tehranians find themselves dazed by the swift imposition of a Western urban life style upon their rural traditions. For visitors, the two most visible symptoms of this cultural confusion are revealed in the insanity of the city's drivers and the repugnant male attitude toward Western women.

Beneath the streamlined skyscrapers, torrents of unmuffled traffic defy every rule of the road. Tehranian drivers make Parisian motorists actually appear courteous and skilled. They seem to find great sport in coming as close as possible to the petrified pedestrian. Each time we crossed a street and discovered ourselves still in one piece, we heaved a sigh of relief. But this was short-lived, for once safely ensconced on the sidewalk, we had to confront a nonstop barrage of sexual harassment.

Silhouetted against the contemporary backdrop of bistros and boutiques, Iranian women enshrouded within the black veil of the "chaderi" live a life little touched by the modernity of their surroundings. Cloistered from puberty, they remain fettered by the strictures of orthodox Islam. By contrast, the female visitor from the West is visibly more liberated and thus seen as fair game.

Despite her modest attire, Marzi was relentlessly bothered as Persian men barged into her, grabbing, pinching, or goosing and then running on. Their compatriots in the street would roar with amusement at the spectacle, ready to intervene should I object. Infuriated, Marzi was just about ready to head for home. I understood her pique when an overlander told us that Pakistanis were even more aggressive. Was it worth it to put up with this nonsense?

Our patience exhausted, Marzi learned how best to cope with the situation after watching the response of a young local woman to a crusty old man who had just fingered her. Bearing dark red streaks on his cheek where her nails had blazed a path, the culprit slunk away, utterly humiliated. Nary a bystander laughed.

Subsequently wielding our sharp-edged can opener whenever venturing out, Marzi brandished it menacingly before her. The change was dramatic. Most men who approached would take note of the weapon and back off. One fool, however, disregarded the threat and continued his advance,' only to be sent howling, having paid a painful price.

I was proud of Marzi and relieved of the anxiety of having to act as her bodyguard. It was this spirit of independence that made Marzi such a superb traveler.

The tensions that are incorporated into the overland experience tear many a relationship to pieces. But Marzi and I had learned some time ago that it was senseless to thrust the frustrations built of external factors upon each other. Most obstacles became joint projects which we tackled together; the challenges we faced on the road would actually serve to strengthen our bond.

Of all the conservative Moslem territory on our route, why did Tehran generate the most unrelieved sexual anguish for overlanders? A primary factor was the confusion of identity induced by the onrush of "Westernization" which the country's oil wealth has brought. Persian men began to seek a "modern" sex life in a society of medieval mores where any erotic act with a female outside of marriage was almost unheard of. Nevertheless, they continued to define a "good woman" as an Islamic virgin or virtuous wife kept chaste behind the chaderi. Their own women out of bounds, Iranian men focused on those they believed "free," and Western females became the target.

The cultural trauma of an ancient order exposed so quickly to the affluence (and thus desirability) of Western ways is perhaps most demonstrably exhibited by the wives of the Tehranian upper class. Many of these women, displaying mini-skirts beneath see-through chaderis, walk the streets of the city without harassment.

The local male's image of panting foreign females is doubtless influenced by Tehran's cinematic staple of low-budget European quasi–James Bond epics. The scantily clad women of this genre are invariably portrayed as sex objects, thus typecasting all young Western women in the mind-set of repressed Persians. And, of course, the urban tension of this grossly overexpanded metropolis only aggravates the obnoxious behavior of the men. Add all these ingredients to an exceedingly aggressive society and you have an anxiety-charged atmosphere for non-Islamic females.

An already uncomfortable situtation is aggravated by some insensitive Western women who make things worse for their sister overlanders by wearing "comfortable" garb which, while fine in Europe, is downright provocative here. Seeing them parade angered us, for it only reinforced the stereotype. When a Persian, living in a society where the veil is still the norm, glimpses a braless foreigner in a transparent blouse, he simply loses control.

We took refuge from the streetside madness within the confines of the Amir Kabir, the "travelers'" hotel in Tehran. While not the cleanest inn on our route, it was surely one of the most colorful and bizarre. Almost all overlanders moving in either direction would spend a night here, and the lobby was a potpourri of Westerners decked out in a dazzling bevy of saris, sarongs, turbans, and baggy trousers.

Here, returning travelers and those who embarked from Australia sat into the wee hours of the morning spinning tales of remarkable adventures. They volunteered invaluable advice on black markets, lodging, eateries to avoid at all cost, and worthwhile excursions off the beaten path. As we listened, we each kept a hawk-eye on food purchased from the adjoining café lest our snacks fall prey to the innkeeper's pet goat. This evil-smelling scavenger wandered tirelessly around the lounge in search of any tidbit he could pilfer. Oblivious to innumerable plans for a mutton barbecue to be held in his honor, the shaggy creature continued his omnivorous ways.

A few of the travelers sat silently, dull eyes prominent in emaciated faces. Some had succumbed to the ravages of dysentery or hepatitis. Others had become strung out on easy-to-obtain hard drugs, surviving until they somehow garnered sufficient funds to return home. Those who had not kicked the habit moved rapidly through Persia, where the penalty for possession could mean the firing squad. I should hasten to add that the vast majority of overlanders never indulged in anything more potent than hashish.

Rather than head east immediately, we reserved seats on a bus bound eight hours south through the desert to Isfahan. Though initially reluctant to spend extra time in Iran, we based this decision upon the reports of overlanders met in the Amir Kabir who raved about the ancient city. They assured Marzi that she was unlikely to experience abuse there, and indeed, they were right. Isfahan was free of the urban mania which had made Tehran so insufferable. Here Marzi was able to sheathe her can opener, for the men did no more than stare. Furthermore, the town was small enough to walk everywhere, with few rampaging autos to dodge. The sole hazard we encountered here was spitting.

Constantly in the Orient, one hears a local plumb the very depths of his being to bring up his best. While some travelers referred to this as the "Asian cough," I dubbed it the "Sound of Mucus." The guttural hacking "chaaach," audible for considerable distances, served as a warning. Whenever we heard it while strolling under a window, we ducked and ran.

In a more pleasant vein, Isfahan's Royal Square combined the most stunning shrines and vibrant bazaars. Its Royal Mosque, the Masjid-i-Shah, outshone the famous works of Islamic architecture we had observed in Istanbul. The dome's hypnotic mosaic transported us into a flowing web of turquoise and gold—a hallucinogenic experience for which no drugs were necessary. Inside, a guide ushered me to an inscription beneath the cupola. "Observe the presence of Allah," he intoned, ceremoniously stamping his foot. In response, the ornate walls of the Masjid-i-Shah vibrated with a percussive echo a holy seven times.

Just opposite the mosque, the profusion of aromas from spices to camel dung and the din of hammered metal disclosed that we had reached the central core of Persia's once great commercial empire, the Isfahan Bazaar. Here skilled craftsmen deafened the ear but delighted the eye with elaborately embellished copper, brass, and silverware. Nearby, sack after sack of pungent spices was unloaded from the backs of hard-working camels and donkeys. In the fabric market merchants vigorously hawked cottons speckled with the region's brilliantly printed paisleys. One could not even begin to compare this multisensory hurly-burly with the synthetic sterility of Western Muzak malls.

Retracing our steps to Tehran, we lost no time booking a connecting coach for Islam's second holiest city, Meshad. After the bus tortuously wound its way up through the Elburz Mountains, our wild-eyed driver reaffirmed his masculinity by roaring his vehicle down a roller-coaster grade to the Caspian Sea. Then we reentered the vastness of burning desert sands.

Most passengers were pious pilgrims who had scrupulously saved for this once-in-a-lifetime "hajj." (Meshad posed an attainable alternative for those too poor to make the distant journey to Mecca.) Uncannily at intervals, as if tuned directly to each other, the faithful would confound us by crying out a prayer in perfect unison.

Because virtually every pilgrim started his journey with a child on his lap, it did not take long for litter to accumulate and foul odors to pervade the bus. Soon the children were laid down helter-skelter in the filthy aisle. When the bus halted for a dinner break, we watched in horror as the prostrate youngsters were trampled underfoot in the elders' stampede for the door.

In the blighted tea house, a crowd gathered around to watch me insert a contact lens. A magician? Madman? Since many Persians believe in the "evil eye," a few spectators no doubt saw me as an agent of Satan.

Indeed the evil eye must have exerted some influence, for I almost lost my money and passport at this pitstop. The toilet was typical of public facilities, a small hole piled high with excrement. Heeding nature's call despite the unpleasantness, I rolled up my trouser legs and entered the flooded stall. Then, aghast, I saw my leather money pouch slide off its unbuckled belt, dropping within a few millimeters of the fetid hole. Had the pouch fallen in, I might well have left it. To add insult to injury, the facility's "cleaning lady" had the audacity to demand a few rials for her services!

Back on board, we noticed the men attentively rewrapping their turbans. As is well known, that coiled cloth protects the head from the sun. But at mealtimes it easily unravels for napkin service. And when desert dust stops up the sinuses, the turban awaits its expulsion. In this age of specialized gadgetry, the handy turban remains unchallenged for versatility.

When we arrived at the Meshad terminal, chaos prevailed. While the pilgrims pushed and clawed to retrieve their luggage, petty salesmen and beggars virtually bowled each other over in an effort to get at the newcomers. Having heard that hotel rates soar during the summer pilgrimage season, we made an end run around the shouting mob and lit out for the local campgrounds.

Suddenly we were intercepted by a well-dressed young Persian. Politely introducing himself and bidding us welcome, Aziz promised to help us find a reasonably priced room. Though he did not look like one of the typical hotel touts who constantly badgered us whenever they saw our packs, we remained skeptical nonetheless.

Aziz accompanied us to a hotel run by a friend's father. Spying the spacious lobby furnished with expensively upholstered sofas and chairs, we informed him that we could not afford such posh accommodations. But Aziz whispered a few words into the manager's ear, and, as if by magic, we were enthroned in palatial quarters at a bargain-basement rate.

Our Persian friend then offered to take us on a sightseeing tour of holy Meshad. He escorted us to the sacred Mosque of Gawharshad, where crowds of enraptured pilgrims thronged the grounds outside the gates. Famed throughout the Islamic realm, the mosque has a resplendent gold-leaf dome and is said to be absolutely sumptuous within. But only Moslems may enter. We were fortunate to be in the presence of Aziz. Some overlanders, seen as "infidels," told of being stoned and spat upon here.

Our "guided tour" continued next—surprise, surprise—to an older brother's carpet emporium. Aziz explained, "I was certain that while in Meshad, you'd want to see the famous Persian carpets. Meshad is the center for the finest rugs and all visitors want to buy one. Believe me, my friends, I have not brought you because of my brother. This shop deals with only the most skilled weavers in the country! And naturally, since you are with me, you will get a special price."

Ah well, having been suckered here, we saw no harm in looking. The proprietor congenially poured some tea before showing his wares. Dazzling us with a cornucopia of exquisite rugs, he almost convinced us to strike a bargain. "Just think of the profit you'll make by selling a century-old masterpiece such as this in America."

Luckily, our better judgment prevailed. Realizing our ignorance of carpet quality, we knew we could be easily conned.

As we later discovered from fellow travelers, other Meshad families, giving hoteliers kickbacks from resultant sales, use similar ploys to lure potential buyers into their shops. This approach is often successful, too, judging from the number of people we met on the road who blindly bought carpets. But an ability to assess standards of workmanship was crucial. A knowledgeable importer later revealed that trucks are sometimes driven over new rugs to make them appear antique!

We did learn something from our visit to the shop. Aziz's brother explained why some of the older carpets, whose complex mazes staggered the mind, were more valuable than those recently produced. Many tribal women, addicted to opium, wove timeless works of art, called "smokers' carpets," through the aura of their narcotic haze. Today, it is eminently understandable that few weavers risk smoking, for the authoritarian Shah of Iran has banned the drug. And to flout his edict is to jeopardize one's life.

Shah Mohammed Reza Pahlevi has reigned for more than thirty years. From the Turkish to the Afghan border, we saw posters of His Eminence and family displayed everywhere: office walls, restaurants, hotels, and people's homes. This visible image is symbolic of the Shah's absolute personal rule. If it leads one to feel that the Shah is watching over all, that sensation is not groundless, for SAVAK—his secret police—do indeed keep close surveillance over every level of Iranian society. I watched Persians shudder at the very mention of anything relating to politics and ultimately refrained from broaching the subject.

Even students avoided controversy. Encircled by a high wall, Tehran University resembles a fortress. When we sought to meet well-informed Persians here, armed guards at the gate advised us that visitors required an entry permit issued by the government. An Iranian friend in the States later commented, "The very last place you would discover what students are thinking about politically is the university."

Persians' fears of being suspected of opposing the regime are understandable. Reliable sources estimate that up to a hundred thousand political prisoners suffer every conceivable manner of torture, deprivation, and humiliation in the SAVAK's dungeons. During a goodwill visit to Washington, the Shah acknowledged that "psychological torture is sometimes utilized to protect Iran from being overrun by Communists. Remember, we are situated precariously on the Soviet border." Other measures employed by SAVAK, according to Amnesty International, include electric canes and probes, shock treatment, ultrasound-wave earphones, plus a de Sade compendium of centuries' proven sexual and physical bestialities.

In our journeys beyond Tehran we were stunned by how little of the annual windfall from the country's immense petroleum revenues had filtered down. The glaring poverty we would witness in Afghanistan and Nepal was at least rationalizable in light of their few natural resources; in an oil-rich nation like Iran it was reprehensible.

Some have prospered, as the space-age skyscrapers and gaudy abodes of Tehran attest. But Persians we observed in the rural sectors still resided in earthen huts without decent water supplies or sanitary facilities. Better than half of the people exist at a bare subsistence level and three-quarters of the populace remain illiterate. Most have never seen a doctor—there is but one physician for every eight thousand Iranians, and the majority of these practices in Tehran. The average peasant's annual income is $125; some are starving. I'm still haunted by the sight of children grazing on grass during a school recess. Little wonder the average Persian life expectancy is but thirty-eight years.

Despite the grotesque social and economic inequities in this land of "black gold," the Shah has managed to fund the strongest military force in western Asia. More than half the Iranian budget is allocated for arms purchases and military expenditures.

The Shah has perpetuated his rule over the years thanks in large part to the political and economic leverage of multinational corporations. A Senate investigating committee has recently revealed that, during a 1953 uprising, the despot retained power only through the timely intervention of the Central Intelligence Agency. At the time of our visit to Iran, we noted with no small irony that the U.S. ambassador was Richard Helms, formerly head of the CIA. Only in the most repressive of police states would such an appointment not be protested.

American investors have found a fertile field in Persia's sands, with the Shah's climate of law and order much to their liking. Prominent concerns that have sown their capital here in addition to the oil companies, are Bank of America, General Motors, Anaconda Copper, and Dow Chemical, to name just a few. To assure that "our man in Iran" remains on the throne, the United States has shipped the Shah sophisticated weaponry to the tune of eight billion dollars from 1972 to 1974 and an ever-escalating figure since then. Recently, the Shah signed a twenty-million-dollar trade pact with Washington.

But apparently the weaponry and commercial favors are not enough. There are currently over one thousand American military advisers in Iran. Guerrilla activity has already begun. If the Persian people should rebel, will the United States intervene to support a despotic regime, as in Viet Nam?

The wonders of Isfahan and the affability of our "guide" Aziz (regardless of motivation) enabled us, after the hassles of Tehran, to leave Persia with at least some positive feelings. But due to the sexual indignities heaped upon Marzi and the culture's general aggressiveness, we departed somewhat bitter. Still, one could not help but sympathize with the Iranian people, for we too felt the oppressive climate of fear in which they live.

How liberating was the insanity of Afghanistan!

AFGHANISTAN

Arabian Knights Spring to Life

Layers of civilization peeled away as we crossed the Afghan border. We found ourselves in an ancient untamed land where rugged nomads still pledge allegiance to their tribe rather than to a nation. They roam the harsh terrain of desert and mountain in this Texas-sized country, maintaining traditional dress and a way of life little changed over the centuries. We had heard some astounding stories from fellow travelers about Afghanistan, but personal experiences would more than fulfill our wildest expectations.

First there was the tricky question of obtaining a visa. A coup d'etat had just ousted the Afghan monarch. The new regime, under the leadership of the former king's brother-in-law, ushered in a change of attitude toward overlanders. General Doud's initial (if only) show of reform was to make things difficult for "immoral hippies" who had set an allegedly "bad example" for Afghan children. A hippy being any Westerner sporting long hair, all visitors were required to be acceptably shorn before a visa would be granted.

In Ankara, a tall young Afghan Embassy functionary turned me away, telling me not to come back until I got a haircut. I complied, but on returning was told that the hair had not been cropped close enough. Having no wish to submit to a crewcut, I pointed out that if the rules applied equally to all, his own hair style would deny him access to his country. The official laughed agreeably and went to confer with his superior.

We showed the consular boss our professional credentials and sufficient cash to cover our stay in Afghanistan. The dignitary proceeded to leaf through the pages of a huge tome filled with mug shots of young Westerners booted out of Afghanistan following the coup. He accused them all of being "immoral hash pushers." Only upon our righteous assertion that we had no intention of peddling dope did he finally acquiesce.

Crossing over to the Afghan customs shed, we found the officials out to lunch. Three hours later, they staggered back. These bureaucrats were not in the least concerned with the length of my hair. They were looking for dope, as an agreement had been reached with the Shah to keep Afghan hashish from being smuggled into Iran. The officials themselves had just returned from a smoke and were so stoned they had no idea whether we were coming or going!

"You have hashish?" the immigration chief demanded, thinking us Persia-bound. Though I assured him we had just arrived, he dispatched his expert, an elfin man with enormous twinkling eyes and a long white beard, to conduct a thorough search of our bags. The underling scrunched down on all fours and his nose began to twitch spasmodically as he circled our packs. He sniffed and sniffed until called off by his chief, who had at long last concluded that we had just entered Afghanistan.

The head honcho stamped us in, sternly admonishing, "Listen well. I inform you of Afghan law. Hashish is forbidden. The black market illegal. You must use the banks for . . ."

Just then, an impetuous youth in a skullcap interrupted, bellowing like a side-show barker, "Change mun-ee? Hashish?"

As the little boy tugged at my trousers, hand outstretched, the official, convulsed with hysterics, rolled on the ground until tears streamed down his face. His authoritarian facade broken, the chief unearthed a hash chillum and passed it all around.

The driver of a decrepit minibus had been snoring away the hours waiting for us to fill up his vehicle. As there was no bank at the border, the Westerners told him he would be paid in Herat, where we could secure Afghan currency. The driver immediately demanded a ridiculous sum in U.S. dollars, arguing that his bus was the only transport to town. Refusing to be conned, we all remained steadfastly on board, giving him nothing. Finally, he swore vehemently, turned the archaic motor over, and off we chugged for Herat.

For me, Herat surely ranks among the world's most fascinating cities. Once a walled village, its crumbling clay ramparts flank the outskirts of the town. Within, camel trains and mule teams stir the dusty byways. There are few automobiles and the only taxis are horse-drawn "tongas." During the fifteenth century Herat was a great cultural mecca, the home of the famous romantic poet, Jami, and the artist, Bihzad, who meticulously painted exquisite miniatures with a one-haired brush. For the residents of Herat's squat earthen huts, the way of life has changed but little since the time of Bihzad and Jami.

Sheltered by the sun in the shadow of a decaying mud fortress, merchants cry out their sales pitches in Char Suq Bazaar. Imposingly bearded tribesmen wander in. Many bear antiquated flintlocks which their ancestors had spirited away as booty from the plundered bodies of British cavalrymen. They have come here to trade their tanned hides and wives' weavings for provisions essential to their nomadic life style.

The bazaar, situated next to the venerable Friday Mosque, was a beehive of commercial activity. A heady fragrance of spices and fruits filled the air in competition with malodorous open drains. The colorful traditional attire of the participants and kiosks exhibiting finely crafted filigree silverware, silk looms, and the products of karakul sheep, re-created a medieval atmosphere. Here overlanders could acquire beautifully embroidered cotton shirts and oversized trousers perfect for the desert heat selling for one to two dollars. For a few cents extra, I was fitted for a tailor-made pair of pants. This proved a mistake as, after a few washings they shrank nearly to the knee.

The famous Afghan sheepskin coat also could be had for a song ($20, relative to $175 in the States). Some buyers were unlucky enough to choose a coat which had been cured in urine. The confluence of so many odors in the bazaar made it next to impossible for an unwary customer to detect anything wrong on the spot. This was no ploy to swindle foreigners; curing has traditionally been accomplished in this way and the Afghans do not mind. But imagine the chagrin of the Westerner who sends her beautiful coat home only to later find . . .

The tall, dark Afghan men, whose Semitic characteristics and garb seemed to create a contemporary biblical spectacle which even Cecil B. De Mille could not improve, were considered the most handsome men in Asia by admiring female overlanders. Most sported "Omar Sharif" mustaches or long, flowing beards. They were usually outfitted in loose-fitting cotton trousers with oversize collarless shirts worn under brightly colored tunics.

Crowned with a turban or karakul cap, these rugged warriors looked perfectly capable of handling any and all perilous situtations, which one must if he is to survive in this harsh land. As for Afghan women, I cannot describe their physical allure, for we could not "see" them.

Entering the bazaar, we were astounded by the ghostly presence of animated tents whooshing past us. These seeming apparitions, we discovered, were Afghan women, cloaked in the most severe "chaderi" we were to encounter in Islamic Asia.

Horrified yet intrigued by the anonymity of the chaderi, Marzi tried one on for size. The heavy cotton serge draped shapelessly from her head, falling in folds like a monk's habit to her feet. I could not see her eyes through the finely crocheted mesh inset and Marzi could barely make out the outline of her surroundings. How Afghan women, their vision partially obscured, gallivant through the marketplace with such dexterity remains a mystery to us.

Until 1959 all Afghan women were legally required to wear the chaderi in public. A Peace Corps volunteer confided that some men still refuse their wives permission to ever remove the chaderi, even at home. It was hardly surprising to learn from a Western doctor based here that after several years of peering through that prison of veil, an Afghan woman's eyesight may become seriously impaired.

Although a mother may describe a prospective bride to her son, most men never look upon their mate until after taking the marriage vows. But in a society where the groom still pays a bride-price to his future father-in-law, conjugal negotiations are concerned not with beauty but with the grim realities of a woman's role in the Afghan order of things. "Is she a tireless worker?" "Is she built for bearing children?"

Affluent merchants have been known to pay enormous sums for the hand of a woman reputed to be a strong worker and of fertile lineage. Although most Afghans are too poor to take more than one spouse, well-to-do men may legally purchase as many wives as they desire.

What accounts for the ludicrous spectacle of thoroughly concealed and cloistered women? My own conclusions are based upon a situation that only changed within the century as a semblance of law and order was brought to most parts of this untamed country (a situation which probably persists to this day in some of the more isolated regions, where there are still rumors of slave trade). Greater numbers were considered a crucial necessity for tribes constantly in conflict with others over pasture land and stock. Hence the importance of women as childbearers and workers—the most valued of private property. Raids to abduct the youngest and strongest women led to the custom of veiling and confinement, initially as a "preventive measure." An extreme double standard of role easily evolved from this, and Islamic law provided the legal rationale for women as beasts of burden. Interestingly enough, when an Afghan woman recently strode down the singular street of a small community without her chaderi, she was stoned by other females who screamed that she was a "harlot." Even the victims are trapped by their own conditioning.

Despite the treatment of local women as eighth-class citizens, Marzi experienced little sexual intimidation in Afghanistan. The vaunted dignity of Afghan men is the chief restraining factor.

Furthermore, in this most orthodox of Islamic societies there is little homosexual taboo and men have long enjoyed an outlet outside of marriage in troupes of young dancing boys who "perform" from region to region. Also, Western films are heavily censored by the Afghan government.

We had not been in Herat more than five minutes when a small boy approached us, whispering "Hashish, hashish?" Nodding, we were escorted to his father's tea shop where the elder Afghan bade us relax for a "taste." After a few tokes, we felt our heads lift-off, bound for Allah's Pleasure Gardens. We then bartered briefly, happily shelling out a mere two dollars for fifty grams of moist, black "afghani," freshly harvested from the renowned fields of Afghanistan's northeast. This was cannabis to be cherished, for smoking quality of this caliber is unknown outside of Afghanistan (as precious hash oils tend to dry out in transit).

Later we were strolling with a couple of overlanders, when a mustachioed jack-in-the-box in a jeweled turban came bounding up. The little fellow breathlessly declared that, as manager of the government-operated Tourist Board's new restaurant, he was inviting us for dinner. He pointed to a freshly painted sign which preened, "Enjoy Dining on Typical Afghan Food, in a Typical Afghan Setting, with Typical Afghan Entertainment." Glancing at the posted menu, we asked why the prices, too, were not typical (sixty cents for a full meal instead of the normal thirty cents). Choking with laughter, he sputtered, "Because you are typical tourists!"

We decided to spend that "outrageous" sum as we were curious to hear some live Afghan music. But when I informed the proprietor that we would return after a smoke in our hotel, a look of true anguish crossed his face. Fearing that we would change our minds and he would lose the restaurant's only clientele (for most overlanders would not dream of paying more than the standard prices), he hurriedly entreated, "You come to our kitchen and we all smoke together." So we four Westerners, the manager, and two musicians crammed into a tiny mud hut behind the restaurant, joining a beaming toothless old cook around a huge "hubble-bubble" (hookah).

To our chagrin, the grizzled old man hacked and spat up phlegm before and after each toke. Envisioning TB, we nonetheless took our turn inhaling the harsh substance, not wishing to appear impolite.

The hash was super-potent, so heightening our appetites that we virtually inhaled the shish-kebab dinner that followed. Coming up for air, I met the ever-smiling countenance of one musician whose huge eyes and drooping mustache made him seem a refugee from a Mack Sennett comedy. He plucked a beautifully carved Afghan lute, whose rhythmic sound resembled a cross between a mandolin and a sitar. His accompanist beat a resonant sheepskin drum. The musicians themselves were so stoned that, entranced by their own music, they began to sing and dance. All of us, manager included, rose dizzily to our feet and joined them.

One insane evening! Turned on by the Tourist Board of a government which saw Western longhairs as a "corrupting influence" because they smoked dope!

The primary drawback with smoking potent Afghan hash is that one becomes hungry for everything. Many Western travelers subsequently throw caution to the winds, disastrous in a country where sanitary habits are neither widely practiced nor known. Plenty of overlanders succumb to the ravages of amebic dysentery as a result of their appetite overruling their head. Some, forgetting that hashish is pressed with *both* hands, eat unbaked cannabis fresh from the harvest, and suffer the distressing consequences.

No matter how cautious, however, a traveler cannot completely control the cleanliness of everything ingested. Almost all overlanders, particularly in Afghanistan and India, get a little sick from time to time. Indeed, to pass something solid in Afghanistan may be genuine cause for celebration. Thus the bowel function assumes such inordinate importance that it becomes a leading topic of conversation wherever overlanders gather. Talk about camaraderie of the road!

But we found such dialogue chiefly pragmatic. If someone was ill, it was vital to find out where and what he had been eating. Unfortunately, such advice was not necessarily foolproof: though a cook or waiter might be careful one day, sanitary precautions might be neglected on another.

An arid wind, which gusted irritating grit into our eyes and up our noses, ultimately sent us packing. Since ahead lay a torrid sixteen-hour ride to Kabul, we decided to stop halfway, overnighting in Kandahar, Afghanistan's second largest city. The first leg of the trip was hot and exhausting, the scenery nothing but sand. To add to the tedium, we were treated to the guttural, grating voice of a singing bus driver who droned the same dirge the entire length of the journey. He was accompanied by the discordant, high-pitched chirping of two birds carried by one of the passengers. Every few hours we would take prayer breaks during which the Moslem faithful would leave the bus, face Mecca, and give praise while kneeling on special rugs. I assumed they were beseeching Allah for silence.

At one point, the bus came to a halt in the middle of the most desolate country imaginable. A wild-eyed old man, whose silvery beard extended to his waist, climbed aboard long enough to walk through the aisle collecting money. The passengers dug into their pouches and gave freely. We gathered that he was a wayfaring mystic, a "mullah" who subsisted solely on such contributions. But as we pulled away, another question arose. For as far as the eye could see, there was not a blade of grass, let alone an oasis, camel, or shaded shelter.

"How does he survive?" we asked the Afghan seated in front.

"He is a mullah, and Allah protects him," the tribesman replied.

Riding off, we watched this enigmatic holy man grow smaller and smaller until he became merely a dot on a sea of sand.

We paused at "chai khanas," small teahouses set at distant intervals along the highway, for delightful jasminelike light tea and three-foot-long strips of unleavened Afghan bread called "nan." Though hot food was sometimes available, the oppressive heat and swarming flies put a damper on our appetites. Visions of a frosty cold drink danced before us, but we could hardly hope for refrigeration in the middle of the desert. Then, as if by order, the chai khana's proprietor ushered us over to a covered earthenware cask from which he fished out a cool Coca-Cola.

Although the chai khanas had no restrooms, the men would pile out of the bus, line up facing the vehicle-turned-urinal, and unabashedly relieve themselves on the spot. Alas for the women, not even a tree stood to afford some modicum of modesty. Marzi soon learned that long skirts, instead of pants, were a must on a journey of any length.

At one teahouse we witnessed a peculiar incident. The oasis doubled as a police post with a direct telephone line to Kandahar. A uniformed militia man called one of the chai khana's patrons over to the telephone. Apparently the tribesman had heard of this miraculous talking machine before, but had never used one. The bearded nomad spoke into the earpiece and shrugged his shoulders when unable to hear the reply. Hurling the antiquated receiver at the soldier, the warrior spat and strode away.

Arriving finally in Kandahar, we ambled around the town, finding it not half as interesting as Herat. In the market, a spindly tout spied us and came on with a rush, arms flapping like a chicken, inquiring, "Your bakery, your bakery?"

"Oh, it's my bakery you want," I humored him. "Well, I've only just arrived and haven't had time to set up shop." It finally dawned on me that he was trying to entice us to an enterprise called "Your Bakery."

As we entered the rickety wooden-framed structure, we inhaled an aroma of fresh pies and biscuits. "Aha," exulted the wizened baker behind the counter, "you have come for the 'special cookie.'"

We understood, paid him the equivalent of seven cents, and trotted off to a hotel with two cookies each. One of these sugary hash pastries would have been more than sufficient; the phantasmagoric lights and patterns lasted well into the next morning as we caught the bus for Kabul.

The construction of a much-needed highway from Herat to Kabul was spurred by competition between the two superpowers for political clout in Afghanistan. An uncharacteristically calculating Afghan king asked the United States to foot the bill and provide engineers for the Herat-to-Kandahar stretch while he simultaneously requested Russian aid to finish the job. Today an excellent road links the country's three major cities, cutting traveling time in half.

Riding from Kandahar to Kabul, we felt thrust into a medieval milieu. Between endless reaches of sand, we would sight lonely oases through the glare of a merciless sun. Nomad camps, roughly a dozen squat black tents made from irregularly sewn patches of tattered goat's-hair cloth, were pitched alongside a shallow pond of precious water. Desert palms shaded the pond, their greenery a relief for our sun-sore eyes.

Burnt-ocher fortresses dwarfed the primitive mud huts of permanent settlements situated at the larger oases. To this very day, these earthen-fortress ramparts serve a vital function. Without them, village peasants would be utterly vulnerable to marauding bandits on camelback who still terrorize the people of the Afghan hinterlands. Acknowledging the danger, the American Embassy in Kabul warns travelers to stay off the highways at night, for the Afghan military cannot insure protection from these bands of itinerant thieves.

Since the bus stopped just outside the city limits of Kabul, we had to hail a taxi into town. The coach's most unusual passenger introduced himself, and since he spoke Parsi, generously offered to help us bargain for a reasonable rate. Mustafa was a black Moslem from Nigeria's Hausa tribe, who claimed to have traveled many a time in Islamic western Asia. He warned us to get out of Afghanistan soon, having heard from some soldiers that a counter-coup was imminent. Fortunately, he had been misinformed.

I wanted to ask what inspired and supported his wanderings. But the Nigerian quickly struck a good bargain with a taxi driver and we were off.

Later in Peshawar, Pakistan, the mystery of Mustafa came unraveled. On the front page of an English-language daily was the African's picture. He had been arrested by Pakistani troops and accused of running guns to rebellious Baluchi tribesmen (fighting to make their territory part of Afghanistan). The government prosecutor had asked the death penalty. While I can't say for certain, given the Pakistani concern over "Baluchistan," I assume Mustafa was hanged.

The mile-high city of Kabul is surrounded by protective mountains which glistened almost purple in the twilight. During the fifth century impregnable walls were built around the city to further discourage invasion. Our first day in the capital we were startled by the explosion of a cannon from atop the rugged escarpment. This was the "Noon Gun," we were informed, traditionally fired at midday. During the late nineteenth century prisoners were strapped onto its mammoth muzzle and blasted to smithereens in the savage spirit of the Afghan past.

Kabul is a city of contradictions, a sophisticated diplomatic center newly grafted onto a land where time has stood still. Its fascination lies in this dichotomy, as the following confrontation along ambassador row reveals. Though this recently paved thoroughfare is lined with the cubistic space-age architecture of foreign embassies and residences, we saw a diplomat's limousine vying with a camel caravan for the right of way. Appropriately enough, the camels held their ground.

Seething, sprawling Kabul Bazaar jumps straight from the pages of Kipling. On more than one occasion we were nearly bowled over by overburdened donkeys bearing steaming heaps of manure to market. But caught up in the excitement of nineteenth-century imagery, who could watch where he was stepping? For Kabul Bazaar presented an unending spectacle of turbaned herbalists proffering frothy folk remedies, as well as dexterous jugglers and magicians who captivated their audience. Equally entertaining were the everyday marketeers. Bakers kneading nan into long strips, the delicious aroma of bread fresh from the charcoal ovens; butchers lethargically yet hopelessly shooing flies from slabs of meat hanging on wooden posts. In the craft section we were particularly struck by one dignified old carpenter. While hand-turning a table's spindleleg, he expertly carved a decorative design with a primitive adz clenched in the vise of his feet.

Like Kabul itself, the bazaar affords an amusing glimpse into the bewildering import of modernity. One emporium doing a bang-up business displayed an array of Western-style toilets which would do Halsey Taylor proud. This struck us as odd, for few Kabulians have indoor plumbing. Invited to one middle-class merchant's home, we learned that sit-down toilets have become a real status symbol among upwardly mobile Afghans, for there the shiny porcelain sat, proudly exhibited in the center of the living room!

Browsing through a well-stocked store, we struck up a conversation with a university-educated shopkeeper. This blossomed into a friendship and while in Kabul we visited Ahmed regularly. Trusting our discretion, he discussed Afghanistan's political plight, vehemently criticizing the government.

When I asked Ahmed about the Doud regime's plans to stimulate development in a nation ranked among the three poorest on earth, he spat. "May I remind you that General Doud is our former king's brother-in-law. He is also a Mohammadzais by blood. His clan has ruled my country like a feudal barony for nearly two centuries. When Doud tired of playing second fiddle to the king, he pulled a coup in the name of 'progress.' You ask me about Doud's reforms to date and his promise to transform Afghanistan into an 'oasis of affluence.' Well, the only changes I've seen around here are the expulsion of the hippies and an edict to paint all taxis black. A Mohammadzais is a Mohammadzais and Afghanistan remains in the Dark Ages. But I can assure you, my friend, that one day we will oust the tyrant."

Ahmed's words were not empty rhetoric. He was a sympathizer of the left-wing Khalq political party which came violently to power in an April 1978 coup. General Doud and several prominent Mohammadzais were killed in the uprising. Khalq leaders have vowed to modernize Afghanistan—a Herculean task, as Ahmed had noted.

"Since the postwar UN immunization campaigns, our food supply has been outstripped by our increase in population," Ahmed told us. "Lands which could barely sustain our populace a few decades ago can't possibly provide a subsistence for the numbers we have now."

Was anything being done about family size?

"Well, as we say in Afghanistan, my wife eats the tablet," Ahmed boasted. "But few other women do. Even with all the international health teams giving inoculations, this country is so poor that half the children still die before the age of five. So men feel a need to have many. Besides, the mullahs are opposed to contraception and they are very influential."

"What about those condoms I saw for sale at the market?"

He roared with laughter. "Most people buy those as balloons for their children.

"Ignorance is Afghanistan's gravest problem," he added in a more

53

serious vein. "Ninety per cent of our people cannot read or write. Still worse, did you know that eight out of ten members of our present legislature are illiterate? Now you understand why progress here has been so slow.

"Please keep what I say to yourself," he cautioned. "The situation is still very tight here and those openly critical have difficulties."

Marzi and I only came to realize just how "tight" the political situation was when we later received a letter in Kathmandu from Louis, an adventurous Frenchman we had met earlier in Kabul. He had journeyed from Mozar-i-Sharif to visit a rural village, for as an anthropology student, he was interested in observing traditionalist strongholds. Suspicious troops posted near the hamlet, wondering what sort of European would want to explore such an "untouristic" site, arrested him as a "spy." Louis was sent under armed guard to Kabul, where an embarrassed colonel, trying to salvage some dignity, altered the accusation to "hashish smoker" (a charge that might be leveled at nearly every Afghan male over the age of eight).

During the day, Louis's jailers would break out a huge hubble-bubble and turn him on! At night he was released and put up in a better class of hotel than he had frequented while free. But the bust proved costly; after three days of "incarceration" our Gallic friend was ordered to buy an air ticket to Paris. He was refused permission to fly anywhere in the Orient, for fear that some confused Afghan consul might issue him another visa. Prior to parting, his apologetic keepers, the colonel included, embraced Louis, giving him a going-away present of leather boots. Stitched into their soles was a pound of the finest Afghan hash.

Louis had recommended that we opt for a little greater comfort by spending more than the usual overlanders' thirty cents a night for lodging in Kabul. Yet although we "broke the bank," spending close to a dollar, the "palace" we chose proved deceiving. We awoke covered from head to foot with a "red rash." The itching became unbearable, the symptoms soon metamorphosing into hundreds of individual pustules. Painfully aware that some tiny visitors had spent the night with us, we hurried to see a doctor.

The sight at Kabul's hospital, the premier medical center of the country, was mind-blowing. Flies buzzed in and out, groans pierced the air, and emergency operations were performed behind skimpy cotton screens. The overcrowded facility was apparently the best this poor country could afford. We watched as two fierce-looking brothers drew knives, insisting that they, too, be permitted into the room where their sister was to remove her chaderi for an examination. They intended to make dead certain that no doctor would "take advantage" of her.

Finally a physician saw us and prescribed tranquilizers to minimize that unrelenting impulse to scratch. In a few days the "red plague" disappeared. Luckily, nowhere else did we experience the nightmare of bedbugs.

We moved immediately to another hotel and treated ourselves to the luxury of showers heated by firewood. Hot showers?! I had almost forgotten what they were like. Actually, given the heat up to now, cold water had been perfectly adequate. Kabul's altitude, however, brought some frigid mornings and the hot showers were truly appreciated. Ah, the comforts of home!

Islamic Asia's two most dramatic attractions, the Bamian Valley and the Lakes of Band-i-Amir, lie well off the beaten path. An enterprising Afghan with a minibus sought paying passengers for a tour of this isolated region. We signed on, the alternative being a perilous perch on the roof of a local bus for sixteen grueling hours.

Jolting along unpaved washboard, it took the better part of a day for our van to reach the Bamian Valley. But we were rewarded en route with scenes from an unlikely juxtaposition of stark plains, green wooded valleys, and the saw-toothed mountains of the Hindu Kush. We stopped at chai khanas to savor a delightful tea brewed in huge samovars, while craggy, battle-scarred nomads tied up their camels and paused to relax over hubble-bubbles rented by the teahouse. Several smoked hashish from ornately carved chillums, inhaling so vigorously that flames shot forth from the bowl. Hash smoking remains an integral part of life in this devout Islamic society where alcohol is strictly forbidden by religious law.

As we continued our journey, camps of Kouchi nomads with

their camel caravans and flocks of karakul sheep broke the solitude of arid emptiness. Roughly two and a half million Kouchis still follow the good weather, with only their black goat-rag tents to shelter them from seasonal extremes ranging from scorching sun and blowing sand to freezing cold and gusting snows.

Many Kouchi bands trek better than a thousand miles every year. It is a life for only the fittest. A boy who reaches adulthood (here at age twelve) has his masculinity affirmed by the bequest of a gun. To our surprise, most of the nomadic women wore brightly colored dresses sans veil. Formidable Kouchi warriors, certain no invaders would dare raid their camp, would never stoop to the indignity of enveloping their women behind the chaderi. They view their settled brethren as cowards and Kouchi women are indeed the most independent of all Afghan females. Relatively speaking, I should hasten to add.

The oasis of Bamian consists of little more than a few dozen mud huts, but within easy walking distance stands an awesome sight. Watching over all are two colossal Buddhas carved into red sandstone cliffs. The taller, partially defaced by the invading hordes of Genghis Khan, stands an imposing 172 feet in height. Its companion, designed somewhat curiously with feminine features, rises 113 feet from its base. These gigantic mud statues were created sometime between the second and fifth centuries, when thousands of Buddhist monks lived in what must have been an important religious enclave. Their order resided in a network of caverns hollowed out behind the Buddha.

Carefully climbing the ancient pathways that connect one story of caves with another, we passed religious frescoes painted during Bamian's golden age of Buddhism. A steep, winding footpath took us gasping to the summit, where a narrow causeway linked the cliff's interior with the very crown of the taller Buddha's head. The climb had been well worth the effort. Stepping out onto the head, we beheld a panoramic view of the surrounding valley, whose sandstone red contrasted brilliantly with an undulating green irrigated plain. A multitude of caves pocketed the hillsides, housing poor Bamian peasants. And across the far horizon, the sun reflected desert sands twinkling like stars on a clear night.

We were surprised to note how cool the dried mud walls of Bamian's only budget hotel kept our room during the heat of the day. Its aged innkeeper had quite a reputation among overlanders, and Marzi was not caught unaware. Many unsuspecting female visitors had been invited to enjoy the "best possible view of the Buddhas" from the roof. As his unwary guest would survey the vista, the dirty old man would sneak up stealthily from behind and squeeze her breasts. He is rumored to simultaneously squeal, "Now, do you see the Buddha?"

Seeking greater profits for his journey, our driver turned his vehicle into a public transport. He rounded up any nomads, along with their goats and chickens, who were bound for caravans in the vicinity of Band-i-Amir. The minibus became so congested that some of the passengers chose to ride on the roof. Protesting to no avail, we were no better off than on public transport, yet at several times the cost.

On the periphery of Bamian's settlements, a lorry cut us off, nearly killing all of us, and I caught a flash of the infamous Afghan temper. Overtaking the truck, our minibus repaid the courtesy. Both drivers jammed on the brakes, leaped out of their vehicles, and started swinging at one another. Basically, they fought with their feet, an Afghan martial art that I had seen previously in Herat when two tribesmen settled a difference of opinion in the time-honored way. A large, enthusiastic crowd gathered, cheering on the combatants until the truck driver, bloodied, scurried off in defeat. Our champion strutted back to the minibus, received congratulations from his countrymen, zealously lit his chillum, and roared out of town.

Leaving the fertile vale of the Bamian, we drove for three draining hours through a pitiless wasteland. During a pause to cool down an overheated radiator, I climbed on the roof to see if the contents of our packs were still intact. It could have been worse; only a flashlight had been removed from the exterior zippered pouches. I timidly queried, "All right, which of you took the flashlight?"

The Afghans on the roof howled with laughter. One Goliath proclaimed that he had not stolen it, because he had no use for a "torch." This only served to increase their mirth and I was hardly going to challenge these leathery warriors any further.

Sand, sand, sand! As the van coasted down a small plateau, Marzi and I begged our driver to stop, for we were transfixed by the baffling sight ahead. Framed on three sides by desert and barren bluffs were five bodies of water, turquoise and transparent as the Caribbean. A mirage? No, these were the Lakes of Band-i-Amir. Despite the scorching daytime heat, the waters, flowing from underground streams, were arctic to the touch. The encompassing hillsides, a prism of golds, yellows, and reds, were strikingly reflected in the clear waters below.

The only human inhabitants in the vicinity lived in a small, earthen village that could not have housed more than three dozen residents. They were Mongoloid in appearance, the product of centuries of barbarian invasion.

For overnighting visitors, the sole accommodations consisted of "tent hotels." The proprietor of one of these canvas hostelries offered free sleeping quarters if we promised to take all our meals in his circuslike headquarters tent.

During the evening repast of eggs and potatoes, the corpulent manager with a Charlie Chan mustache provided entertainment, energetically wrestling his beanpole cousin. Just as we were about to turn in for the night, the proprietor called me aside.

"My cousin, he no speak English. He want to sleep with your woman."

"Then who will I sleep with?" I joked.

"With me!" he leered.

Ask a silly question . . .

At Band-i-Amir, it was necessary to don our sweaters for the first time in Asia. Despite several layers of clothing plus the covering of a sleeping bag, our teeth chattered as evening desert temperatures plummeted to freezing. What a contrast to the bake-oven conditions of the day!

Returning to Kabul, our driver confided that he was distraught with the political dictum banning the annual festivities commemorating the king's birthday. The event he would miss in particular was the championship "buzkasi" tournament. The carcass of a newly decapitated goat served as the ball for this rough-and-tumble game of polo contested by two teams numbering upward of a hundred horsemen each. Because there were few restrictions on the players, buzkasi was played ferociously with no holds barred. Death among participants and spectators was not uncommon, for the wildly charging horses smashed into each other at headlong gallops. What more fitting national pastime could there be in this cruel land where only the hardiest survive?

From Kabul, the road leading to the Pakistani border was a prodigious feat of engineering, bisecting breathtaking gorges. We raced blindly around hairpin turns, marveling at torrents of water which cascaded into streams of rapids rushing light-years below.

Our adventures in wild Afghanistan were drawing to a close. Ahead lay the legendary Khyber Pass.

PAKISTAN

Warriors of the Khyber Pass

Pakistan has a horrendous reputation among overlanders. Alarming tales of drug entrapment, baiting by baksheesh-seeking bureaucrats, and infuriating sexual confrontations led us to give this country short shrift. We were wary of even the few days we had to spend in transit through the narrow Pakistani corridor to India. After all, we wished no repeat of Tehran.

At the Pakistani side of the border with Afghanistan, officials scrutinized immunization cards. This was the first such examination since we had entered Asia, and a few foolish Westerners, who having earlier spurned smallpox or cholera vaccinations, were given a choice of returning to Afghanistan or being immunized on the spot. We actually had met several people who boasted that they need not bother getting any shots. This was incredibly stupid, for smallpox and cholera epidemics are commonplace in this part of the world. Their reward for such calculated negligence was inoculation by Pakistani health aides repeatedly wielding the same unsterilized hypodermic syringes. We later learned that some travelers contracted serum hepatitis through these contaminated needles.

Before entering the customs shed, we were surrounded by mobs of men anxiously pushing each other aside, hoping to sell us black-market rupees. That any transaction with these independent money-changers was illicit seemed quite a joke, yet customs officials gave our bags more than a cursory search for illegal currency. Of course, they knew what was going on right outside their door. But later in India we would discover that the luggage check served purposes other than mere lip service to the "law."

To reach Peshawar, the major trade center in the northwestern part of the country, one must first ascend the infamous Khyber Pass, historic scene of bloodcurdling hostilities between turbulent native Pathans and imperial England's foot soldiers. A network of old British fortresses, besieged and twice abandoned to the onslaught of warriors, stood moldering within view as our bus zigzagged its way up through the pass. It took little imagination to conjure up images of bearded, heavily turbaned Pathans drawing a deadly rifle bead as they lay in wait to ambush the retreating redcoats.

Our bus had been driven recklessly enough while on the right side of the road in Afghanistan. Now the myopic driver moved his unwieldy vintage coach over to unaccustomed left-hand drive. We closed our eyes as the bus wheezed to many a sudden stop on sharp switchbacks, halting face to face with oncoming vehicles. No guard rails afforded any protection from a precipitous drop of hundreds of feet over the embankment.

All through the Pass we saw armed tribesmen, some carrying archaic muskets doubtlessly captured by their ancestors during the savage fighting of the last century. Atop the Pass flourishes one of the world's largest illegal gun markets. The ornate weapons sold here are not merely decorative, for blood feuds and smuggling are still a way of life in this region. The bellicose Pathans thumb their noses at central authority, and helpless Pakistani governors have thrown up their hands, in essence conceding the Khyber to the audacious smugglers. We would later be shocked to discover that a one-rupee "road tax" assessed all travelers at the border is in reality "protection money" turned over by the government to the Pathans in order to guarantee safe passage for those crossing the Pass.

Historically, all those entering the Khyber Pass who refused to offer tribute paid with their lives.

Immediately after arriving in Peshawar, we hopped on a tonga headed for the railway station to catch the night train for Lahore. While we waited on the platform, at least a hundred Pakistanis converged to stare at us. They meant no harm, being either curious or eager to practice their English. What made the situation uncomfortable was that this boisterous, milling mob kept pushing closer and closer until they were virtually on top of us.

We would repeatedly see this phenomenon in Pakistan and India. Westerners simply are not an ordinary sight and arouse as much curiosity as "moon men." Furthermore, the Western sense of "personal space" is not shared in these drastically overpopulated regions where it is perfectly acceptable etiquette to eyeball someone from a distance of six inches. My initial reaction to a scrawny Pakistani who thrust his curry-breathed face into mine to gawk was to demand, "Why are you staring at me?"

"I no staring you." He smiled. "I just looking you." I thereafter refrained from anger and in time became accustomed to the vicissitudes of Oriental curiosity.

Finally, the train steamed in and the scene that followed left us aghast. Before we could even pick up our bags to board, a torrent of screaming Pakistanis inundated the platform. They hurled themselves acrobatically through the windows of the train and those unable to fit inside laid siege to the roof. Forget it, there was no way we could or would get on that train. We understood third-class rail in India to be crowded, but this was ridiculous. Standing within any proximity of the car, one could be trampled to death or smothered once inside.

Forlornly watching the train puff off, we had strong doubts about continuing. If Pakistani transport was like this, I could not begin to imagine Indian trains. Just then, the stationmaster appeared. "The evening train is always packed during the pilgrimage season. It connects with another westbound for Mecca. In the morning you can catch the express to Lahore."

"Why didn't you tell us when we bought the tickets?"

He shrugged. "You didn't ask."

The stationmaster pointed out a government hash shop. We declined, having already heard about this ploy to sucker overlanders into buying hash–perfectly legal, followed by a bust for "possession" on the train. The railway detectives made a good living in bribes from this enterprise which they no doubt shared with their friendly agent, the stationmaster.

We returned the next morning with several other overlanders, buying second-class tickets for a few cents more. Greeting us was a porter who, having observed our consternation the previous afternoon, happily announced that this train too would be thronged. Fairly licking his lips, he promised to secure seats for us–for a few rupees, of course.

The train chugged in absolutely empty and few passengers boarded. As we found our own seats, the cagey porter demanded payment. We ignored his pleas for "baksheesh," that all-purpose word for a bribe, gratuity, or charity heard throughout the East. Seeing the train ready to depart, he cried, "Look! I making sure this compartment only for Europeans." We replied that we had nothing against traveling with Pakistanis. Whining "You promised baksheesh" to the very last, he finally leaped to the platform as the train got underway.

The view from the window struck us with incredulity. Green, green, green–how welcome after so many months of seeing nothing but bleached desert and barren mountain. It was as if we were watching an epic black-and-white movie into which someone had suddenly spliced living color.

Adding to the sense of transition, fewer and fewer camels appeared as beasts of burden, replaced by sleek black water buffalo. We passed many a field, watching this creature wallow his huge body in the mud. It was hard to fault his squalid habits, for the humidity in central Pakistan was more oppressive than any we had yet experienced. The drink vendor did record business in our compartment. During the twelve-hour ride, we drank fourteen king-sized bottles of soft drinks apiece, but perspired so profusely that we never even had to empty our bladders.

This part of the country had recently been ravaged by the worst flooding in years. Ten million had been left homeless as twenty thousand square miles were under water. We could see miserable multitudes lining the few roads left intact. The scene resembled newsreel footage of war-torn Europe, the tragic spector of refugees carrying what few belongings they could, fleeing their flooded homes. Some managed to save their Brahmin bulls. These strange-looking creatures with a hump where one would expect shoulders carted entire families on heavily laden wagons down the road to emergency centers set up by the Red Cross and U.S. AID. Thousands of peasants had already starved; many more would die en route.

At one point, the train stopped and four army officers aiding in the evacuation joined us. Purchasing food from insistent vendors outside the window, they amicably invited us to sample some highly seasoned nuts. One soldier spied Marzi, a "southpaw," writing in her diary and jokingly inquired, "And with what hand do you take your food?"

The officers were anxious to discuss their country's problems, pinning the blame for economic misery (including natural disasters) squarely on India. They emphatically related that they felt very pro-American because of the large U.S. contributions of aid for flood relief and, more importantly, U.S. support during the recent war with India. They vowed that there would again come a time when Pakistan would be strong enough to recover Bangladesh and Kashmir, arguing that only a final defeat of India could put the nation back on its feet. In the face of their vehemence, I felt it useless to argue that perhaps there were other national priorities.

The train pulled into a rural junction and a skeletal one-legged girl hobbled aboard. Silently holding out her hand, eyes pleading, she passed me a tattered letter in typescript. "My parents dead from cholera. I have no one. Please feed me." Although I knew pitiable children were hired to beg on a commission basis, this girl was obviously in bad shape. As I dug for a few rupees, one of the soldiers barked an order and she struggled agonizingly out of the coach.

"These beggars are a national disgrace," the officer said, scowling. The train pulled away, leaving her squatting in the dust.

The decaying, thousand-year-old metropolis of Lahore is a bewildering yet intriguing jumble of architecture from the Mogul Empire and the colonial era, intermittently festooned with tumble-down shanties. Wagons drawn by lethargic water buffalo and ponderous Brahmin bulls made headway by mechanized traffic impossible. On more than one occasion, when the streets were hopelessly clogged, our undaunted motorized richshaw drivers took to the sidewalks, scattering panicked pedestrians like tenpins.

In the evenings, Lahore's flickering streetlamps revealed the tragedy of thousands of peasant families who had migrated here in search of El Dorado. Leaving behind worn-out lands which would no longer support their burgeoning numbers, they had come to the city in the hope of making a livelihood. But there is little industry in Lahore and few find employment. Homeless, they chose the streetside for their bed, and from our hotel window we watched the pavement stir with desperate human forms.

Lahore, our first exposure to third-world urban tragedy, was a shocker. No written account can adequately convey its horror. And although we were to see scenes like this repeated in nearly every other Asian and African city we visited, we never really grew accustomed to it.

Finding the black market in Lahore posed no difficulty. There were scores of money-changers standing conveniently right outside the banks! We bargained with one dhoti-clad, hook-nosed man for a while and, dissatisfied with his "final offer," turned to another. The first changer menacingly shoved the second aside, shouting out a better rate. We curtly informed him that we wouldn't deal with someone as nasty as he, even at five times the rate. Hearing this, he went absolutely berserk, screaming and yelling at us and scratching at the face of his competitor. When it became obvious to all that he was spoiling for a fight, a group of Pakistani men intervened, forcibly leading the would-be combatant away and apologizing for his behavior.

We reached an agreement with the second money-changer, a well-dressed young man who said he needed a solid currency for a proposed move to London.' After I wished him well, he startled me by exclaiming, "Thank you, my darling." I would be called "my dear" or "my darling" regularly in Pakistan and India. Was this a bastardized form of colonial-era affectation or merely a misinterpretation of the dialogue in imported films?

Leaving the frenzy of the city's center, we opted for the tranquillity of sumptuous Shalimar Gardens where two Pakistani university students engaged us in conversation. Like most Moslem males in this part of the world, they had sex on the brain and posed the usual question: "Your sister or your wife?" Then, disclosing that Pakistani marriages were customarily arranged by parents, they peppered me with questions concerning Western courtship. "In America, when you see pretty girl you like, you make love right away?"

I shifted the discussion to politics, only to hear yet another scathing diatribe against India.

Out of historical interest we visited the Red Fort, a one-time residence of Shah Jahan. An energetic Pakistani, excitedly bobbing his head up and down, cornered us and introduced himself as Hussein, a hypnotist from Karachi. After escorting us around the grounds our "guide" insisted on treating us to soft drinks and ice cream. Marzi and I glanced at each other thinking: How long will it be before he puts the bite on us? But at the gate to the fort, Hussein bowed and wished us well, stating what pleasure he had showing foreign guests around a national monument.

Such kindness! Maybe in our short stay we had been lucky, for most female overlanders could not get through Pakistan quickly enough, encountering an unremitting onslaught of sexual torment which rivaled even the worst incidents of Tehran. But on the road one's conclusions are usually the sum total of one's experiences. We left Pakistan with generally positive feelings and tremendous compassion for its poverty-stricken millions.

INDIA

Bureaucrats, Beggars, Baksheesh

"Bloody idiots."

"Rip-off artists."

"Untrustworthy bastards."

Even the most sympathetic travelers have applied such expletives to Indians from time to time. A majority of overlanders idealize India as the Ultimate Destination . . . and wind up hating it. Why?

To the impoverished Indian, all Westerners appear conspicuously affluent and foreigners are unceasingly assailed by beggars. The exigencies of survival in India have driven the venerable game of con artistry to new heights—or should I say depths. Be they peddlers, postal employees, bankers, or bureaucrats, the cagiest of the Orient's schemers see Western visitors as a gift from the gods with a bottomless reserve of rupees ready to be plucked like an orange from a tree. They feel no sense of wrongdoing in tricking a traveler out of a few rupees. After all, he won't miss it.

Outraged by nonstop attempts to swindle us in every conceivable manner, yet at the same time trying to empathize with the plight of Indian poverty, we continuously strove to both understand the cause of this aggravation and cope with it. But to say that our tolerance was sorely tried would be an understatement.

Westerners who have never been to India tend to envision it in those stereotypical terms manufactured by "gurus," Hollywood, and the Indian Tourist Board. My own personal notion was distilled from accounts of the pacific revolution for independence led by that "paragon of exemplary tranquillity," Mahatma Gandhi. That is to say, I expected to encounter a spiritual, docile, easygoing populace. I couldn't have been more wrong.

But any explanation for the unrelenting aggressiveness of Indian society cannot be solely rooted in the country's terrible poverty. Afghanistan and Nepal have a poorer overall standard of living, yet in these cultures people relate to each other with a pride and dignity not to be found in India. Indeed, to even begin to understand what I had experienced in the subcontinent, it was necessary to examine its heritage of caste and the legacy of colonialism.

For hundreds of years, Indian society has been torn asunder by the rigidity of the Hindu caste system. At birth, each Indian's role is strictly defined by his family's rank and he is obliged to act in accordance with its prescribed limits. There are more than two thousand castes within the subcontinent, each with its own rules of behavior. These include restrictions on intermarriage, occupation, and physical and sometimes even visual contact. Perched at the top of the ladder, the Brahmins use the lower castes unmercifully, exploiting the products of their labor and their very lives. Each higher caste, in turn, lords its status over those "beneath them."

At the lowest rung of the Hindu hierarchy are the "untouchables," or literally, "outcastes." Roughly one of every ten Indians, a doomed sixty million, is cursed from conception with "untouchability." Because they are denied even the least desirable of jobs, familial survival begets tragedy; we commonly observed children who had been mutilated by their parents in order to appear more pitiable when begging.

British colonialism both reinforced and exacerbated the fragmentation of Indian society by superimposing "class" over caste. Not until the ascension of Gandhi was the caste system seriously questioned. Despite the Indian Parliament's postindependence political gesture of technically outlawing caste barriers, social conditions have changed little since the days of the Raj and caste distinctions are still widely recognized. In a society so divided, any measure of cooperation and efficiency is difficult to find, as members of different castes simply do not work well (if at all) together.

Apart from the mind-numbing poverty, I was most disturbed by the subcontinent's entrenched colonial legacy of class distinction between European and Indian. Since the authoritarian days of the British Raj, Westerners have been defined as "high caste" and many Indians still actually expect Caucasians to treat them as inferiors. Unfortunately, to act with courtesy and consideration only confuses that pattern of behavior so rigorously instilled by the British.

After several irritating encounters, it became apparent that whenever we were patient or soft-spoken, we were either served last or ignored. Only when we raised our voices were we treated with any measure of dignity. Some overlanders came to enjoy playing the sneering, superior colonial and these got along quite well in India. Marzi and I found such behavior an anathema and were often taken advantage of because we refused to perennially wield the imperial swagger stick.

Nowhere in the third world did we find a bureaucratic boondoggle to rival that of India. That the overpadded civil service, requiring at least three men to do the job of one, accomplishes anything is a small miracle indeed. Considering the magnitude of India's problems, this is nothing short of catastrophic. For us, it meant hours, sometimes days, of standing in queues for train reservations, extending our visas, even leaving the country. And since corruption is perhaps more blatant here than anywhere else on the overland route, we readily realized that the only sure path through the bureaucratic morass was the tender of a little baksheesh. Almost any matter, official or otherwise, could be expedited by a bribe. Expedited, that is, after first placating the ego of the petty civil servant in charge. In remembrance of the racism of the Raj, these functionaries delight in throwing roadblocks into a foreigner's path which can only be removed by a proper show of subservience and, of course, baksheesh.

Our personal introduction to Indian bureaucratic corruption

came, appropriately enough, right at the border customs station. Having encountered only male customs inspectors in the Islamic nations, we thought we were playing it smart by hiding in Marzi's bra five hundred black-market rupees, bought in Kabul Bazaar. To our amazement, we were greeted by a stern-eyed inspectress who gave Marzi a voracious frisking. My heart sank as the inspectress haughtily summoned Marzi into a back room. Drawing a curtain, the official pushed at Marzi's blouse, hissing, "I know what you've got in there." Despite her apprehension, Marzi could barely stifle a humorous reply. But humor leaped quickly back to horror when the inquisitor ordered, "All right—put the rupees on the desk and remove your dress." Marzi complied and was the object of so thorough a body search that "intense" would be too light a word.

Standing outside, I miserably paced the floor, envisioning Marzi's certain incarceration in the local equivalent of the "Black Hole of Calcutta." The same nightmarish thought, of course, ran concurrently through Marzi's mind. How naive we were then.

"What do you want to do with this?" gruffly demanded the crusty bureaucrat, pointing at the five 100-rupee notes (ten dollars each) and two one-rupee bills.

"I'd like to keep it," replied a shaking Marzi.

"What *do* you want to do with it?"

Now Marzi was beginning to get the message. She sheepishly offered the two one-rupee notes (worth ten cents apiece). Officials come cheap in this part of the world, but not that cheap.

The bureaucrat threw a near tantrum, stamping her feet and angrily waving the two small bills away. Harshly enunciating each word, she reiterated, "WHAT DO YOU WANT TO DO WITH IT?"

Marzi finally handed over a 100-rupee note. Like a cat pouncing on a mouse, the official snatched the bill and in one motion stuffed it down her sari, adding conspiratorially, "Let's keep this little matter to ourselves."

Surprised to see Marzi return, I was even more startled when the inspectress grabbed my crotch and began to feel around. Traveling in Moslem Asia for the last several months, I had seen few local women's faces, yet here was a female bureaucrat giving my genitals a more intense search than a doctor checking for a hernia. During the next few hours the insatiable inspectress deftly probed a backlog of overlanders, supplementing her income handsomely in the process. Prior to parting, she whispered confidentially to us all, "If you have any more black-market currency or hashish you would like to bring in, just pay me a little baksheesh."

In the border city of Amritsar, Marzi and I hopped aboard a bicycle-powered rickshaw to find a clean hotel we had been told about. The driver transported us clear across town, stopping at a hovel of an inn for local transients. "This one good hotel, sahib." Of course, it was not the hotel we had asked for; he no doubt got a commission for channeling travelers here. We angrily started to get out of the rickshaw but the driver pleadingly promised to take us post-haste to our intended destination.

Under a baking sun, we meandered from one part of town to the other, repeatedly asking the driver if he knew where he was going. His response gradually changed from the affirmative to "Maybe, sure." At length, he pedaled us to another crumbling shanty. "This number-one hotel." Furious, we left the carriage, growing even more irate when he tried to double the fare. We had certainly been taken for a ride!

I refused to pay the driver anything, and as he screamed venomously at us a mob mushroomed from the sidewalks. Immensely amused, some bystanders shouted that we pay nothing; others sided with the driver. Meanwhile the sun beat madly on this sideshow. Desperate to get in some shade, we threw the original fare into the rickshaw and indignantly strode away.

During our stay in India almost every rickshaw driver tried to cheat us in one way or another. But our anger was greatly tempered by the strenuous nature of their occupation and its skimpy rewards. It was agonizing to watch a malnourished driver pedal an entire obese family of wealthier Indians around for sizable distances. I recall the telling instance of being delayed at an overturned garbage can in Amritsar's most affluent district, while our driver sifted through the refuse. Finding a foil-wrapped bouillon cube, he asked what it was. On learning it was edible, he grinned, ecstatic at the discovery of such a treasure.

Amritsar is the home of the holiest shrine of the Sikh people, the Golden Temple. From Kabul to Burma, some of the craftiest businessmen are the hard-driving Sikhs, whose religion, an amalgam of Hinduism and Islam, enables them to operate commercially in areas where merchants of these rival faiths would not be welcome. (I should underscore that the majority of Sikhs, like most of the Indian populace, are very poor.) Forbidden by religious law to cut their hair, Sikh men are distinguished by the huge turban that balloons from their forehead and the colorful sheath into which they roll their beard.

The Sikh Golden Temple rests amid a quagmire of misery. Layered in gold leaf and glittering like the tropical sun through an afternoon haze, the structure is encircled by an enormous stinking pool of stagnant water in which some truly pious pilgrims immerse themselves. Within the shrine, even the poorest Sikh is obliged to offer contributions of either food or money. I found it impossible to reconcile the juxtaposition of this opulent temple with its environs of abject degradation.

To reach the lush valley of the Kashmir, we squeezed into an overcrowded bus whose close-quartered wooden seats and low ceiling were better suited for pygmies. Three hours north of Amritsar, our antiquated transport squealed to a stop behind a long line of traffic. Every passenger sought to discover the source of the delay for himself, simultaneously bolting for the single exit. Arms flailed, elbows punished, fists pummeled, and somehow the bus emptied without loss of life or limb. The rush was certainly uncalled for, as we were destined to remain here for five hours. A drainage dike had burst, flooding a bridge.

Within three hours, the damage was repaired, yet no one could move. Lorries and buses were stacked up for miles on both sides, but the bridge could be crossed by only one vehicle at a time. The only equitable solution was to alternate the movement of transport from either direction. But the soldiers who had mended the dike lay back motionless in their truck, while confused drivers on either side stared blankly across at each other.

At length, a lorry from the opposite end started over the bridge and the traffic behind followed. The vehicles in our line sat passively for two full hours, waiting until the snarl in the opposite lane petered out. No one thought of directing traffic in an alternating pattern; no driver paused to let his opposite through. "Fair play" bore no relation to the "etiquette of survival" in this impoverished society.

Finally our driver started his engine and all passengers tried to enter the tiny door at once. One elderly lady who lost her balance was shoved off the steps. Dazed, she slowly picked herself up, returning to push at the rear of the throng. Nothing warranted this insane grappling, as all seats on this coach were reserved. I initially tried to justify this behavior in terms of a desperate, overcrowded populace groping for a sense of individualized turf, but on seeing it repeatedly throughout India, my tolerance began to wane.

We soon ascended a ribbon road threading some magnificent mountain scenery reminiscent of Vermont. The driving was fast and crazy, and we held our breath as the bus began a sharp descent into the Kashmir Valley. Making a welcome stop at a roadside restaurant, we ordered some curried rice.

I almost broke a tooth on tiny stones camouflaged by the rice kernels. Raw rice in India is often mixed with minuscule pebbles to make it weigh more prior to sale in the market. In the more expensive restaurants, a cook carefully sifts through the grains, but not in budget eateries. What an absurd way to get our minerals!

The spicy curry sauce called for a beverage. Of course, tepid tap water was strictly off limits. Indian tea, famous worldwide, proved surprisingly unpalatable here. Boiled and boiled for hours in huge kettles until harsh, it was usually brewed together with sickeningly sweet, condensed milk.

The only alternative was Coke. Although bottled under international safety standards, the soft drink posed a health hazard in India. Some merchants were experts in removing bottlecaps without leaving any telltale dent. Half the cola was then poured into an empty bottle and both subsequently filled to the brim with tap water, the caps carefully replaced. We had to shake each bottle, hoping to find a satisfactory quotient of fizz. Otherwise, instant amebic dysentery!

We finally entered one of the subcontinent's most fertile regions, the Kashmir. India and Pakistan, chronically short of food, covet the

Kashmir and have often fought for control of this rich vale. On the bus I sat next to an outspoken Kashmiri engineer who cursed the Indian soldiers we saw stationed there.

"The Indians are always condemning colonialism, yet they have treated us no better than a colony. When a more powerful nation robs the fruit of our harvests and gives us nothing in return, that's colonialism, pure and simple. I'm not ecstatic about the Pakistanis either, but at least they are Moslems like us. That's why when the Indian government tries to persuade the world that there's democracy up here and holds a plebiscite, we Kashmiris vote to join Pakistan every time. To tell you the truth, we would prefer independence. We are productive enough to go it alone and it's high time we controlled our own destiny."

Filled with propaganda from the Indian Tourist Board, we looked forward to what we thought would be a romantic interlude on board a houseboat in Srinagar, the Kashmiri capital. Moored on twin lakes, houseboats ranged from luxurious two-story yachts to moldy, decrepit floating shanties. We planned to opt for something in between, a place to relax after a hectic period of overlanding. But arriving at the bus terminal, we were set upon by dozens of touts representing various boats. Though I told them firmly that I already knew where we wanted to stay, several nonetheless collared us and proceeded to take off in opposite directions.

"Sahib, my boat best."

"No, sahib, mine is finest."

Exasperated, I finally used the Hindi expletive "jow" ("fuck off") which served to disperse them. "Jow" regrettably became an integral part of my vocabulary throughout our stay in India. It was not always so effective.

My image of Srinagar stemmed from posters in Amritsar's Indian Tourist Board depicting a translucent Dal Lake in whose reflection shimmered the foothills of the Himalayas. The mountains which encompass the valley are indeed beautiful, but Dal Lake is disgustingly polluted. I tried to forget that dishes from our houseboat's kitchen were washed in that water. Paddling around in a "shikara" (a gondola with a sunroof), we rowed past floating islands of tomatoes, cucumbers, and other vegetables, whose produce was reaped by landless peasants. Their crumbling shacks, a vivid contrast to the tourist area, revealed a squalor surprising in a region so productive. The Kashmiri engineer's bitter commentary echoed in my memory.

Our first morning in Srinagar, we were awakened at five o'clock by a commotion in the living room. There two perfume peddlers were arguing loudly with each other over, we assume, the right to get first crack at us. We ordered them out; no easy matter, for they obstinately swore they had been told we wanted to buy some scent. But no sooner were they out the door than other shikara-borne merchants bombarded us, hawking a profusion of goods from touristy knickknacks to dope. As most wouldn't take "no" for an answer and hovered around screaming sales pitches, I finally got rid of them by inviting them to return that afternoon. We knew the word would spread and naturally we had no intention of being present. Later the keeper of our floating "bazaar" cheerfully informed me that at the appointed hour two dozen salesmen crowded our doorstep. Pandemonium reigned, some merchants being tossed by their rivals into the drink.

There was one insistent hustler I could not turn away so brusquely. Only nine years old, he already had acquired a remarkable rudimentary knowledge of English, French, German, Dutch, and Bengali. His father dead, he helped support a mother and three younger brothers through his precocious enterprising as a tout for a local craftsman. Yet the pennies he earned on commission were insufficient to cover his protruding ribs.

Tired of the tourist bottleneck, we left the commercial trappings of Srinagar in search of the traditional Kashmir. We found it, trekking from the placid village of Pahalgam into the foothills of the Himalayas. At seven thousand feet, no tourist bustle, no choking fumes, no persistent peddlers. Following the switchbacks of a mud trail which linked villages in the hinterlands, we breathed the piny air of evergreen forests and drank from cool, sparkling Himalayan streams. A trio of shepherds engaged our attention in the rolling softness of a mountain meadow. Shearing sheep in preindustrial manner, they locked their squirming lambs in the vise-grip of their knees and carefully trimmed the wool with an elongated scissors.

Late in the afternoon we were drenched in a driving rainstorm. Climbing up a muddy embankment to a wooden shack, we met a stunning Kashmiri peasant woman, who invited us to share the shelter of her roof. She spoke no English, but her disarming smile bade us welcome. Disappearing for a short while, she reemerged bearing freshly roasted corn. We could appreciate this sacrifice, for she doubtless had little food to spare. During our stay in the valley we met other Kashmiris of similar warmth and relaxed hospitality. It would be most difficult to make the transition to teeming, pushy Hindu Delhi, an unpleasant city under any circumstances.

Back in Srinagar, we tried to secure a special discount concession for train connections to Delhi. But it took better than half a day to obtain the appropriate forms from the Office of the Divisional Commercial Superintendent. Once inside his office, the superintendent made us wait and wait, treating us with sneering insolence.

The next morning I joined the rear of a seemingly endless queue for third-class reservations. After a full day of jostling for position with Indians who thought nothing of entering the line in the middle, I finally reached the ticket window only to be told, "Reservations finished." Fellow overlanders had explained what to do in this event. First I returned to the snobbish bureaucrat who granted the concession and woefully pleaded my predicament, groveling within reason. Then I offered a few rupees "to expedite" issuance of a ticket from his "official quota." All this performed, the superintendent, reveling in his authority, initialed a paper approving our reservations. The following day, I staggered for hours in that interminable booking queue to certify confirmation. Utterly exhausted, I was little prepared for the ordeal of Indian third-class rail.

Our reserved sleeping berths were metal planks that folded up during the day. That was fine. I unrolled my sleeping bag and drifted into a deep slumber. Until 3 A.M., that is, when an old man began intoning nasal-soprano prayers, a performance he repeated for the next three hours. At 4 A.M. someone across the aisle turned on a transistor radio full blast, and we were "treated" to the high-pitched screeching of modern Indian music. (Contrary to popular Western conception, the classical music of Ravi Shankar and Ali Akbar Khan is seldom heard in India.)

At 6 A.M. new passengers entered the railway car–and they kept coming and coming and coming and coming! How can I describe the hordes of people who descended upon our car? When the coach was overflowing, another multitude climbed up to the roof. Inside, passengers were wedged onto each other's laps, on every conceivable bit of floor space, even up on the overhead luggage racks. Screaming babies and crowing roosters added to the din. Absolutely unbelievable!

Because the conductor had no room to enter the car, most of the passengers were able to ride without a ticket. Our "reserved seat" quickly became a misnomer. In the ensuing chaos, one mustachioed youth kept crawling onto my lap as he endeavored to force more space for himself. I first asked him politely to move off me and finally resorted to shoving him off the knee that he crushed with his full weight. Even this did not dissuade him. I grew so enraged that I threw a punch, missing his head by at least a foot. Undaunted, he moved onto someone else's lap. I had not struck anyone since boyhood–an indication of the psychological impact of such cramped quarters.

The British built a fine railway system in India, but it was not designed to hold nearly so many passengers. Since the nation is too poor to add any rolling stock, virtually every third-class passenger on major runs endures such conditions. We had to watch our possessions carefully, as many travelers are ripped off in the congested mayhem. I was told of one overlander who, wedged next to the open window of a train entering Calcutta, was victimized when a thief standing on the platform reached inside and yanked off his spectacles!

Originally we had planned to take these trains across northern India to Varanasi (Benares), then north to Nepal. But finally arriving in Delhi and discovering in amazement that our limbs and gear were still intact, we resolved to spend more for a better class of transport. India was the only part of Asia where public transportation proved uncomfortable. (In retrospect, traveling a year later in central Africa, an Indian train would have seemed downright luxurious.)

Western travelers often suffer the hardship of third-class rail and other discomforts because they become absurdly stingy in the Orient. Living miserly becomes a fetish—overlanders are always comparing what they have paid for this and that. Because all prices are relative, it was easy to lose perspective and fall into a pattern of self-denial, especially when one realized how little it actually took to get by.

Haggling induces parsimony. There are usually two ranges of prices quoted in Asia: one for the local and another for the Westerner. In the ethos of bargaining, a customer is seen as a fool if he pays more than the going rate. Most overlanders would therefore refuse out of principle to pay any sum above the acknowledged norm. We, too, overdid it, stupidly rejecting some exquisite articles of indigenous craftsmanship or an extra measure of comfort in order to save the few cents we thought we were being cheated. The inanity of quibbling over pennies hit home only when I returned to the West, spending more for necessities in the course of a day than I had in a week's time in the Orient. I then swore that if I should ever return to the Orient, I would not make things so hard on myself to save next to nothing. But back in Asia the following year, this vow was largely forgotten once I was again seduced by the spirit of bargaining.

Although the old quarter of Delhi was vastly more intriguing than the capital's modern industrial and diplomatic center, it was here that we were exposed for the first time to the heart-rending despair of the Indian city. Delhi, Bombay, Calcutta, and Madras sprout quantitatively the worst urban poverty. Hundreds of thousands of destitute Indians live out their entire lives on the sidewalks, for they have no other home. They are born, eat, defecate, sleep, grow "old," and die along filthy roadways; no facet of their lives is concealed from public view. Their clothes are rags, their water supply the open drain, their will to survive bludgeoned by an aura of hopelessness.

In visible abundance were purposefully mutilated children, whose eye had been plucked out or hand cut off by their parents. Swarms of such wretched urchins with distended bellies stood begging on toothpick legs. In the rare instance when no one else was around, I would give "baksheesh." Otherwise it was impossible, as others would see and haunt us all day.

An almost inexcusable tragedy: in a land where protein is scarce and malnutrition the norm, there exists an estimated three hundred fifty million cows—one for every two Indians. These pampered beasts roam everywhere, tying up traffic on busy boulevards or leaning luxuriously under shade trees. Around them scurry emaciated human street dwellers, wondering how to scare up their next meal.

Since cows are sacred to the Hindu, they are not slaughtered. All that sorely needed protein on the hoof goes to waste, for consumption of beef is illegal in India. Perhaps our most ghastly revelation here was the goodly sum set aside annually by the political order for the feed and lodging of aging cattle! Obviously, the ruling Hindu hierarchy has far more reverence for its cows than its people.

Another terrible absurdity: Delhi's numerous Western beggars. These were primarily French, but there were also quite a few Americans and English. Their clothes in tatters, their bed the street, most had been reduced to a life of panhandling, having spent all their money on easily accessible hard drugs. The outrageous spector of these Westerners cadging rupees among millions born to poverty touched a raw nerve.

Overlanders got a real taste of India's pervasive corruption in banks and post offices. When buying rupees legally in the banks, I came to expect being short-changed. Counting out the money, I would hold my hand in front of the teller who, without changing expression, would ultimately drop a withheld bill into my palm. Happened every time!

Because a stamp would almost assuredly be removed and resold, it was foolish to post anything other than an airgram from India. If a clerk could successfully pocket the proceeds of a few international airmail stamps, he would make the equivalent of his daily wages. Some Westerners were unwitting enough to try sending parcels home. The contents could usually be found the next day on the black market.

I noticed page after page of advertisements for spouses in the local English-language daily. European physical characteristics like light complexions were emphasized in describing prospective brides. This reminded me of the black Caribbean, where one is judged on the basis of "good" (i.e., European) hair, nose, lips, etc. The legacy of racism is universal. In India it adds to the division of caste and class.

The Indian film industry cranks out more movies than any other country in the world. (Some overlanders made a little cash serving as Western "hippy" extras in Bombay-based productions.) One evening we decided to attend a standard three-hour color extravaganza. In the style of a Douglas Fairbanks epic but completely devoid of the flair, there was action aplenty. The good guys and villains were as one-dimensional as comic-strip characters. Whenever the hero was about to kiss the heroine, lips tantalizingly inches apart, they would burst rhapsodically into song.

The audience loved every minute of it, cheering their favorites. During slapstick comedic interludes the theater rocked with laughter—one of the few times I witnessed Indians enjoying themselves with unrestrained gusto. Films of the internationally renowned Bengali director, Satyagit Ray, which depict the brutal realities of Indian life, do not make money in his native land. Not surprisingly, Indian audiences seek the entertainment of escape.

Deciding that third-class trains were for masochists only, we were distraught to discover that first-class rail fare costs virtually as much as an air ticket. (Second class existed only on a few lines and has recently been merged with third.) On a hotel bulletin board, we spotted a sign advertising a bus from London that was looking for passengers. It offered a ride all the way to Kathmandu for ten dollars, the equivalent of third-class fare. The driver planned to stop at the places we hoped to visit en route, so while we had qualms about following someone else's schedule, the bus still seemed like a decent alternative to the agony of Indian trains.

Our first stop was Agra, site of the Taj Mahal. During the seventeenth century the powerful Islamic ruler Shah Jahan resided with his favorite wife, Mumtaz Mahal, in Agra's impressive Red Fort palace. Mumtaz Mahal died in childbirth, and overcome by grief, Shah Jahan ordered the construction of the Taj in memorium. Prior to visiting the Taj, we frankly anticipated some degree of disappointment, for most ballyhooed "wonders of the world" have been oversold. The Taj, however, is the exception – the quintessence of architectural beauty. No prose, poetry, or photograph even remotely captures its essence.

But now, after four hundred years, this majestic homage to romantic love is cruelly threatened. A commercial firm with tremendous political clout plans to construct a cement factory in the vicinity and environmental experts predict its polluted effluence will blacken and eat away the Taj's radiant white marble. Despite considerable international concern, the Indian government has thus far taken no action to protect its most extraordinary monument.

What a contrast is the Taj to the miserable hovels that serve as home for millions of rural Indians. People, people, people, everywhere. Yet the Indian government has recently cut back funds for family planning while spending three billion dollars on atomic-bomb research (more than the government allocates for much-needed housing). Indeed, most of the educated Indians we discussed this with expressed greater interest in their country's new nuclear might than in the prospect of economic reform.

Every time we got off the bus in rural villages, throngs of people gathered around to gawk at the unusual sight of two-dozen Caucasians. Soon the familiar round of questions heard throughout India would commence in earnest. "What is your name?" "What time is it?" "What is the purpose of your visit to India?" When one was satisfied, another Indian who had been listening would step up with the very same questions, followed by yet another until we were ready to scream. We soon learned that these were the only English phrases they knew. Almost any answer, as long as it acknowledged the inquirer, would suffice.

During an overnight stay in a small town, one of our fellow passengers suffering from an acute asthma attack made the mistake of visiting a local doctor. Without taking the patient's medical history, the physician advanced with a syringe. Our friend fled, learning later that this was apparently normal procedure. Accustomed to waves of UN inoculation teams, Indian patients do not believe they are getting their money's worth of care unless they receive an injection. We resolved, thereafter, to seek medical aid only in major cities.

Our bus, carrying twenty-four young Britishers, was commanded by a foppish little tyrant in RAF shorts named Colin and driven by a half-witted, quick-tempered Cockney, Mike. We never managed to see the fabled erotic temples of Khajuraho, as Mike got lost taking a "shortcut." Because the bus had broken down in Turkey for a month, our "leaders" were anxious to make up time. When we reached Varanasi (Benares), India's most fascinating city, Colin wanted to shoot straight on through. The passengers were disgruntled but made no attempt to alter the plan. Marzi and I subsequently spent half the night building enough of a fire under the heretofore intimidated Britons to have them demand en masse the right to spend some time there.

I know it is terrible to generalize, but sometimes it comes in handy. Marzi and I had by now developed stereotypes of various nationalities as overlanders. It was often hard to believe that young British travelers were the descendants of imperialists who built the Empire. They were pleasant and fairly knowledgeable, but so malleable as to be continually pushed around and conned by locals. Those on the bus certainly fell in line with this. Contrarily, the French were by far the rudest, most aggressive and insensitive of travelers. Most cared little for Oriental culture, their primary interest being drugs. Nevertheless, our closest friends on the overland route were French (I know, so much for the logic of generality). Germans were a real mix: some earnest and aware, others brutally pushy—epitomizing the stereotype. Australians and New Zealanders, though not particularly interested in Asiatic culture, were nonetheless plucky adventurers who often dared go far off the beaten path.

American travelers provided the real surprise. I had seen black Caribbean porters ordered around by American tourists acting like plantation owners in the antebellum South. Young Americans were the loudest and most ignorant of travelers in Europe. But the overland route in Asia attracted Yanks who were both culturally aware and interested. They were often so painfully sensitive of the Ugly American image that they would go overboard with caution rather than risk any possible insult to Eastern tradition. Of all overlanders, Americans were generally the best informed. Canadians were virtually indistinguishable from Americans, albeit sometimes more naive.

Colin was incensed that we had "stirred up" his passengers and offered to return our money if we would get off the bus. I declined, and to Colin's chagrin, his charges refused to leave Varanasi until they had a proper look.

Varanasi, India's holiest city, simultaneously repels and intrigues the foreign visitor. It was here that we were most infuriatingly badgered by beggars and con artists. And although the noxious mingle of excrement and charcoal is an odor common to all parts of the subcontinent, in Varanasi the stench of raw sewage is undiluted. It really amused me to think that, back home, the true function of Indian incense had never occurred to me.

Adding to the environmental discomforts, our hotel was simply awful—filthy and encompassed by a malodorous pig wallow. (The only alternative budget lodging had no vacancy.) Evenings, the city was invaded by hordes of little flying bugs that caught in our food, clothing, eyes, and hair. Nonetheless, our endurance of such tribulations was more than rewarded by a tour of this sacred city.

At dawn, we hired an outrigger and paddled down the Ganges. As we sailed along the river bank, our nostrils twitched with the acrid smoke of corpses burning in fiery cremation "ghats." Indian Hindus believe that if a man dies in Benares and his ashes are scattered on the holy Ganges, he will be spared the suffering of another earthly incarnation. Drifting downstream, we observed scores of devotees who bathed in the river's sacred waters while others brushed their teeth, meditated, or shat squatting along the banks. Then, to our horror, we were nearly upended by the carcass of a floating cow.

Returning to the shore, we passed through one of the most

squalid slums imaginable. The sidewalks were littered with bodies. Stepping over some I wondered: sleeping or dead? The luckier inhabitants lived in shacks or cardboard boxes. Mothers with sunken eyes sat in alleys checking their children's hair for lice.

Amid this anguish, self-ordained "holy men" preyed upon the pious pilgrims. Westerners too were targets, for many guru groupies flock to Benares. Thinking us gullible ashramites, a loincloth-clad "fakir," matted hair down his chest, smeared some sacred river mud on Marzi's forehead and held out his hand, asking "Rupees for my blessing."

All day long, we were followed by salesmen peddling beads, flowers, peacock feather fans, noisemakers, and the like. One particularly tenacious merchant hawked flutes, trailing us unsuccessfully for hours, playing the same ear-splitting sequence of notes. At a cluster of temples five miles from central Varanasi where Gautama Buddha preached his first sermon, the tranquillity was shattered by this same flute peddler; he truly earned his "jow."

We crossed the Ganges by ferry at Patna, watchful for the pickpockets who roamed the crowded boat. A few hours from the Nepalese border, the bus completely lost its suspension. Its rear end careening wildly, the coach knocked a rickshaw driver off the road. Colin ordered Mike to drive on without checking to see if the cyclist was all right. We were livid—this was the last straw. It also was the last gasp for the dilapidated bus. Despite Colin's pleading, Mike wisely refused to drive up the steep mountain roads leading to Kathmandu.

Pulling into a "small town" (well, relatively, the countryside is so crowded that even the less "important" towns teem with people), Colin and Mike quickly booked a room in the hamlet's only hotel. The passengers, as usual, were left to fend for themselves. A paunchy, dhoti-clad Indian at the desk announced that he would find us a vacancy. He led all twenty-four passengers up and down the same staircase three times until we called a halt to this charade, as it was perfectly obvious that there were no empty rooms. Then the fat man revealed that he was merely a guest. He opened the door of his room and offered Marzi a share of his bunk, already occupied by his three snoring mates. We trooped off to sleep in the bus.

We were happy to leave the bus, but the passengers who had ridden all the way from London had either packed or purchased too much to carry. They proceeded to hold a riotous impromptu auction to sell their excess socks, underwear, heavy coats, sweaters, bathrobes, and anything else they could no longer use or carry. At least a hundred Indians participated, bidding fast and furiously even for the most useless items. This being the tropics, most of the heavier clothing was unwearable, but because it was Western, it was deemed desirable. How ironic to have the tables reversed: Indians buying souvenirs from Westerners!

En route to the Nepalese border on a local bus, I thought about the few travelers I had met who maintained their zeal for India. Most of them had spent the majority of their time in non-Hindu areas or ashrams. Catholic Goa, the former Portuguese colony, was a popular tropical "beach scene," where Indian tourists flocked by the busload to watch young Westerners swimming nude. "See the hippies," proclaimed Bombay-based tourist agencies. Another favorite spot for travelers was the cool Kulu Valley, basically Moslem like the Kashmir. Dharamasala, home of the Dalai Lama, with a sizable Tibetan populace, also attracted many overlanders.

But Hindu India would sorely strain the tolerance and patience of a saint. A handful of travelers who spent long periods of time there claimed they became accustomed to the constant conning, dearth of dignity, bureaucratic tangle, baksheeshing, and requisite screaming and ordering. Almost as a corollary, they also became inured to the misery.

Some Westerners lived in ashrams, meditating behind walls which shut out the realities of Indian life. Their religious panacea rang particularly false in this setting: true, man may not live "by bread alone," but here it was abundantly clear that he could not live without it. It was difficult to justify the spiritual pilgrimage of sons and daughters of well-to-do Western familes to a land sapped of spirit. Gurus bringing "peace of mind" to the alienated affluent of the West appeared even more suspect after our visit to India. If the gurus truly sought to bring tranquillity to mankind, they would offer their "god-given" teachings to the people most in need of it, their own.

India and China were on the same economic footing in 1948. Thanks to socialist revolution and planning in a culture "right" for it, China has accomplished the momentous task of feeding and bringing a decent standard of living to its people. Until I traveled in the subcontinent, I naively believed that India's hope for salvation lay in the Chinese model. But the fragmentation of Indian culture far transcends the Marxist notion of class. With caste so deeply inscribed on the Indian psyche, revolutionary change on the order of China seems inconceivable.

While an Indian rail strike was being celebrated in Western leftist papers, Marzi and I knew it would come to naught. Members of the lower castes felt no sense of solidarity with one another and their militancy quickly fizzled—exemplary of the political scene in microcosm. Indeed, even the 1977 elections were deceptive, for the political coalition that ousted the Gandhi government is dominated by a status-quo-oriented, ofttimes reactionary, right wing. Thus the future of India appears frighteningly clear: more people, starvation, and misery. Hardly a catalyst for social change, as hungry people think only of their stomachs.

This chapter may seem unduly harsh to those who have never visited India. I have made an effort not to pull any punches, to write without apologia as I saw the subcontinent. I entered India filled with compassion for its poverty-stricken masses, but departed callous and irate. Upon realizing I had actually grown accustomed to stepping over body-strewn sidewalks and barking orders to get something accomplished, I knew it was imperative to leave. Only distance and time would enable me to reevaluate my experiences with greater feeling and understanding.

It had been easy to sit around the university discussing with radicals an all too logical blueprint for social change in impoverished nations. But India taught me that each society is the unique product of hundreds of years of political, economic, and philosophic interaction. "International" ideologies of salvation appear inapplicable to a society where the inequities of caste are so deeply ingrained.

Some travel to India to find their guru, to discover "Truth." More than anyplace else, India forced me to rethink ideals of human potential that I now regard as utopian. What I learned here was invaluable but disturbing ... a profound jarring of illusion that left an acid taste.

NEPAL

Trekking the Himalayas

A visit to the Himalayan kingdom of Nepal is a necessary antidote to the misanthropy induced by exposure to India.

Just across the Indian border stood a striking Nepali woman serenely smoking a hash chillum. No one bothered her as she swayed her hips in time to some sensuous melody inside her head. This woman would become symbolic to me of her easygoing countrymen, for there could be no more marked contrast between two neighboring peoples: the perennially pushy, uptight Indians and the proud, hang-loose inhabitants of the majestic Himalayas.

For centuries, Nepal was a forbidden land, off-limits to outsiders. Finally, in 1951, the gates of the tiny kingdom swung open. From small contingents of adventurous mountaineers, the invasion of globetrotters snowballed into an avalanche. Each pilgrim, while seeking his personal version of Shangri-La, disgorged upon Nepal the neuroses of his own chaotic civilization. But thanks to their lengthy period of political and geographical isolation, the Nepalis have maintained a surprising immunity to Western ways. Today, even in well-touristed Kathmandu, the rich culture of the dignified mountain people remains intact.

Virtually all travelers who arrive in Kathmandu via the subcontinent are moved to ask, "Why is Nepal so different from India? After all, half the Nepalis are Hindus."

Perhaps the Himalayan barrier which has sheltered the kingdom from external influence has also shielded it from the religious decadence which so dehumanizes its giant neighbor to the south. Or it may be that an infusion of ancient animism has softened the strictures of Nepalese Hinduism and Buddhism. Although Hindu caste does exist, its social and economic consequences are not nearly so debilitating as in India. And despite Nepal's diverse mix of faiths and peoples, religious and ethnic tensions seem conspicuously absent.

Little Nepal affirms its independence by setting its clocks ten minutes ahead of Indian time. To extend the metaphor, both in temperament and demeanor, this micro-nation is eons ahead of the subcontinent and perhaps for that matter, the rest of the world. Tolerance, in fact, appears to be the cornerstone of human interaction in this legendary land.

The bus which took us from Birganj, on the border, to Kathmandu, was a vintage 1930s model outfitted with wooden benches which we lined with sleeping bags for greater cushioning. Although the leg room between rows was solely for Lilliputians, the driver packed the coach until the passengers were on intimate terms with each other. We had been on the road only an hour when the Nepali on my left drifted into a deep slumber on my shoulder. After a couple of months in India, this did not take me by surprise, but I was startled by his sincere apology upon being shaken awake.

The bus began its eight-thousand-foot climb prior to descent into the Kathmandu Valley. As we rose in elevation, the sticky humidity dropped completely away, replaced by refreshing mountain air. The distant face of the Himalayan range appeared almost close enough to touch; yet even at our elevation, a substantial portion of its lofty snow caps was enveloped in the clouded heavens. It was as if the mountains teased, "If you really want to be taken by my full beauty, come closer still." That would have to wait, for few peaks are visible from the low-lying valley of Kathmandu.

Even the most jaded of overlanders are smitten by Kathmandu. They come expecting typical third-world urban blight: characterless high-rises ringed by festering shanties. No semblance of planning, no traffic controls, no distinctive identity. Just a chaotic mishmash of the impoverished old and the alien new which is utterly without rhyme or reason.

Kathmandu, however, has retained the charm of its time-worn architecture. Its imposing skyline is uncluttered by hulking steel-and-glass monoliths and its environs are free of depressing cardboard-and-tin hovels. Archaic yet solid stone abodes house the populace. Several families may live under one roof, but they are well protected from the elements. Most of the streets are in reality unpaved lanes, impassable for Kathmandu's few autos but perfect for rickshaws, pushcarts, and (sigh) pedestrians. In sum, this distinctly Nepalese capital strikes one less as a city than a close-knit assemblage of peasant villages.

Living among the awesome Himalayas has long inspired a sense of the divine, and the significance the Nepalis attach to the spiritual is inescapable in Kathmandu. Renting bicycles, it was impossible for us to pedal in any direction for more than five minutes without scenting the tantalizing aroma of joss sticks. As often as not, we would trace the fragrance to some petite, exquisitely carved stone altar, where we would be held spellbound by the intrigue and intensity of solemn ceremonial rites.

Without question, Kathmandu maintains more shrines per acre than any other Eastern city. Yet its temples are not outlandishly opulent; they appropriately mirror the simplicity of life at the roof of the world. In fact, daily life is played out within the temple walls. Children frolic and women sew among statues of animist deities dating from long before the coming of the Buddha.

As we approached a shrine in a plaza of temples, Marzi and I suddenly had a chilling suspicion that someone, or something, was spying on us. Sure enough. From high atop a rectangular watchtower, hawkish eyes painted on all four sides scrutinized the behavior of Nepalese Buddhists—and us. A massive rotunda at the base of the tower was reputed to retain some fragment of the Buddha's body. These immense "stupas" are found in other Asian societies, but nowhere are they as impressive as in Nepal. Although the holy master has bequeathed stupas with all-seeing eyes, we could well understand why he charitably denied them a nose.

Kathmandu literally ranks as the world's dirtiest city. Given the absence of a sewage system through much of the town, streets function as the municipal outhouse. I always wore shoes rather than my usual sandals in Kathmandu, as (particularly after a rain) it was difficult to discern whether one was stepping in mud or excreta. I remember climbing one temple's staircase for a better view of a religious shrine, only to catch a whiff of an all-too-familiar stench. Looking down, I observed a queue of men waiting in turn to anoint the temple's wall. I imagined this to be a strange rite of sanctification—the Nepalese counterpart of baptism.

Nonetheless, the city's unique atmosphere and congenial residents soon muted such sights and smells. After a while I became acclimated and managed to tune out the unpleasant superficialities—something I was never able to do in India, where I noticed every aspect of filth.

Although Nepal stands with Haiti as the two poorest nations on earth, the Nepalis are too proud to beg (the only cadgers I saw in Kathmandu were Indians). Even the most malnourished Nepali in tattered rags displayed an unshakable sense of self-worth extraordinary under the circumstances. Competition and conspicuous consumption have only recently been introduced into this harsh mountainous environment where an ancient code of honor and respect holds sway.

Our guest house was a popular haven for rurally based Peace Corps volunteers on leave in Kathmandu. We struck up a friendship with Ken and Paula, a New England couple in their late twenties, who served as a public-health team in a Sherpa village. Nepal is considered a hardship post for Peace Corps stationed outside Kathmandu; no electricity, telecommunications, or medical facilities in the hinterlands. When we met, Ken was recovering from injuries sustained in a fall. He had been carried in agonizing pain for three days by Sherpa stretcher-bearers down a treacherous footpath from his mountain village to the nearest road.

Ken and Paula had decided to extend their work in the village a third year, for the volunteers felt they were accomplishing a good deal in the way of preventive health. But one "malady" they couldn't prevent was pregnancy, as this telling anecdote reveals.

"We felt ensnared in a vicious circle," Paula related. "For some time, health units like ours had been helping to reduce infant mortality. But with more mouths to feed, the peasants' terraces no longer produced enough food. So families started clearing vegetation for new fields, which in mountainous terrain is disastrous. When the rains came, the soils washed away.

"The only logical solution seemed to be family planning. Fortunately, the village elders gave us their blessing and we proceeded to wrangle birth-control pills from AID. But we should have known that foisting pills to be taken daily upon illiterate village women was doomed from the beginning.

"Then Ken hit upon a brainstorm. Since every family knows how to use an abacus, he thought, why not distribute some arranged according to a woman's fertility cycle? Each day on the cycle would be represented by a colored bead. We planned green beads for 'go ahead' days and red beads to signify abstinence.

"Well it seemed like a good idea ... but turned into a total fiasco. When husbands wanted to make love on 'red days,' they simply pulled down a green bead!"

We were lucky to be in Nepal for "Diwali," the Festival of Lights. Throughout Kathmandu, bazaars bleated and baa-ed with thousands of goats and lambs, many imported from Chinese Tibet. Meanwhile, priests supervised the painting of the city's hundreds of religious shrines. Beneath the multitiered umbrella-roofed pagodas of Durbar Square, the spiritual heart of Kathmandu, the grotesque rock-carved image of Hanuman, the ferocious monkey god, was splashed in hideous hues, its canine teeth inflamed with monstrous menace awaiting the mayhem to come.

At neighborhood temples as well as the Hanuman Dhoka, holy

men accepted animal offerings from the devout. We trembled in anticipation alongside the sinister shrine of the monkey god, watching a priest corral a terrified lamb that sensed a violent end at hand. While the struggling animal thrashed, his executioner reached for a gleaming ceremonial knife and deftly slit the jugular. The priest held the still-kicking carcass over the voracious mouth for the stone simian to drink, great clots of blood gushing from the artery, splattering the sacrosanct altar.

Queasy at first, Marzi and I passed by so many scenes of slaughter that we thought we had grown inured to the carnage. We were quite unprepared for the grisly climax of Nepalese Diwali.

About to enter our hotel, we were swept into a sea of festive Nepalis hell-bent for Durbar Square. There we squeezed into a crowd in the courtyard of a great pagoda where thousands of revelers had turned out for the royal ceremonies. The Nepalese Parliament stood at attention while quarter-ton water buffalo were led before a shirtless, barrel-chested muscleman. Gripped by an electric tension, the crowd lapsed into a deadly silence. Buffalo tethered helplessly before him, the Gurkha strongman raised his razor-sharp khukuri sword. With one clean blow, the royal butcher cleaved head from massive body. The crowd roared.

As blood from the severed head spurted into a sacred vessel, three of the king's ministers daubed their right hand into the brackish fluids and, to the fanfare of royal buglers, swathed a crimson stain upon the flag of Nepal. This ceremony was repeated after each of some two-dozen decapitations.

Despite appearances, Diwali is hardly a celebration of savagery. Sacrificed to insure the favor of the gods in the year to come, these animals provide the only taste of flesh many Nepalis will enjoy in the course of a year. In a populace so bereft of protein, this is most appreciated and one may draw an analogy of sorts to our Thanksgiving. Incidentally, meat from the royal buffalo is divided among the citizenry, making the festival of Diwali truly a feast.

A few Westerners who had been in Kathmandu before were surprised to find the hash shops closed. Under pressure from Nixon and Willy Brandt, King Birendra had ordered these government establishments shut down. Nonetheless, grass and hash were still cheap and easily accessible throughout Nepal. One astute Nepali provided a big bucket of grass free in the center of his restaurant. Patrons would sample the powerful cannabis, thereby increasing their appetite and intake of the establishment's cookery.

For overlanders recovering from the ofttimes inedibly seasoned curries of India, Kathmandu was a real foodfest. Some Peace Corps and other Westerners have taught shrewd local entrepreneurs to cater to travelers' tastes and, for a few cents, one can dine on everything from water-buffalo cheeseburgers ("buff burgers") to chocolate cake to enchiladas. While I truly enjoyed a change of diet to Western dishes after months of local cuisine, I was also painfully aware of the damage so much Western influence may eventually have on Nepal.

The King is pushing for still more tourism and delayed his coronation until a new luxury hotel could be completed. Japanese businessmen have already constructed a plush lodge (fifty dollars per person a night) at the foot of Mount Everest, replete with oxygen masks. Isolated for so long, Nepalese culture has thus far shown resilience in the face of its numerous visitors (most of whom fly in). But how long will it be until the material "bounties" of Western life are construed as a better way?

Plastered everywhere in Kathmandu are laughable posters of King Birendra. Dressed in a comical cape, he looks like a chubby, bespectacled Clark Kent in ill-fitting Superman garb. Although educated at Eton and Harvard, the young Birendra maintains the mystique among his subjects that hereditary Nepalese monarchs are gods, the reincarnations of Vishnu.

Sandwiched between India (which would, for "strategic reasons," like to annex Nepal) and China, the King must walk a political tightrope to maintain Nepalese independence. Under the circumstances, he has done well in international diplomacy. Birendra's domestic policy, however, is a tragic dud consisting of mere rhetoric. Admittedly, with little in the way of natural resources, the monarch does not have much revenue to bring a better life to his people. Yet he seems to have made next to no effort. Sanitation is terrible, the vast majority of the populace illiterate, and malnutrition (and related diseases) takes a fearful toll. Nonetheless, the king is revered as sacred by his countrymen, and within Nepal religion is paramount.

On the outskirts of Kathmandu, we visited a Tibetan refugee camp. This village was established by the Nepalese and Swiss governments for those who fled their homeland when Tibet was declared an integral part of China. Sitting in my academic womb, I had sympathized with the Chinese action. Poverty-stricken Tibetans had historically toiled under semifeudal conditions. Their leader, the Dalai Lama, appeared to be little more than a spiritual despot. Furthermore, after seeing the pernicious influences of organized religion in India, Latin America, and the Moslem world, I harbored little sympathy for supporters of a theocracy.

All such conclusions evaporated after spending some time in the Tibetan camp. My change of heart was not prompted by any political discussion nor could it in any sense be characterized as "intellectual." I do not mean to be jargonistic but the vibrations of the Tibetans were quite unlike any other unspoken form of communication encountered before. The perpetual bliss etched on their faces, far deeper than mere surface emotion, reflected something very special about these people—a "presence" even a skeptic like myself had to acknowledge. My wariness of what I could not rationalize in intellectual terms utterly collapsed in the refugee camp. While I believe that the majority of Tibetans are better off materially under Chinese rule, I now must question the trade-off: the loss of that intangible sense of inner serenity still found in a few small refugee settlements outside of Tibet.

The Himalayas seduce—wondrous peaks generating a magnetism impossible to ignore. Having seen them from afar, the viewer feels compelled to become one with them. The ego is jolted when one gazes at those colossi of stone and realizes just how insignificant he really is. I suspect that is why some climb the Himalayas, to reaffirm their egos—their "superiority" over nature. Others seek the fulfillment of unity with natural forces that only a trek into the Himalayas can convey.

95

Although the hike to the Mount Everest base camp is the most popular excursion for visitors, our Peace Corps friends convinced us that more majestic vistas lay in store for trekkers threading the Annapurna Range on the fabled Jomoson Trail. To reach the trailhead, we embarked upon a full day's bus ride to the central mountain town of Pokhara. Snaking along a ravine of the Trisuli River, the new Chinese-built highway was bounded by a steep vertical wall of craggy shale which spewed chunks of rock in our midst.

About halfway to Pokhara, one slide reached near-avalanche proportions, obstructing our passage. Just when it looked as if the bus would have to return to Kathmandu, a crew of peasants emerged from between the crevices and energetically cleared the way. This would happen at least a half-dozen times en route, and I came to appreciate the vigilance with which these industrious villagers maintained their road. They were proud of it, for prior to its construction in the sixties, Kathmandu Bazaar was an arduous and time-consuming trek through high valleys.

Pokhara marked the road's end. Venturing on foot further west into the Himalayas led one into a world apart—the legendary land of the yak and yeti. Primed for the experience, Marzi and I were ready to strike off toward the Tibetan frontier, when unseasonably heavy rains poured down, delaying our start. Looking up dejectedly, all we could see was a swamp of grim clouds concealing the glaciered giants of Annapurna. The chill rain continued for three days, placing a damper on our spirits. Then at last we awoke to behold everything we had expected ... and more. There they stood, the imperious diamond peaks of Dhaulagiri, Machapuchare, and the three Annapurnas, piercing through a soft bed of cloud to dwarf all else in view. Inspired, we hoisted our packs and ascended.

On the slippery trails of the lower reaches, the land is lush, the people poor but reasonably healthy. Outside the clusters of clay huts, brilliant hibiscus emblazoned the pastoral green with dollops of crimson. Above loomed the snow-cone summit of 25,000-foot Machapuchare, revered by the Nepalis as a benign protector.

We lodged in a stone hut erected for trekkers and visiting officials. Laughing children tumbled at our feet, curious yet unafraid, while their hospitable elders made us feel at home. The warmth of these villagers almost anchored us here, but after a few days the Himalayas beckoned.

Back on the trail, I stopped to inspect a blister on my foot and, unlacing the boot, felt something disturbingly damp. Blood! At first I thought a sharp stone had penetrated the sole of my shoe, but it was something far more vile. At the spur of my heel sucked a brown-black two-inch leech, bloated with my blood. I knew that to pull the leech off was unthinkable, for it could cause infection. Marzi reminded me that table salt was said to do the trick. But dousing the disgusting creature with salt didn't help at all. It simply refused to come unhinged; in nauseating frustration, I prepared to wait until it had drunk its fill and fell off.

Then I remembered a scene from *The Bridge On The River Kwai* in which William Holden burned the buggers off with a cigarette butt. Bravo—chalk up another one for Hollywood! In vengeance, I cut the loathsome leech in two, whereupon each segment crawled away, no doubt lusting for new victims.

Thankfully, as we climbed to higher elevations, the leeches disappeared. The once gentle terrain grew starker, the vegetation all but vanishing into hills of flinty scree. Up and down wound the worn path of centuries' foot travel, becoming increasingly precipitous. We didn't mind the going up so much as the going down, for our weak sinews were strangers to such stress and our uncallused toes, which had known only the freedom of sandals for months, were now thrust cruelly against the abrasive leather tips of our boots. Yet we hardly complained, for the astounding Himalayan scapes more than made up for the rigors of our trek.

Every step further up the Jomoson seems to bring out more remarkable detail and color from the constantly changing vistas. The pressure of the altitude coupled with the grandeur of the environment and the crispness of the pure alpine air creates an intoxicating sensation. We became stoned simply by breathing. The gestalt is unbelievable. A natural high!

"Namaste," barefoot Sherpas greeted us as we trekked. They exhibited their vaunted agility and strength, somehow bearing loads weighing upward of a hundred pounds on their backs, held secure by a strap which bit 'deeply into their foreheads. Vertigo-stricken, Marzi and I crossed bridges of swaying bamboo vines on all fours; sure-footed Sherpas toting heavy burdens waltzed across with the assurance of a Wallenda. Once we scurried to the edge of the trail to make room for four wiry mountain men. Carrying on their shoulders an aged holy woman enthroned on a finely carved settee, they told us they had been descending for nearly a week on a pilgrimage to a sacred shrine! What stamina!

We arrived late one afternoon at a village teahouse where affluent, porter-assisted hikers sat drinking two-dollar Coca-Colas cooled by a kerosene icebox. The refrigerator and the Cokes had been hauled up here by Sherpas at the behest of a crafty innkeeper who was making a fortune from the few pampered parties who broke their journeys here. We watched Americans and Germans carelessly toss their imperishable refuse out the door. I could just hear them returning home with their tales of "unspoiled Himalayas."

Treating ourselves to a stay in this unusually plush way station, we were torn from slumber about midnight by the excited voices of the tourists. Creeping outside to see what all the excitement was about, we were greeted by an unforgettable sight. On the clearest night in memory, stars luminous against jet-black sky, a full moon beamed over glistening snow peaks as we were enveloped by the entire Annapurna Range. A surreal super-planetarium! I motioned Marzi away from the village and into the welcome solitude of the trail, for this was a spectacle to share only with someone special.

The beauty of the Himalayas lies not merely in the mountains themselves. Hardy peasants terrace these penurious environs for a subsistence, yet they betray neither animosity nor envy toward the more affluent Western visitor. Sherpa homes stand two stories high, constructed of fitted stone with gracefully sloping slate gray roofs. Firewood, fodder, tools, and livestock are stored on the ground floor, while the entire family squeezes into a single room on the upper story warmed by a cheery hearth. The Sherpa's most important domestic animal is the hairy yak, which, in addition to being a beast of burden, is a source of wool and leather for clothing, milk and meat for food, and dung for fuel. In a region of few trees, the ripe aroma of dung cooking cakes always let us know on the trail when a village was close at hand.

It was not only the friendliness extended to us in these mountain hamlets, but the respectful, relaxed manner in which Nepalis related to each other that were most impressive. Though their environment is one of the toughest to be found anywhere, the Sherpa endures with dignity. Nepal is hardly the eden of *Lost Horizon;* infant mortality is high, the life span short. In the rocky terrain above the tree line, cultivators are hard-pressed to provide enough for all. But while UN statistics show Nepalese peasants to be among the poorest people on earth, there should be another yardstick for measuring wealth beyond the material.

At the last village on our trek, we watched children gleefully riding hand-pushed wooden ferris wheels set against the awesome backdrop of Annapurna. A wandering band of minstrels stopped by and were invited to drink "chang," the strong home brew from fermented potatoes which tastes somewhat like sweet beer. Then the itinerant musicians played their elaborately decorated string instruments, accompanied by the villagers singing haunting traditional verse. As the final strains faded into the valley below, backs to the mountains, we began our descent to that other world of material comfort, competition, and crowded anonymity.

BURMA

Smugglers' Nirvana

Although we had originally planned to go no further east than India, our experiences in Nepal proved so intriguing that we felt compelled to visit Southeast Asia. Realizing how rewarding and inexpenseive overland travel could be, and how much of the world we had yet to explore, to return home now was unthinkable.

Still ridiculously close-fisted, we chose to fly the Union of Burma Airlines from Kathmandu to Rangoon because it offered a savings of five dollars over other carriers. The "meal" served inflight revealed how that fly-by-night airline made up the difference: a bread-and-butter sandwich and a smashed banana. Nonetheless, our ascent from Kathmandu more than compensated for any culinary quirks. As we approached twenty thousand feet, the breathtaking peaks of the highest Himalayas could still be seen soaring way above us—what an intoxicating sensation from the windows of an airborne plane.

The Burmese government had forbidden entrance or exit by land transport across its borders, leaving us no choice but to fly into the capital, Rangoon. Not that we would have opted for overlanding either frontier even if permitted, for anyone venturing within Burma's unpacified extremities would be exposed to considerable risk. In the steamy lowlands near Bangladesh, a bloody insurrection led by pro-secessionist tribal forces flares. Concurrently on the eastern frontier, a secret struggle over opium perpetuates the strife of several decades in a region infamously known as the Golden Triangle. Here, at the remote, rain-forested confluence of Burma, Thailand, and Laos, Burmese national troops have been waging a seemingly endless guerrilla campaign against a formidable remnant of Kuomintang regulars. The prize for the victor: control of Burma's lucrative narcotics trade.

Burma was an unknown entity on our itinerary. Because foreigners could only obtain seven-day visas, few travelers disembarked here. Most flew directly on to Bangkok. Just two years prior to our visit, tourists were allowed no more than a twenty-four-hour stopover in Rangoon. I knew that Burma was politically xenophobic, not wishing to have much contact with the outside world. But as travelers interested in traditional societies, Marzi and I would profit from this minimal exposure to the West, for Burma's self-imposed hibernation has preserved a culture largely unscathed by external influences.

Burma would have proven prohibitively expensive for budget overlanders like ourselves were it not for the most incredible black-market exchange rates to be found this side of Uganda. Because Burmese currency is next to worthless in international trade, travelers who bartered with money dealers in India or Thailand rather than changing at the offical bank rate in Rangoon could increase their dollar's purchasing power of "kyat" at least fourfold. Certainly such exchanges were illicit, but they made Burma accessible for the most impecunious traveler. Any moral qualms we initially harbored were blown away inside Burma, where we saw the black market function openly as an astoundingly integral part of everyday transactions.

After our near-disastrous encounter with the Indian customs inspectress, we weren't about to gamble and smuggle kyats into

Rangoon. Instead, we took fellow travelers' advice, purchasing our legal allotment of an imperial quart of liquor and a carton of European cigarettes. The airport's immigration captain, eyeing our duty-free goods, grinned knowingly: "You'll find the best market for those at the 'Y.' "

And indeed we did. At the entrance to the YMCA we were immediately surrounded by a bevy of Burmese students who proceeded to hold an auction for the rights to our imported treasures. Bidding a price several times higher than our original investment, a young wheeler-dealer sped off to the bazaar to unload his valuable cargo for an even greater return.

"Blood" spattered the sidewalks of Rangoon. We initially imagined some terrible accident, until I remembered seeing a similar stain on the streets of Delhi. Burmese must chew more betal nut per capita than any other nationality, as red spittle paints the pavement everywhere. "Pan," as it is called in this part of the world, is a mild narcotic which, after prolonged years of chewing, rots the teeth black. This hideous habit was countered by the allure of native Burmese dress. Both men and women wore delightful form-clinging sarongs, or "longyis," as the male wrap-arounds are called here. Made of light, bright cotton, they were both colorful and completely compatible with Southeast Asia's sultry climes.

The ancient Shwe Dagon Pagoda, whose bell-shaped, gold-leaf spire stands 368 feet over the city, is the only distinctive feature of decrepit Rangoon. In a perpetual state of disrepair since the Second World War, its crumbling colonial manors dwarf stucco shacks on pot-holed streets. This is an apt reflection of the declining Burmese economy under the sixteen-year reign of its military governors.

Burmese isolation from the rest of the world has been costly. True, the country has remained distinctly Burmese—this is the only country I have ever visited where there is no Coca-Cola. But mismanagement by the corrupt military regime and insufficient production of necessary mechanized equipment (difficult to import due to tariff restrictions and little foreign exchange) have led to industrial stagnation and overall economic shambles.

The monocled, silver-haired stationmaster who booked our reservations for Mandalay, though understandably reluctant to criticize the current bureaucracy, nonetheless spoke nostalgically of the past. Like so many men in privileged positions we had encountered in India and Pakistan, he pined for the "good old days" of the British Raj, when everything "ran like clockwork," lazy workers were "promptly terminated," and inept officials "cashiered."

We counted out our considerable surplus of black-market kyats, worthless outside of Burma and impossible to redeem, and decided to treat ourselves to first-class fare. As the train started to roll, our fellow Burmese passengers bolted the doors and windows of our compartment. When I asked why, they warned me of the thieves who lurked in the dark of the night at local junctions or switching points. As the train slowed, the thugs would pounce through any open windows, heave out a drowsing passenger's luggage and quickly disappear into the thick teak forests.

Our Burmese traveling companions, hungry for news of the outside world, eagerly asked us about our country. Although they lived under an authoritarian government, these Burmese and others we would meet were most open in their complaints of present-day inefficiencies. But when I inquired if there existed any organized political opposition, they sadly shrugged their shoulders.

At one stop an elderly, buttery-faced Burmese with a full set of gold teeth bought us some food wrapped in a banana leaf from a vendor outside our window. It was a delicious spicy mix of chicken and rice, "panthy khowsey." The other passengers purchased prawns and crayfish so highly peppered that they glowed infra-red. A whistle blew and we had no time to buy a beverage to cool our mouths. Noting our distress, our seat mate thoughtfully poured cups of tea from his flask.

A family in the coach had packed their own supper in an ingenious multipan container held together with a metal skewer that ran through the center of each round receptacle. One compartment would hold tea, another rice, a third fish, a fourth sauce, etc. The family thereby partook of a five-course home-cooked meal.

The train chugged lazily alongside lush paddy fields, bounded by dense tropical forests. At least Burma has no food-staple shortage, maintaining a high enough rice yield to feed its populace. For the first time since Istanbul, we saw no sign of malnutrition, though some undoubtedly exists in the hinterlands. But while most have an adequate diet, the Burmese peasantry could hardly be called prosperous.

Shortly after the breaking of the dawn, we could see many peasants wading or fishing in the flooded paddies adjacent to bamboo homes raised by pencil-thin stilts over the water. Although they didn't have much in the way of material goods, each family had its own private fish pond and swimming hole. The irrigated yards also functioned as baths. Peering into this green serenity, one could spy modest young women pulling sarongs up over their breasts and pouring water over their lustrous black hair.

In contrast to the countryside, dusty Mandalay simply did not live up to the exotic Hope-Crosby "road picture" image. At least not during the day. The streets were near deserted. We wandered in and out of the town's wooden frame stores. No customers. Clerks sat idly fanning themselves, listening to radios. We found one salesman stretched across his counter, snoring contentedly. Strange.

For a city of better than a quarter-million inhabitants and the commercial capital of central Burma, Mandalay was incomprehensibly quiet. Downright dead. We speculated. Certainly there were no suburban markets to lure away all the shoppers. Nor were we here on any national or religious holiday.

Marzi and I knew that after strongman Ne Win and his military cronies seized power in 1962, they declared Burma a "socialist state" and nationalized the country's factories and stores. Only the government shops were authorized to sell consumer products. "So"—I gesticulated to the empty storefronts—"where are all your shoppers? What the hell is going on?"

As the sun went down, the feverish glow of a thousand kerosene lamps illuminated a town suddenly sprung to life. Once-empty avenues sprouted umbrella-topped tables crammed with merchandise ranging from aspirins to zippers. Impassioned bargain hunters milled about, haggling boisterously. Food vendors peddled rice cakes and sweets on every corner. A troupe of jesters performed. Incredulous, we watched all Mandalay being transformed into a gigantic flea market, and an illegal one at that.

Browsing at a display of watches from Japan, pharmaceuticals from China, and American cosmetics, we recognized its salesman as the Burmese who had treated us on the train. About to say hello, we were held in check by the determined approach of a square-shouldered soldier, who strode up to the elderly gent and began a heated discussion with him. We figured the merchant had seen his last daylight, that he was about to be busted for selling goods unlawfully.

Suddenly, seeing us staring at him, the salesman flashed a smile of recognition and affably waved us over. He then introduced us to "My son, the captain."

After some small talk, Marzi's inquisitiveness got the better of her. She blurted out, "I thought by law only government shops could sell merchandise like this."

Father and son exchanged amused expressions. "Yes," the old man admitted slyly with a twinkle in his eye, "that is the law."

Since neither of them seemed reluctant to discuss the matter, I continued: "Won't you get in trouble for selling here? Why don't the people shop at the government stores? Can't they be arrested for buying from you?"

The captain patiently explained: "After being taken over by the government, the factories didn't turn out enough goods and the quality of what they did manufacture was poor. The situation got even worse when inflation upped prices beyond most people's means. So out of necessity, we started importing from Thailand the merchandise you see here."

"Do you mean 'import,' or 'smuggle,'" I countered, surprising myself with uncharacteristic bravado.

The merchant cheerily responded, "In Burma, we say 'import.' How else do you think we could meet our people's needs?"

"And the authorities don't interfere?"

"Never. If they even tried, I'm certain there would be a full-scale riot. All of Burma would be upset—there are markets like this one, smaller but similar, in almost every town. In any event, the authorities are hardly going to slit their own financial throats."

"What do you mean?" I asked, a little slow on the uptake.

"Since the army came to power in Burma, many officers have invested heavily in the 'import' business. You see, Burma is a poor country and even our leaders' salaries could use a boost." Father and son laughed.

As customers converged, we said good-bye, leaving with the distinct impression that the captain had put his father in business.

Apparently what may well be the world's biggest black market still isn't sufficiently stocked to satisfy Burma's demand for consumer basics. On the street, in restaurants, in the foyers of hotels, Burmese would cordially draw us aside and, pointing to my shirt or Marzi's dress, request in stage whispers, "You sell shirt, dress, have soap, lipstick, jockey shorts? I give you many kyat." But nothing we owned brought as much attention as our blue jeans.

A worldwide phenomenon, blue jeans were in great demand here and everywhere else in Asia. The heavy cotton denim was hardly suited for Burma's sticky humidity. Nonetheless, isolated Burmese youth had for years heard via the international grapevine about the "mystique" attached to jeans, and they became one of the most sought-after commodities on the black market.

Monstrous white-stone effigies of mythical lion-dragons serve as watchdogs to deter the forces of evil from climbing the seventeen hundred steps of Mandalay Hill. I wish they had deterred us. Despite the awful humidity and a nondescript series of sculpted shrines, we dragged ourselves ever upward, spurred on by the "must see" ravings of a guidebook. Like a highly hyped movie which disappoints, we stuck with it, thinking this has got to get better.

As we ascended, I noticed that the once-standing statues of the Buddha had given way to sitting Buddhas and thence to prostrate images of the Master. Could this have been intentional? Surely the relaxed countenance of the reclining Buddha at the summit reflected a knowledge superior to those of us foolish mortals who stood gasping stupidly at his feet, contemplating the long, hot trip down.

No such regrets mar our memories of a sojourn to the rustic village of Pagan. Thanks again to the paranoid Burmese government's policy of isolation, the ruins of Pagan remain a super star of antiquity little celebrated by the outside world. Some archeologists consider Pagan's medley of five thousand venerable shrines and temples to be on a par with the fabled ruins of Cambodia's Angkor Wat. We went to see for ourselves, discovering a bucolic scene of green paddies rimmed by imposing stone remnants of an extraordinary twelfth-century civilization.

Lodging at a basic, bamboo-walled hotel, we asked about hiring a guide who could tell us something about the ruins and were rewarded when the manager paired us with Aye. An intense man in his late twenties, Aye disclosed with typical Burmese candor that he had been a history student at Rangoon University until his wife ran off with all of his money and worldly possessions. This was no sob story to gain baksheesh, for although he was struggling to repay a debt, Aye later refused our every offer to give him a gratuity.

Aye spent the better part of two days escorting us by tonga to the most noteworthy of the temples. His rendition of their historic and religious function filled my imagination with colorful images of an ancient civilization which technologically and organizationally far eclipsed any to be found in medieval Europe. With Aye's assistance, we scaled the roofs of several pagodas for a panorama of Pagan's fertile fields, broken by heaps of stone shrines in varying states of decay. Some pagodas were wonderfully preserved, exhibiting the finest examples of Buddhist sculpture and frescoes we were to see in the Orient.

Dusk was a memorable experience. We sat atop an ornate shrine, overlooking the sluggish Irrawaddy, and saw that sacred river afire with the blaze of the setting sun. Slowly the Irrawaddy triumphed, swallowing the golden-orange flames, leaving nothing but the darkness.

For once our timing was perfect. That evening Aye invited us to a special event held but once a year in Pagan, "Pwes"—or, as dubbed by British colonials, "Burmese Opera." Guided only by the light of

Aye's torch for an interminable hour down a dark jungle trail, and hoping not to disturb any cobras, we finally breached an opening in the bush. There waited half of Pagan, impatient for the show to begin. Children played noisily before a makeshift stage illuminated by oil lanterns. But when the curtains parted they quieted down, giving the performers their rapt attention.

Aye ushered us to the rear of the dais where we were introduced to the director of the opera company, one of Burma's most famous dancers. He invited us to take a seat right on stage and humbly promised to dance especially well in honor of our presence.

"Opera" is more aptly termed Burmese vaudeville. Humorous satirical sketches mocking modern mores are coupled with traditional dance and song. The performers travel all over the country, annually visiting rural villages and small towns. The orchestra of drums, gongs, and shrill flutes really earns its pay, for Pwes lasts from dusk until the sunrise.

The lead dancer amused and awed the audience with choreography both comic and classical. He executed acrobatic leaps as well as stylized hand and foot movements with the grace of a Burmese jungle cat. The star was accompanied by lithe ballerinas with flowing black hair. Poured into lengthy gowns which tightly followed their form until widening at their feet, these lovely dancers conveyed the most poetic of body messages. Adopting an array of precarious stances, they somehow billowed out their gowns with a gentle kicking motion to the throb of a demanding drum.

During comedic interludes, the cast engaged in exuberant banter with the audience. Villagers shouted with relish, responding to the thespians' antics, and the comedians picked on some of the hecklers for lighthearted humor. About four o'clock in the morning, one comic caught me nodding and proceeded to mimic me, all in good fun.

With the dawning of the day, Pwes drew to a close and the entire company came over to bid us good-bye. The audience shouldered their dozing children and trudged wearily home to steal a couple hours of sleep before returning to their routine of the paddies. We too left bleary-eyed, yet pleased to have savored such a rare taste of traditional Burma.

Just as we were falling in love with Burma, our seven-day visa expired. I felt like a suitor jilted and wanted to stay on, but alas, no extensions. Flying to Bangkok, I recaptured visions of Burma: delicate, sarong-clad young women bathing in sparkling rice paddies; longyi-wrapped men vigorously chewing betel nut; and matronly women smoking stout stogies as they haggled over prices. Most of all I thought of Aye, truly a master historian who wanted so desperately to return to the university, yet was penniless. How many other Ayes were there? Then, recalling the serenity of Pagan, where peasants tilled the soil beneath the stone legacy of their past, I vowed someday to return, hopefully to get to know the people and to spend more time exploring the many distinctive temples.

A year later, I read in disbelief that a severe earthquake had destroyed many of Pagan's wondrous monuments. A reporter on the scene noted that after the rubble of ancient pagodas was cleared away, peasants returning to work their fields seemed in near shock, no longer able to gaze upon the spires of shrines which for so long had served as the spiritual protectors of their village.

THAILAND

Los Angelesization of the East

When the door of the air-conditioned jet opened, I was nearly bowled over by the blast furnace of Bangkok. The heavy atmosphere, fairly dripping with humidity, added to my discomfort as I had eaten something in Burma that was wreaking havoc with my system. Ah well, I reassured myself, in two bus rides we would arrive at a comfortable hotel.

As we rode the airport bus to the city, Marzi looked at me aghast. "You're turning green."

"I can hold on," I replied without much conviction.

We transferred to a local bus packed with Thai commuters. At two and a half cents a ride, most Thais get through the constant traffic snarl of this Oriental Los Angeles on these fume-spewing vehicles. The buses are always so crowded that it is impossible to fall.

We stood wedged against a window between two seats. With my backpack burning into my shoulders, perspiration pouring from my forehead, and a tidal wave of nausea rolling from my gullet upward, I tried the window; it wouldn't budge! Desperately surveying the swaying coach, I noted that there was not one inch upon which to heave without hitting anybody.

I fought and fought, trying to concentrate on anything else; miraculously, the regurgitory wave subsided. After forty-five minutes of agony, we reached our destination. I clawed my way to the exit, inhaling the refreshing outdoor air I had initially found so oppressive.

This typical abdominal malady of the Orient thankfully disappeared twenty-four hours later, the recovery no doubt aided by the most luxurious lodging we had enjoyed on the journey thus far. For roughly four dollars, or twice the price of our previous most expensive accommodations, we broke the bank at the fabulous Hotel Malaysia. The bite of that "exorbitant" rate was healed by extras unheard of at other budget inns along the overland trail: air-conditioning, a double bed with clean white linens, constant hot water for showers, plus access to a swimming pool and sundeck! After enduring spartan accommodations for months, we found the "Malaysia" a veritable palace.

We felt compelled to ask the desk clerk how, in a country with a higher cost of living than those we had already visited, the "Malaysia" could offer so much for so little. He smiled suspiciously, then disclosed the secret.

"In past, our guests were U.S. GI's. They come from Saigon and Udon—come here for rest and play. We charge them plenty. When Vietnam finish, soldiers go home, and hotel empty. Same like other hotels."

He spread his arms out, palms upward, as if to lend credibility to his tale. But "hotel empty" did not wash, so I pointed to the No Vacancy sign and asked how business could be so bad if this six-story high-rise was filled?

"Business no bad," he cackled. "Business now very good. I not finished with story. With soldiers gone, no guests here, and I lose job. But we have Chinese owner. Chinese very smart. He see young 'forengi' like you. He see many. Then he bring down price. Many come like you. I get job back. Owner now rich man. Everybody happy."

Indeed.

Only the comfort of the "Malaysia" made a stay of any length tolerable in this steaming, modern city. To hear one another, Marzi and I had to shout above the commotion of freeways crawling with traffic. After months in traditional Asiatic settings, culture shock was induced by avenues of Manhattanesque skyscrapers, smooth-cheeked Beau Brummels in fashionable suits, as well as Suzy Wongs wearing deep décolletage and thigh-high mini-skirts. With our sinuses smarting from petro-pollution, we struggled to remember that we were still in the Orient.

But the worst was yet to come. At the "Malaysia," we met a bushy-bearded traveler named John who promised to "show us the town." John had once been stationed at the air-force base in Udon and knew Bangkok well from "R & R" forays. Now claiming to be a member of Vietnam Veterans Against the War, this overlander wanted to revisit some of his old haunts in Bangkok.

As John guided us about the tourist district, we came face to face with the image of Colonel Sanders under the red-and-white awning of a Kentucky Fried Chicken joint! The goateed Colonel spouted a quote in Thai calligraphy no doubt extolling the virtues of "finger-lickin' good." Before the day was through, Bangkok would provide us with a full "food tour of America"—including pizza, sub, and hamburger emporiums.

"There are even more fast-food outlets here now than before," John told us. "The big difference is that I see mainly Thais eating in them." Without question, the American military presence had taught Thais to become "junk-food junkies."

John also explained why we kept hearing rock-and-roll and country and western music fulminating from every corner. "Some of my lifer buddies told me that when they first got here, there were no 'groovy sounds,' only soft female voices singing very Oriental melodies. Enter the PX and imported hot wax for the bar scenes. You won't hear much that's distinctly Thai today."

At dinner, John asked us if we would like to see a little of

112

Bangkok's infamous "nightlife." Marzi perceptively took a pass and John led me to the Patpong district, or what he lustfully called "The Promised Land." Although most of the clubs John once knew were still operating, he withdrew from the first, instructing, "This one is no longer for us—strictly for Oriental businessmen, say from Japan, Taiwan, or Singapore. How do I know? See the girls on the poster—they're Yanks or Europeans."

We walked down a few doors. A dazzling young Thai with luminous hair down to her waist greeted us at the bar. She sat on John's lap while he bought drinks at American prices. Disco music pounding from a jukebox, a go-go dancer shed her clothes to the drools of middle-aged tourists who were similarly being hustled for drinks by the "B-girls."

We made the rounds of a few bars, the same monotonous scene. It left me bored—and depressed. John reminisced, "These places used to be packed and there were two girls for every soldier."

To John and other servicemen here in the sixties, Bangkok was synonymous with sex. Entertainment was geared to the soldiers' libidos, and prostitution grew into a major enterprise. But with the America pull-out leaving just a few military "advisers," hundreds of prostitutes and their pimps fell upon hard times (although the increasing tourist trade may well pick up the slack). As we headed back to our hotel, every block hissed with pimps' promises of cut-rate erotic joy, "Want fuckee-fuckee! Nice girl, clean—big tits! Suck and fuck, eight dollars, all night, twelve dollars!"

Entering the "Malaysia," John asked "room service" to send him an evening's company. Since sex is free and easy on the overland route I was surprised to note how many other young Westerners in the hotel purchased the services of Thai prostitutes, risking an antibiotic-resistant strain of gonorrhea which the troops had imported from Vietnam.

John rationalized, "Why? Well, for one thing the girls are young and truly beautiful and they don't rush you like hardened whores back home. There is also an enticement factor—the mystery of the Orient and all that shit. Most Asian societies are so conservative that you go out of your mind looking at beautiful women you can't approach. I don't think it's any different than paying for the plea-sure of a massage, sauna, or anything else that feels good. I slip on a rubber and don't worry. Anyway, the girls make more money doing this than other work."

Not all Thais agree. I began to notice hostile stares, and ven-omous spitting that went on behind the backs of American men escorting Thai women. Thailand is one of the few third-world countries which has never been subjected to colonial rule. To main-tain independence, Thais have often had to compromise themselves, politically and otherwise. This has historically been borne of neces-sity, but not without feeling. Consequently, I found many Thais sullen, though not aggressively hostile, in relating to Westerners. Some refused to speak English, even though they knew how. In fact, Thailand was the only country where we experienced consider-able communication problems—an understandable response after many years' exposure to the American military.

Aside from its long-standing independence, one reason for Thai-land's relative prosperity is the business acumen of its merchants. The Thai business community's greatest coup is to package an image of Bangkok to thousands of affluent tourists as something other than a basically Western, insufferably hot metropolis with an abnormal number of bordellos. The most ballyhooed of the tourist teasers is a boat ride through the city's wide klongs (canals) to the "exotic" floating market. At one time, Bangkok was considered the "Venice of the East," but most of its canals have been filled in and paved to accommodate the city's polluting proliferation of motor vehicles.

The floating market is a tourist rip-off, consisting of waterborne fruit hucksters hawking produce at five times the normal price. But for us, there were some illuminating sights. Under the opulent Bangkok skyline thousands of destitute scavengers dwell in tin-roofed cardboard shanties with floors of stinking mud. The canals of Thailand's number-one tourist attraction serve as their water supply, bathtub, and toilet. While the misery of Indian cities lies open for the world to see, the poverty of Bangkok is disguised by the glitter of skyscrapers, nightclubs, and freeways.

After the magnificent Buddhist shrines of Nepal and Burma, Siamese "wats" seemed hideously gaudy—well suited to the tastes of today's Bangkok. The more famous wats were deluged with Western tour groups, with few worshipers in view. We were about to completely write off any other "tourist attractions" when a fellow overlander heartily recommended a visit to the "Snake Farm."

Death from snakebite is a major cause of concern in a nation reputed to have more species of poisonous serpents than any other. The only hope for saving the life of a victim of one of the more venomous reptiles is the quick administration of antitoxin. Clinics in the rural areas are furnished with this vital serum from snakes "milked" at Bangkok's Pasteur Institute.

We watched in awe as herpetologists descended into open-air concrete pits to extract venom from six beautiful yet lethal black-and-yellow-banded kraits, which were bound together in colorful knots that the scientists unraveled with the utmost care. Grasping a struggling snake firmly by the back of the head and under the jaw, the fearless Thais forced fangs against a glass receptacle, issuing forth a flow of phlegm-gray venom into the cup. Then to resuscitate the reptile, the handlers inserted a tube nearly full length and proceeded to pour a nourishing liquid down the hatch. After repeating this process with slender pit vipers whose virulent poison attacks the nervous center, the scientists entered the dank pit of the master of serpents, the king cobra, which, at sixteen feet, is the world's longest poisonous snake and one of the deadliest.

The expert handlers manipulated these spectacular snakes with startling ease, staying always just outside striking range and even playfully pushing the hoods of menacing cobras down from behind. This lent credence to the notion that most victims of snakebite are those who inadvertently tread upon the reptile. Virtually blind and deaf, the dozen or so snakes in each pit were unable, even after being irritated by handling, to successfully strike the men at relatively close quarters. Nonetheless, when one of the thick-as-a-rope king cobras got away for an instant and started crawling up the stairs of the pit toward the open gate, the spectators (myself included) quickly scattered.

Although it was possible to go directly from Bangkok to Vientiane, we decided to wend our way through rural Thailand, thereby entering Laos via its northwest frontier. Between Bangkok and Thailand's "second city," Chiang Mai, the terrain is basically flat, and we soon wearied of endless rice paddies. The roads, however, were exceptional, and the modern coach made good time. We were amazed to observe how developed and prosperous the countryside was relative to that of the Oriental societies we had previously visited. The peasantry in this region actually looked well fed and housed.

Chiang Mai has served for centuries as the trading center for outlying hill tribes. We had heard stories of wealthy visitors paying astronomical sums for "Jungle Tours" to villages where the inhabitants were being exhibited for a cut. That was more than enough to dissuade us; we would see plenty of noncommercialized tribal peoples in Laos.

I had read accounts of foreigners falling in love with "Chiang Mai Village" prior to the Second World War. The Thai Tourist Board is still fond of quoting from this literature. But a quick look at the town punctures any illusions of tranquillity. The influence of the contemporary West has blasted into Chiang Mai with typhoon force; amiable street stalls have yielded to plasticky boutiques and bicycle pedicabs have been replaced by thundering motorbikes. Except for hill-tribe people, all of Chiang Mai is on "business time." This is no sleepy town.

Chiang Mai's only link to the past lies in its heritage of expert silversmiths and fine silk weavers. Ironically, these skilled craftsmen have become increasingly dependent upon tourist dollars for the survival of their art. The upper-class Thais who could afford their creations prefer the status of imported goods.

En route to Laos we caught an early-morning bus to the jungle outpost of Fang. Tiring of monotonous paddies, I was just about to pick up a book when the rice fields suddenly disappeared into a great mouth of matted rain forest which proceeded to devour everything in sight until halted by a river. There, at Tha Ton dock, we made the acquaintance of one of the more unusual overlanders, a sixty-year-old Israeli.

Born in Marseille, Henri had fought against the Nazis with the French underground. Arriving in Israel in 1948, he became a captain in the merchant marine. Now retired, he had never lost his love of travel. Henri's only complaint was that he was restricted from Moslem countries like Malaysia and Indonesia because of his Israeli passport. He traveled by public transport, ate as we did in the "peoples'" restaurants, and resided in budget hotels—a living testimonial that the spirit of overlanding knows no bounds of age.

Our most memorable adventure in Thailand was a trip up the Wang River, a tributary of the Mekong. I was edgy at first, as three submachine-gun-armed Thai soldiers accompanied the boat. The northeast has long been economically neglected by the rest of the country, and leftist guerrillas have found a fertile base of support here. This region was also infested with cutthroat opium smugglers and bandits.

A motorized outrigger carried us through a sequence of seething, swirling rapids, which a month earlier had capsized this same boat. At one point the captain ordered us to disembark and walk through the thick jungle shoreline while he navigated a particularly perilous stretch of white water.

Back on board, we enjoyed the luxuriant profusion of reptilian vines and elephantine leaves which hung over the banks. Several times, the outrigger put in at lonely bamboo dwellings crowned with thatch to take on peasants carting baskets of bananas and other produce to the market at Chiang Rai, the northern terminus. When the motor was cut and we drifted slowly in to makeshift docks, we grew uneasy. The soldiers, wary of an ambush, would release their safeties and survey the surrounding jungle. Then returning to the mainstream, our fears abated as we sliced deeper into that splendorous world of green.

Northeast Thailand was the antithesis of the rest of the country: relatively unpopulated, basically uncultivated rain forest where few Thais owned vehicles and time was measured by the season rather than the clock. The easygoing peasants were a breed apart from their aggressive southern cousins.

For a brief period in Chiang Mai and Bangkok, we had reentered the modern world. Now we found ourselves back in the ancient Orient, where revolutionary forces were trying to usher in the twentieth century. We reached the northern border of Chiang Khong and scanned the infamous muddy Mekong that separated us from war-torn Laos. It was dusk, but from a point overlooking the Laotian shoreline, a glint of light sparked from a sentry's bayonet.

LAOS

Opium and Fratricide

We were ferried across the Mekong in a leaky canoe which had just about filled to the bailing point when we touched Laotian shore. Finding the customs offical snoring contentedly, we unceremoniously slammed our packs on his desk. He awoke in terror and instinctively groped for his rifle. Truly sorry, we apologized. Regaining his composure, he sluggishly stamped us in and directed us up a path that led to the frontier town of Ban Houei Sai.

The people of Ban Houei Sai spanned a vivid visual spectrum of races. A few were golden brown like the Thais, others a deep bronze similar to the Burmese of Pagan. Also present were some females who indulged my fantasies with their delicately sculpted faces, café-au-lait complexions, and lithe figures. From their features, it seemed evident that the French penchant for sexual fraternization with colonial subjects had been enthusiastically embraced even in this remote backwater. But propagation was about the only tangible contribution the French made to this once sleepy landlocked nation of primeval jungles, gentle tribespeople, and opium poppies.

119

"Once sleepy," that is, for when we arrived here, a cease-fire had just been declared after years of bloody civil strife. Under the terms of the armistice, a coalition of Pathet Lao communists, royalists loyal to Crown Prince Souvanna Phouma, and representatives of a right-wing military clique was to govern. No one familiar with the situation held any illusions that the three bitter adversaries would maintain their shaky unity for long. On pacifist grounds, we wished, however skeptically, that political differences could somehow be resolved without further bloodshed. If not, we fervently hoped that hostilities would be kept under wraps, at least until after our departure.

In the general store which also functioned as Ban Houei Sai's bank and bar, we met a balding Danish physician employed by the United Nations who insisted that we join him for a beer. Conversation soon turned to politics and the doctor left little doubt about his sentiments.

"Your country's foreign policy is insane," he railed. "The CIA decides Prince Phouma is too neutral to its taste and has its cronies in the royalist army stage a coup. Then the generals' regime alienates even some of its allies with its avarice and brutality. The peasants and French-educated intelligentsia—what little there is of it—who had been sitting on the fence started leaning toward the Pathet Lao. Not because of any sudden conversion to communism, mind you, but because they were fed up with the generals' barbarity and ineptitude. At least the PL's were known as competent administrators, free from corruption.

"So how does your CIA respond? They turn three hundred and sixty degrees and plot like hell to put Souvanna Phouma back on the throne. Now the best they can do is this farce of a coalition. But it's too late. The Pathet Lao have the strength to usurp full control of the government whenever the time is ripe. That is, whenever your leaders finally decide they've had enough of butting into other people's affairs and pull out of Southeast Asia."

I reminded him that we were two among thousands of Americans who stood in opposition to U.S. policy.

"Yes, I've read of the demonstrations," he added wearily and broke open another bottle. "I'm sorry. I suppose I've just been here too long and seen too much. You won't be able to get out to places I've worked like the Plain of Jars, but I assure you, my friends, you won't want to. Napalmed children, starvation from defoliated lands, disease rampant in regions we couldn't set foot in due to the intensity of the fighting." The doctor then recited tales of atrocities witnessed during his medical forays and succeeded, intentionally or not, in rekindling our guilt as Americans.

"I'm sick of seeing peasants, who are totally ignorant of what communism or capitalism is all about, disemboweled by the caprice of arrogant politicians who assume they know what's best for the world.

"Forgive me," he said, pouring yet another round. "I'm supposed to be neutral." The Dane laughed caustically and raised his glass in a toast. "Let's drink to neutrality."

We had hoped to make immediate reservations to fly to Luang Prabang, as the road south had been blown up and a river journey on the Mekong would be hazardous since some soldiers were still unaware of the truce. Air being the only transport, the short flight to Luang Prabang was booked for a week. We told the pilot that we were willing to sit in the aisle and, when that failed, tried to grease his palm with a few "kip." Unfortunately, we didn't offer enough, learning later that two Lao merchants succeeded in being seated on the floor of the cockpit.

Thanks to our frugality, we were stuck in this dusty little hamlet which by late afternoon was near deserted. The café-cum-store closed, sojourns into the countryside off-limits, our unventilated room stifling. Clothes clinging to our bodies, we mounted a staircase leading to a Buddhist monastery high above which afforded an unobstructed view of miles of meandering Mekong. The surroundings were so placid it was hard to imagine that a few months earlier, gun sights had been trained on the river from the picturesque lookout.

That evening we discovered that Ban Houei Sai was not such a somnolent town after all. Music from a live band echoed through the town, while well-dressed sons and daughters of war profiteers

121

and generals (the women in mini-skirts, the men in crew-necked sweaters) executed a graceful combination of Western and traditional dance steps in a converted munitions warehouse. The band sported the standard electric guitar but also included a four-foot bamboo drum; the rock singing sounded more tribal than Western—a curious fusion.

Further down the street a more restrained party was under way, sponsored by the U.S. Embassy, local royalist officials, and businessmen. The American ambassador, ironically named Whitehouse, was paying his first visit here since the truce. Liquor flowed freely while the guest of honor and staff were served by tribeswomen attired in full-length black dresses with silver brocade. We crashed the party and enjoyed the hors d'oeuvres—after all, it was our tax money being squandered to prop up these petty tyrants.

Having helped myself to a few drinks, I decided to pop the question. What could I lose? "Mr. Ambassador, could you give a couple of fellow Americans a ride in your jet to Luang Prabang?" The Honorable Whitehouse looked dumbfounded, but the over-dressed Lao to his right, sneering like a villain in a Charlie Chan epic, spat, "This is not the place to ask such a question."

We returned to our tumbledown accommodations to hear over-landers complaining about a creeping bellhop peeping through a hole in the women's john. One huge amazon of an Australian promised, "I'll fix him good," and she went hell-bent to the stall. Soon we heard a splash and saw the skinny bellhop tearing down the hall and out the door. The Aussie had urinated in the flush bucket and thrown the contents at the hole.

Not wishing to remain in Houei Sai another five days, we booked a flight for Vientiane. The Houei Sai airport, like the town, was crowded with soldiers. Military planes, now on reconnaissance to "keep the peace," continuously landed and took off. A young soldier meticulously checked Westerners' luggage, ostensibly looking for weapons, but basically just curious to see what unusual items the white foreigners possessed. At one point he waved a Tampax in the air, asking in sign language what it was for. The woman was hard-pressed to describe its function through gesture.

COUNTERCLOCK-
WISE: KOUCHI
NOMADS IN
AFGHAN DESERT;
LAOTIAN
JUNGLE WATER-
FALL; FLOATING
AFRICAN VIL-
LAGE OF
GRANVIL;
TOOTHLIKE
ROCKS CARVED
BY HOT SPRINGS
IN TURKEY

HAND-PUSHED FERRIS
WHEEL IN THE NEPALESE
HIMALAYAS

ABOVE: CAMEROONIAN
DANCERS AT A
FESTIVAL. BELOW:
WANDERING
MINSTRELS ENTERTAIN
AT NEPALI MOUNTAIN
VILLAGES

ABOVE: FIERCE HULI
WIGMAN PLAYING
PIPES OF PAN IN PAPUA
NEW GUINEA. BELOW:
AFGHAN MERCHANT AT
KABUL BAZAAR

SRI LANKAN
PEASANT
SWINGING FROM
MEATHOOKS IN
RITUAL SELF-
TORTURE

PRECEDING PAGE:
KASHMIRI
MERCHANT
HAWKING FLOWERS
AND HASHISH. ABOVE
TRADITIONAL
MASKED
CAMEROONIAN
DANCER

ABOVE:
KATHMANDU'S
STONE EFFIGY OF
HANUMAN, THE
FEROCIOUS
MONKEY GOD.
BELOW: A WITCH
DOCTOR IN
FETISH COSTUME
TERRIFIES
CENTRAL
AFRICAN
VILLAGERS

COUNTERCLOCKWISE:
SHERPAS TREK MILES
TO KATHMANDU
MARKET; A NEW
ARRIVAL TO CAIRO'S
MOUSKIE BAZAAR;
BUSTLING
MARKETPLACE,
VIENTIANE, LAOS

COUNTERCLOCK-
WISE: SIKH
GOLDEN TEMPLE,
AMRITSAR, IN-
DIA; ISLAMIC
SPLENDOR OF IS-
FAHAN, IRAN;
BUDDHIST
STUPA WATCHES
OVER KATH-
MANDU;
BUDDHIST TEM-
PLE IN LUANG
PRABANG

**LEOPARD IN THE
TREES, SERENGETI
GAME RESERVE,
TANZANIA**

The Lao Airlines plane was a 1941 Lockheed prop whose engine the pilot had to prime three times for enough thrust to get it off the ground. We breathed a sigh of relief as the plane barely cleared a jungled hillside. Once at cruising altitude, the Lao pilot—the sole occupant of the cockpit—strode leisurely back to have a word with some retired French officers. While we braced ourselves for a collision or crash, the flight carried on smoothly until the pilot returned to the controls.

The prop bumped and rolled the remainder of that short but memorable flight. A middle-aged Lao, steadying himself against the overhead racks, served warm Fantas to the passengers; we later discovered that he was not an employee of Lao Airlines, merely a bored passenger in search of something to do.

At our hotel we once more crossed paths with Henri, the ageless French-Israeli we had met on our river journey through northern Thailand. "Come with me," he entreated. "Tonight we dine!"

Henri escorted us to the French Officers' Mess, originally established for former foreign legionnaires and now open only, as we would soon discover to our chagrin, to the French-speaking public. Slowly and with great gusto, Henri recited a menu that had us salivating. We started with a flavorful onion soup, following that with escargots and a real prize, the first green salad we considered safe to eat in months. The entrée was chateaubriand, prepared with loving perfection, nicely charred on the outside, delicately pink within, and tender throughout. We washed this down with a carafe of heady Beaujolais. And for dessert, the waiter skillfully served up bananes flambées, accompanied by rich imported café from the Côte d'Ivoire. Needless to say, the French Officers' Mess rated three stars in our book.

After months of stinting, I picked up the tab. I could afford to be generous, a gourmand without guilt, as the bill for the three of us totaled five dollars.

Naturally, Marzi and I returned the very next night. But Henri was not with us and the stuffy Lao waiters, in the spirit of their proper Parisian brethren, took note of our imperfect French and refused to acknowledge our presence. For an uncomfortable hour, they ignored us. Finally, Marzi walked up to the maitre d' and politely asked, "Why will you not serve us?"

He fairly hissed, "English not welcome here. You get out."

Furious at the snub, I overturned a basket of baguettes. That was a mistake, for the enraged maitre d' pursued us out the door, chucking stones in our direction as we beat a hasty retreat. Ah well, Marzi and I consoled ourselves, when traveling in the Orient, one couldn't go wrong with spicy Thai and Lao dishes.

One evening, a young Australian couple prevailed upon us to accompany them to what they repeatedly described only as "a most unusual bar." The infamous (as we later found out) White Rose proved a pathetic scene—the real-life counterpart of Genet's *The Balcony*. Here American military personnel on R & R paid Lao prostitutes to act out their perverse fantasies in front of their buddies.

"Want to see cigarette trick, you pay me only three dollars," entreated a petite whore who couldn't have been more than sixteen. From across the bar, a paunchy American serviceman who was being fellatioed bellowed drunkenly, "Sure, honey, I'll take you up on that."

The young Lao proceeded to light and insert seven cigarettes in her vagina, somehow keeping them going through a studied bump and grind. "And now one in asshole," she added. We left while the soldiers cheered her on.

Vientiane, when we saw it, was still in form and spirit a bastardized French metropolis. A ludicrous imitation Arc de Triomphe towered over the town's Asian marketplace. Well-to-do Laos of mixed French ancestry and Europeans sat leisurely munching croissants and sipping coffee at umbrella-shaded open-air cafés. There were boucheries, patisseries, and boulangeries. Indeed, if it hadn't been for the number of soldiers here, one might scarcely have known a war had been fought, for Vientiane itself was untouched and carried on as a drowsy incarnation of a French provincial town. Every element seemed so familiar yet somewhat misplaced, making me also feel out of kilter and more than a little uneasy.

Luang Prabang proved far more intriguing. Although the French colonials and later the Pathet Lao made Vientiane their administrative headquarters, Luang Prabang remained the heart of Laos for its people. And little wonder. Nestled within the emerald jungles that border the Mekong, the former royal capital is studded with a dazzling mélange of ancient Buddhist wats. Beams of solar lighting streamed from tri-tiered temples plated in gold, casting halos, while pagoda murals portrayed scenes from Buddhist mythology so vividly that I could swear they were in motion. After the more recently constructed, crassly commercial wats of Thailand, the shrines here were a revelation.

Historic site of kings' coronations and royal weddings, Luang Prabang is also a city holy to Laotian Buddhists. Countless monks have journeyed here over the centuries to take their vows of poverty. In the early morning, we would awaken to the tinkle of temple bells and watch saffron-robed monks line up, bowls under their arms, to accept food donations. Buddhists believe that giving alms to monks will be deemed a plus when they enter the next world. By religious law, begging is forbidden and the monks' sole subsistence is based upon charity. All Buddhist males are expected to briefly join a monastic order at least once. Because they are only permitted to eat before twelve noon, some of the mischievous younger boys could be seen sneaking rice in the late afternoon.

In keeping with the haute cuisine of Vientiane, the residents of Luang Prabang prepare their own gourmet specialties. Grasshoppers, grubs, and beetles, impaled by the dozen on thin slivers of bamboo, hopped and flopped while tribeswomen carefully inspected and bargained for the juiciest. Nearby, shoppers haggled over barbecued bats, geckos in gravy, smoked snakes, and assorted intestines of unknown origin. One cherubic Meo matron proudly clutched by the tail her pièce de résistance, a struggling field mouse.

In a more serious vein, these tidbits were true delicacies to a people for whom protein was so scarce. The havoc of war was one reason for local food shortages, an emphasis upon the cultivation of opium another. Journalists had alleged that few parcels of foodstuffs donated by international relief organizations for free distribution reached their destination due to the pervasive corruption. Proof positive lay in the Luang Prabang marketplace where bags of rice being hawked had clearly stenciled upon them "A Gift from the People of the United States."

Because Luang Prabang was the major trading center of central Laos, its market painted a colorful, if tragic tabloid of the region in microcosm, for hundreds of Laos came from far and wide to peddle their wares here. Among them were many hill-tribe people in full traditional regalia. Perhaps the most striking of these were the Meo women, with their embroidered black dresses and silver yokes of familial wealth worn about their necks.

Also conspicuous were scores of soldiers—it seemed half the men in town were in uniform. Most had been conscripted by whichever army controlled their district. The stupidity of the vicious ideological warfare imposed upon them was perhaps most apparent in the marketplace, where Mao-jacketed Pathet Lao troops leisurely shopped alongside olive-fatigued royalist regulars.

From a far corner of the market, we heard a husky voice call out to us in fractured English, "Hey, Yank, want good dope? I got Buddha sticks, sixty kip (ten cents); smack—very pure shit; 'O'—I got smoothest smoke."

We traced the voice to a frail, fair-skinned Lao in blue jeans and a UCLA T-shirt. No, he wasn't kidding. Displayed before us on a long rickety table were innumerable packets of dope, hard and soft.

"How can you sell this stuff so openly?" I asked the Lao.

"What you mean? 'O' is our number-one export ever since the French bring it from India one hundred fifty years ago. Look 'round here—every Meo man smoke." Indeed, at all hours Marzi and I had seen tribesmen staggering up and down the back lanes of the town in what I now realized was a narcotic stupor.

The dope dealer crumbled a stick of grass and packed it into the bowl of his "bong" for us to sample. With his gaunt features and bloodshot eyes, Jean looked considerably older than his stated thirty years. When asked where he learned English, Jean told us between tokes that his father was a Frenchman who left his Lao mother shortly after the fall of Dienbienphu. Raised a Catholic, Jean was educated by priests who taught him French and a smattering of

English. He attributed his fluency in slang to American friends who, he claimed, were working for U.S. AID.

As we smoked, my tongue loosened and I asked Jean if it didn't bother him to sell addictive drugs.

"I told you," he said irritably, "Every body here take 'O.' In the hill country, all those Meos, they grow poppies for the big land-owners, the royalist generals.

"I buy from generals, sell to Yanks and Aussies. I no feel bad and I say fuck you if you no like what I do—especially you Yanks 'cause your own brothers fly 'O' out for the generals."

"Who?" Marzi asked in disbelief.

"Air America pilots. Air America same CIA airline. They fly poppies to Saigon, keep generals happy, keep Meo from joining Pathet Lao."

"Come on, you're bull-shitting us."

"I no bull shit. You go to airport, see for yourself. Everybody here Luang Prabang know 'bout this—no secret."

We really didn't believe Jean until several days later at the airport Marzi and I witnessed burlap bags bursting with opium poppies being loaded onto props bearing the Air America insignia. Nonetheless, it was hard to fathom any link between Air America and the CIA, for it seemed inconceivable that the U.S. intelligence agency would knowingly contribute to burgeoning drug problems at home.

But when we ultimately returned to the States, little-publicized hearings before the Senate Foreign Relations Committee disclosed that the CIA, through its clandestine airline, had indeed been spiriting the drug to Vietnam in order to assure the loyalty of high-ranking royalists and their Meo sharecroppers. Allegedly, Ky, Thieu, and other bigwigs of the South Vietnamese regime received a cut of future profits and, from Saigon, the narcotic was shipped to heroin-refining factories in European ports like Amsterdam and Marseille. Then the white-powder "smack" was transferred under the auspices of the Mafia to the streets of New York.

By the time testimony was taken before the Senate Foreign Relations Committee, the Pathet Lao had already assumed complete control of Laos and Air America had ceased to function. What truly boggles the mind is the revelation that at the very moment President Nixon was making political hay with his heralded "War on Drugs" and the State Department was economically blackmailing Turkey into cessation of opium cultivation, the CIA was playing a pivotal role in the world narcotics' trade!

As we were about to leave the market, a couple of Australians strode up to Jean and slapped him on the back, exclaiming, "Hey, mate, word has it you got some good candy for us." Jean knew them as steady customers, among the contingent of Western junkies who had domiciled themselves in Laos because opium and heroin were so readily accessible, cheap, and "pure." A small number of these addicts were former travelers, primarily Australians. Cut adrift from their conservative society's protective apron strings, the Aussies had overindulged in the hard stuff with harrowing consequences. Like so many American GIs stationed in Indochina, they would eventually take home a habit only the wealthiest could maintain outside the Orient.

The Aussies purchased a packet of heroin, then asked Jean if he would join them that evening at some place called Wu's. Jean informed us that Wu's was one of the few opium dens left functioning in Luang Prabang. "Three years ago, we had many dens. Then royalist and Pathet Lao both ask money from owners. Those that can't pay have their pipes broken—they finished."

"Why didn't they just buy new pipes?"

"Only pipe good enough for den must be smoked twenty-five, thirty years so insides get buildup for good smoke. Those years pipe must be smoked all-a-time. Very rare. Very expensive. So when soldiers break pipes, dens must close. Now only Wu's and one other left. Wu a China man. He and wife have other business—could afford to pay, so his den still go."

"What's an opium den like?" asked Marzi.

"You both come with me tonight and see."

"But we've never smoked opium."

"You try it once, you like very much."

"That's what I'm worried about."

Our curiosity got the better of us and we met Jean at a Mekong rendezvous for our venture to the den. We had taken Jean's advice not to eat any supper, but thirsty, I had guzzled a Coke. This would come back to haunt me.

As I bowed low to enter the undersized doorway of a squat bamboo hut, a toothless Madame Wu beckoned me to accompany her on a slender wicker bed. The wrinkled Chinese patroness removed a licorice-colored opium plug the size and consistency of a baby Tootsie Roll from an ornate inlaid silver box. Impaling the "O" on a thin bamboo skewer, she rotated it expertly against the flattened portion of a beautifully carved pipe nearly a foot in length. All through this process, Madame Wu held the flame of a kerosene lamp close at hand to keep the drug gummily malleable. Having skillfully achieved the proper spherical shape to fit the pipe exactly, she thrust the opium into the bowl. Then Madame Wu handed me the pipe, and in a guttural voice that belied her skeletal frame, the wizened old woman commanded, "Smoke!"

I inhaled as long as I could, sucking the sweetly harsh substance from the pipe. Veteran addicts like Jean and Madame Wu ingest the entire wad in one breath; it took me three deep tokes. For every pipe I smoked, Madame Wu took in two. She repeated this process when Marzi and Jean took their turn. In between pipes, a teenager Jean identified as Wu's daughter poured some tea. I had thought Madame Wu ancient! How old could she be? Is that the impact "O" has on one's body?

Requiring both hands to push myself from the bed, I knew my equilibrium was no longer in sync. With difficulty, I counted out one hundred kip, or about eighteeen cents, for the six pipes I smoked. Six, Jean said, was sufficient for a novice—and more than enough for me.

Soon after I left the bed I became dizzy and nauseous. Jean told Marzi we should feel free to leave whenever we felt like it, for "O" is a lonely drug and you don't really care if others are around when you're stoned. It was easy to see what he meant. Three Meo customers lay sprawled on straw mats within the den, all obviously in their own private worlds.

Marzi inhaled her six, and when Jean began his tenth pipe, I asked to be excused. As Marzi and I dazedly embarked upon the half-mile hike to our lodge, I perceived time and space in disjointed waves. The effort to walk became tortuous. I drunkenly careened out of control from one side of the street to the other, nearly crashing into rickshaws and bullocks. Marzi, whose senses were less distorted, guided me back to our inn where I lost my Coke and began an intermittent pattern of dry heaving that lasted throughout the night. But my thoughts were sheer liquid dream—an ecstasy of disembodied "floating," delightful when I wasn't throwing up. A novel experience that I resolved never to repeat.

When my brain cleared and my system regained normalcy, I contemplated life in the Meo's "opium culture." It was impossible to imagine how, under the disabling influence of the drug, tribal peasants could till their plots and wrest a viable subsistence for themselves and their families. I was told that they cultivated little other than "O," using their meager allotments from the landlord-generals to buy food in the marketplace. If the harvest was not good, or decimated by the war, these peasants starved.

The Danish physician we had met back in Ban Houei Sai revealed that both the communists and royalists had initially fought for control of the richest opium districts to help finance the war. He noted that under the coalition, poppy fields in Pathet Lao-administered areas were being burned and food crops substituted. Hopefully, this is now taking place in the country at large, although it probably means "cold turkey" for a substantial number of addicts.

Royalist businessmen who ran the cramped Laotian Tourist Board office in Bangkok had zealously promoted visits to "Holy Pakou Caves," an hour's boat ride downstream from Luang Prabang. River travel elsewhere could be dangerous, but a tourist official assured us that this was one Mekong excursion we could undertake without much risk. Since a sail on the Mekong appealed in and of itself, we planned to check out the Buddhist shrine. But in Luang Prabang, military authorities informed us that it was first necessary to obtain police permission so that the soldiers patrolling the area would not mistake our intentions.

Safe passage papers in hand, we hired a motorized outrigger and swept down the murky Mekong. It was easy to see how guerrilla fighters could conceal themselves from aerial surveillance in the thick green growth that blanketed either shore. At abrupt intervals, we sighted gaps in the curtain of vegetation. Pocketed within were petite bamboo settlements, the smoky fragrance of their charcoal braziers adding zest to the otherwise ubiquitous odor of mildewy jungle rot. From our vantage point, Mekong villages, aside from the conspicuous absence of young men, showed little outward evidence of the destruction wreaked upon this area by the war. The peasantry endured. When their huts and fields were burned, they would stoically clear another patch of wilderness and rebuild. Existence went on pretty much as it had long before this decade of terror. Men stood on the banks casting fine mesh nets extending from lengthy fishing poles. Mothers whacked their laundry against the river rocks, keeping an eye on children playing what must be the one universal game, the wheel and the stick.

This tranquil spell was obliterated at military checkpoints. Here teenage soldiers (Pathet Lao or royalist at alternate stations) nervously licked their lips, holding machine guns on us while their military superiors examined our "laissez-passer." We held our breath until they concluded that everything was in order and waved us on. Every now and then the dense forest overgrowth was breached by artillery emplacements. We hoped that no misunderstanding would provoke the firing of the gargantuan guns.

Disembarking, Marzi led the way up stairs carved into the bank leading to the caves. Suddenly she froze. Out of the bush slithered a streamlined olive-brown snake. It was a green tree viper, a deadly poisonous reptile we recognized from our visit to the Bangkok Snake Farm. Like most creatures of the wilds, the snake was more frightened of Marzi than she was of it (which is really saying something) and zipped up the nearest tree. I tried to photograph the serpent, but he blended so well with the foliage that it wasn't worth a shot.

The caves themselves were a farcical rip-off. As advertised, there were effigies of the Buddha—hundreds of them. These crude statuettes were probably strewn around the caverns in recent months by the Tourist Board. But we didn't mind, for the river trip had been most illuminating.

Back in town, some Americans who taught English in the local "Lycee" gave us directions to a fabulous waterfall twelve miles into the bush. We shared a taxi to a comatose Meo village. The road was studded with military checkpoints, once again puncturing any illusion of pacific peasant homesteads. At road's end, we trekked better than a mile through a sea of vegetation. Along the path, psychedelic butterflies fluttered through tree-filtered sunlight. Only the exotic sounds of tropical birds pierced the quiet of the rain forest.

In the sun-splashed jungle a sparkling waterfall churned over obstructing stone and shrubbery, playfully shooting jets of mist from a multitude of heights and angles. Alone in this unspoiled setting, we leisurely undressed and bathed in the refreshing natural pool formed by the falls. No Hollywood fantasy could top this. We smoked some of Jean's "Buddha grass," the finest cannabis this side of Afghanistan—one toke and you really do see the Buddha! There was never a more perfect setting for lovemaking. Later we enjoyed a picnic lunch, watching the water gush over the rocks, reveling in the jungle's silence.

When we returned to the village, our idyllic odyssey was rudely shattered as we stared down the barrel of an M-15. The Pathet Lao officer demanded our passports and police authorization. Scrutinizing the papers, he eyed us and smiled. Noting our relief, he joked with us in French while we waited for a return taxi.

The war had brought an end to bus service between Luang Prabang and Vientiane. The sole land transport running between Laos's two principal towns was a freight truck that supplied a Chinese-owned electric store. The truck made the journey only once a week, but for three dollars we booked passage, hoping to see more of the countryside than was possible from the air.

The trip normally takes eleven hours, but we were informed by the Chinese merchant that the Lao driver set his own pace. His plans were to leave at 6 A.M., drive for two hours, and then inexplicably sleep for a day in a Meo village. The following morning he would set off again and reach Vientiane by late afternoon.

We arrived at the electric store on time, but by 8 A.M. there was no sign of the driver. The Chinese merchant passed by and said to return at ten. We returned but still no truck. "Come back eleven-thirty." At eleven-thirty, "Come back twelve-thirty." At the newly appointed time, "Driver back in hour, go have lunch." We ate something and returned, only to find the truck had left without us. Shades of India! We flew out the next day.

For all our transport problems, Laos proved an eye-opening journey to a land of gentle people ravaged by a savage war which they little understood. The peasants were trapped in a brutal struggle between those who sought to maintain the inequitable and corrupt status quo and those who hoped to usher in radical change with the blood of the alleged "beneficiaries."

MALAYSIA
AND
SINGAPORE

Ethnic Jungles; Urban Jungles

Traveling by rail from Bangkok to Butterworth, Malaysia, I watched Thailand's flat rice paddies give way to a series of eroded limestone mounds rising sharply from the lowlands. Shortly thereafter, tangled arms of jungle sprang up and embraced the train with a shimmering verdant wall on either side, snarled vines intertwining to form a natural canopy.

I sat enraptured, viewing from the comfort of a fan-cooled seat this magnificent rain forest dappled with more hues of green than I had ever dreamed conceivable. I could go on like this forever. . . . In this ecstasy of motion, I was living my own movie—not the vicarious experience of someone else's filmed adventures. I remembered life in the States' with its all too predictable rhythm and regularity. But as an overlander in the Orient, every dawn ushered in an onslaught of new stimuli and events, oftentimes challenging and always novel.

Malaysian immigration officials had been afflicted with some of

Singapore's infectious paranoia of young Westerners. Forewarned, most males took the precaution of pinning up or cutting their hair. At the border, one long-haired American was lectured, "Why do you wear your hair like a girl?" and given a short-term visa. A large "SH" was stamped in bold letters in his passport.

"What does 'SH' stand for?" he meekly inquired.

"Suspected Hippie," snapped the bureaucrat.

At Butterworth, we transferred from the train to a ferry bound for the isle of Penang, two miles from the mainland. A huge banner greeted passengers at the dock: "Spitting is not only illegal, it is disgusting!" Undeterred, a grizzled Chinese man to our right liberally lubricated the gangplank.

Penang mirrors in microcosm Malaysia's rich ethnic diversity. The sole city of any size is predominantly Chinese (they make up 40 per cent of the nation's populace). The countryside is largely Malay (50 percent). Disbursed in both the urban and rural sectors are a small number of Indians (8 per cent). As we would soon discover, there is no love lost between these culturally dissimilar peoples.

Georgetown, Penang's capital, has a distinctive Chinese atmosphere. Outdoor restaurant stalls dot the city's harbor, tri-shaws scuttle through shadowy passageways, and glassy-eyed men stagger away from opium dens. Compared to the sedate Malay towns of the island's interior, Georgetown is highly animated. The hectic mercantile tempo that energizes the city has brought its Chinese citizenry considerable prosperity, as evidenced by the plethora of air-conditioned shops selling expensive Western fashions, jewelry, stereo and photographic equipment. When Penang was a free port, such shops were patronized primarily by tourists. Now many locals can afford these luxuries.

We relished Malaysia's multiethnic cuisine at open-air street stalls where an Oriental smorgasbord cost less than a half dollar per filling entrée. Satay, charcoaled skewers of meat served with a spicy peanut sauce, Malay seafood curries, Indian vegetarian dishes proffered on banana-leaf plates, and a wealth of Chinese concoctions steamed from each cluster of cooking kiosks. The Chinese cuisine held the greatest intrigue, for the cooks at even the tiniest eateries were

135

ceaselessly inventive. While we didn't always know what was sizzling in their woks, the results were invariably delicious.

One Malay I hitched with scornfully told the tale of a Chinese family he knew in Singapore. He claimed that they held the head of a live monkey in the vise of a table opening. The Chinese allegedly cut open the top half of the simian's head like a coconut and scooped out the poor creature's brains. I initially passed this off as typical racist ridicule, but relating this to a Chinese friend in Kuala Lumpur, he cheerfully noted, "It's possible. If the sun shines upon it and it's not human, we will eat it."

Penang's modern movie houses import Western films (although Hong Kong–produced "kung fu" epics are the favorites) and one must book tickets early to be sure of a seat. All the world is movie mad. Most impressions of the West, and hence cultural emulation in Asia and Africa, are byproducts of cinema. This is reinforced by commercials which generally run for a good half-hour prior to showtime. (Canada and the United States are the only two countries I have been where there are usually no ads.) In Penang, ninety-nine per cent of the audience seats itself on time for these glamorous shorts, oohing and aahing at the luxury products advertised. It seemed as if the commercials enjoyed more rapt attention than the feature.

At intermission in cinemas, on tape cassettes as we hitched around the island, in shops and over transistor radios, in fact everywhere we went in Penang, sugar-throated Chinese girls could be heard singing the worst American song lyrics of the fifties. We heard "Puppy Love" and "Teen Angel" enough to be certain that they were near the top of the Malaysian hit parade. This is neither nostalgia nor high camp; they are being aired for the first time here and local teenagers, like their American counterparts of the fifties, take the simple-minded lyrics very seriously.

Soon tiring of city life, we traveled through the island's rural sectors, which were almost exclusively inhabited by Malay. Here we down-shifted precipitously from Chinese urban time to Malay rural time. After some hard traveling, the transition was most welcome. On the quiet beach at Batu Ferringhi, we rented a room for a half dollar in a fisherman's home, built on wooden stilts to keep rain, vermin, and snakes out. I have seen more attractive beaches, but Batu Ferringhi was our first in the Orient and it was nice to relax with fellow overlanders in surroundings of palm trees, sand, and surf. The only drawback was the nauseating odor of drying fish which the wind wafted over from time to time.

Leaving Penang, we found hitchhiking the Malay Peninsula a breeze. The highways were smoothly paved, the scenery lush, and the drivers actually eager to pick us up. Thumbing rides afforded an introduction to local people and the severe ethnic frictions that have rubbed this society raw. Whether we rode with Chinese or Malay, our drivers never missed a chance to denigrate their racial opposites.

The Chinese, often referred to as the "Jews of the Orient," are the most industrious and affluent businessmen in Southeast Asia. The Malays, on the other hand, have traditionally been farmers or fishermen. No longer content with a subsistence livelihood, many Malays are today trying to enter the business arena. But to compete with a people whose mercantile inheritance goes back centuries has been frustrating for the Malays and has endowed them with a powerful sense of envy and loathing toward the Chinese.

The government, dominated by Malays, is attempting to improve the economic status of its own people through a calculated policy of discrimination against the Chinese. The most blatant example of official bias lies in education. Although both English and Malay have been decreed national languages, and university classes are taught for the most part in English, those wishing to go on to higher education are required to pass exams in Malay. So the Chinese must obtain fluency in Malay in order to gain admission to one of the national universities. Preferential treatment is also exhibited by the civil service, which is disproportionately Malay. The government has trod upon the Chinese preserve of business as well, legally obliging firms to train and employ Malays in upper-echelon positions.

Malay efforts to establish their own enterprises have been staunchly resisted by Chinese competitors. Charges by the Malay of "Chinese conspiracy" and "racist monopoly" have a measure of legitimacy, particularly in the link between Chinese wholesalers and shopkeepers who fix prices or unite in other ways to keep merchandise out of the hands of struggling Malay retailers.

In response to these accusations, the Chinese argue that the Malays fail in commerce because they have no "business sense" and are nothing but "shiftless, slow-witted peasants." The Malay deride the Chinese as aggressive, "scheming swindlers." It surprised no one when in 1969 these smoldering passions exploded, setting Kuala Lumpur, the capital, aflame with racial rioting. Although there have been no comparable outbreaks of violence since that upheaval, ethnic antagonisms remain fierce, a bed of dry kindling awaiting a spark that could reignite Malaysia into a bloody racial inferno.

This aura of hostility became immediately apparent when we hitchhiked south from Butterworth. An air-conditioned Mercedes pulled up driven by a Chinese industrial supplier named Lee, accompanied by Sully, one of the firm's Malay sales managers. They both treated us royally, buying us an expensive five-course meal in a posh restaurant and dispensing information on what to see in Malaysia, the economic situation, and local culture. I had planned to discreetly inquire about ethnic grievances, but Lee broached the subject himself.

"You see, all the international journals say we Chinese and Malays don't get along. Look at Sully and me, we are the best of friends." Sully nodded in affirmation.

During a rest stop, Sully excused himself and set off with his prayer rug to pay homage to Allah. Lee motioned us aside. "He always wastes my time with this religious nonsense. You know, the government made me hire him and even after I teach him the ropes five times over, he still can't grasp sales policy. You see, the Malay are slow upstairs and very lazy." Then, forcing a Cheshire grin, Lee welcomed Sully back.

Lee paused at the town of Ipoh to say hello to some relatives. As we waited, Sully growled, "These Chinese have come in and taken over our country. They cheat us and control everything. Someday we will throw them out."

Other Malay and Chinese we rode with expressed similar senti-

138

ments. Both ridiculed the Indian, who, of the three groups, is the poorest and most disadvantaged. (Indians were brought over as indentured labor by British planters who thought the Malay not industrious enough.) It is truly sad that such ethnic tensions threaten to rend the delicate social fabric of one of the few nations of the Orient that is not yet overpopulated and has the capacity to develop a robust economy with its abundant resources of tin, rubber, palm oil, and forests. But it is hard to argue with the government's notion that to "bring the Malay up" to the Chinese level of prosperity and an equitable share of the national economy, some element of privilege is necessary.

That the Chinese are not exactly happy about the outright policies of discrimination is just as easy to understand. There is also some truth to the Chinese contention that without their commercial and technological expertise and industrious character, Malaysia would not be nearly so well off economically. Furthermore, government efforts thus far appear to have improved the lot of the middle- and upper-class Malay without substantially benefiting the lower-income peasantry.

A Communist guerrilla movement, basically comprised of Chinese, has been active since the 1948 "Emergency." While not particularly strong at this point, the guerrillas ironically have the financial backing of some wealthy Chinese businessmen—perhaps as a backlash to the government's policies. I was astounded to hear many of those super-capitalists who gave us a ride in their luxury vehicles boasting with pride of mainland China's achievements. Ethnic identification certainly transcends ideology.

From Ipoh, we caught a ride with a young Chinese couple up a twisting road to the delightfully cool hill station of the Cameron Highlands. During the colonial era, British officials and rubber-plantation owners escaped the humid coastal regions, building a resort here. Today it remains plush, with numerous affluent Chinese vacationers flocking to its gambling casinos.

For us, the attraction of the Highlands lay beyond the gaming tables. Leaving the resort behind, we explored a captivating rain forest whose silence is broken only by the humming of insects and the trill of boldly plumed tropical birds flashing feathers of vermilion, chartreuse, and royal blue. We hiked past crystalline waterfalls cannonading from the swell of recent torrential rains and on one occasion glimpsed an aboriginal Oreng Osli, garbed solely in a G-string, chasing butterflies with a bamboo net. There are few of these primitive original inhabitants of the Malay Peninsula left. Most live in the more remote regions, and the government is trying to integrate them into contemporary society through transient teams of educational and medical personnel. But the Oreng Osli have suffered greatly at the hands of outsiders and cling to their jungle refuge.

In the darkness of these forests lurk tigers, ferocious long-tusked wild boars, and a variety of poisonous snakes. We spotted one of the world's largest constrictors, the reticulated python, coiled around a sturdy limb above our heads. He must have been about twenty feet long and the huge bulge before his first coil indicated that he was in the process of digesting a substantial meal. These snakes' jaws are "elasticized," enabling them to swallow a calf whole. Though attacks on humans are rare and usually in self-defense, we were happy he had already eaten.

As we started down a sloping path leading back to civilization, we heard a drumming overhead and realized a storm had come up. At first, we didn't feel any rain as mammoth leaves above served as our umbrella. Soon it came down hard enough to penetrate to the jungle's floor, making the labyrinth of roots embedded in the trail slippery as ice. Tripping and stumbling, we slid a good deal of the way down. It seemed as if the jungle were purposefully reaching out to give us alien intruders a hard time.

Leaving the refreshing mountain air of the Highlands, we hitched down to the stifling capital of Kuala Lumpur. Only two images of Kuala Lumpur stick in my mind: the railway station, a magnificent monument to the Victorian era with its graceful, undulating arches and, in glaring contrast, the hideous modern National Mosque, which I first mistook for a common railway station. Otherwise Kuala Lumpur is just another Oriental city which has grown much too fast to accommodate its burgeoning traffic and housing problems.

On our first visit to Malaysia, we stayed exclusively on the western shore, for monsoonal rains pelted the east, flooding the roads. The west coast is basically Chinese, while the east coast is primarily inhabited by Malay farmers and fishermen. We greatly regretted that weather kept us from seeing the rest of the country, but good fortune enabled us to return a year later to visit the land of the rural Malay.

In Malay "kampongs" (clusters of wooden houses elevated on stilts) of the east coast, life goes on pretty much as it did during precolonial days. Bounded by wild-flowered tropical forests on three sides and miles of untouched white sand beach on the other, the Malay inhabitants are content to farm or fish for a subsistence. The men claim they have everything they want and see no point to working harder for a surplus.

Islam was a latecomer to this land of animists and in the kampong, the spirit world sometimes still takes precedence over orthodox Islam. Diviners may be accorded as much respect as Moslem priests. Women, in both Malaysia and Indonesia, are not nearly as cloistered as their sisters in Islamic West Asia and the Middle East. Female adults and adolescents wear loose kebaya blouses and comfortable sarongs. They go freely to market unchaperoned and without scrutiny. No sexual hassle for Marzi here.

I met a few former Peace Corps men who found the east coast's atmosphere so simpatico that they stayed on here, teaching in government-run schools for a meager income. Most enjoyed the relaxed atmosphere of rural kampong life. Mornings or late afternoons, they swam the silvery waters of deserted beaches. Weekends, they might hike into verdant jungles teeming with wildlife, or join a local fishing excursion. They helped organize village cockfights and gambled with Chinese shopkeepers in nearby towns. As teachers, the Americans had the high esteem of their neighbors. Pressure for them to be anything more than what they were was completely absent around the kampong.

141

Since Malays have a puritanical outlook on premarital sex, an erotic outlet provided the only problem. Some Western residents "resolved" this with visits to Thai whorehouses across the border. One American converted to the Islam and married a Malay. But Paul had a special problem.

While Marzi rested at the kampong where we stayed as Paul's guest, he and I went into town for a beer at the Chinese saloon. He said he had to talk to someone and after a few rounds discussed his affair with a young Malay married to his neighbor. Melia was thirty years younger than her husband, having been betrothed at age ten. Though Paul had been attracted to Melia for some time, their affair was hardly premeditated. Paul had come over to borrow some palm oil when he found Melia alone. Strongly drawn to each other, they began a most dangerous relationship.

It was a terrible dilemma. Paul loved kampong life, but if they were ever suspected or caught in the act, he would have to leave. Worse still, jealous Malay husbands have been known to use their keen-bladed parangs on those cuckolding them. The kampong is a small "closed society," where everyone knows everyone else's business and gossip is the chief form of entertainment (as it is in most of the world). Paul and Melia lived in constant fear of discovery.

A few months ago I received a letter from Paul. He had tried to break off his affair, but could not face constant impersonal contact with Melia. Paul moved south to Kuantan, but town life did not agree with him and he contracted to teach at a rural school the following year. Having once returned briefly to the States, he could not envision himself ever living in such a pressure cooker after so many years in the kampong. Paul wrote that he often thought about Melia but could not bear the pain of a visit to his former village.

Giant half-ton sea turtles surface annually to lay their eggs on a single patch of east coast Malaysian beach. How and why they find their way to the very same sands remains a mystery. Unfortunately, villagers informed us, we were a few weeks early for turtle season. Still, it was so pretty and peaceful we decided to stay awhile.

Strolling along a picturesque waterfront uncluttered by hotels, I noticed what looked like black rocks on the white sand. As I picked one up, a sticky goo oozed over my hand—a clot of oil. The South China Sea, so inviting from a distance, was polluted by the spillage from petroleum tankers sailing for Singapore. No wonder the residents of the kampong had observed that fewer of the huge turtles were appearing every year.

On the second visit our ticket enabled us to fly to Sarawak, Borneo. Ruled personally for years by a British family whose patriarch was known as "the white Rajah," Sarawak is now a part of the Malaysian federation. We were particularly interested in the Dyak, the "wild men of Borneo," infamous in days gone by as headhunters. Colonial rule had forced many Dyak to give up their warrior ways, but during the Japanese invasion of World War II, the tribesmen delighted in a return to guerrilla warfare. They netted many a Japanese head to redecorate their longhouses.

In Borneo the rivers serve as the roads. Although relatively comfortable launches run between towns, only outriggers service the more remote reaches of the interior. Searching for a Dyak longhouse that retained the customs of the past, Marzi and I set sail down the mighty Rajang, then hired a guide and canoe for a venture up a jungled tributary.

Several sweltering hours of paddling brought us to a structure nearly the length of a football field, elevated on stilts high above the soggy river bank. While some longhouses are said to be inhabited by as many as forty families, a good seventeen resided here. Their shelter's construction was sturdier than it looked and quite functional, with hardwood beams lashed together by sinewy vines, roofs of thatch, and walls of latticed bamboo to provide the utmost in ventilation. Longhouses are aptly named, a single row of partitioned rooms, one per family, fronted by a continuous veranda—the focal point of communal activity.

Although most of the women were bare-breasted, all but the eldest men wore Western dress. There they sat in contrast: aged men with tattooed bodies and wooden ear plugs, wearing loin cloths, reminiscing about their warrior days; youths in Levi's and

143

carefully tailored shirts, anxious to leave the longhouse for the exciting life of the towns.

The elderly "tunenggung" (chief) told us that few of the able-bodied educated men had plans to stay in the longhouse, and that this was the case throughout Sarawak. The tunenggung had served as a governmental representative for his district and had traveled throughout its least accessible regions. He noted that schools, transistor radios, and sojourns to trading post or town had transformed the life style of most of the Dyak and Iban forest peoples. Now longhouse dwellers are impatiently awaiting the arrival of television in Sarawak, due next year (many have installed electronic generators). To find a village which maintained the traditional ways, one would have to walk on foot for weeks through the jungle. The skulls that hung in bamboo ramparts above the common room of most longhouses were but a memory of the past.

On the Malay Peninsula, the aggressiveness of Chinese culture has been tempered through contact with the relaxed Malay. There is no such check in the island-country of Singapore, a pushy, unpleasant Chinese city-state. After independence from Britain, Malay political forces cast Singapore adrift in order to avoid dominance by a Chinese majority—a most astute decision.

I cut my hair short in Kuala Lumpur, preparing to enter this uptight little island with its virulent fear of Western longhairs. Lee Kuan Yew, Singapore's strongman, has correlated Western youth and hair with drugs and immorality. His vigilante squads comb the streets with scissors in search of any hirsute locals who have contracted the disease of "hippyism." This is yet another of dictator Lee's political ploys to maintain uniformity in what is already a conformist society in the extreme.

Many overlanders, to avoid Singapore, leave directly from Penang, hopping a boat over to Sumatra and thus seeing little of Malaysia. We decided to enter Indonesia on a cheap charter flight from Singapore to Djakarta. Despite having heard only negative stories about the island-country, we wanted to see for ourselves.

Bustling Singapore was a rude reintroduction to urban hustle after the unhurried enchantment of Malaysia. Unlike other third-world cities, Singapore is clean, prosperous, and Western in every way. Wealthy tourists are attracted here because Singapore is indeed immaculate, a duty-free port, and has been energetically promoted by its tourist board as "Instant Orient." It seemed more like "Instant America" with its high-rise apartments, glassy office towers, and multistory shopping malls.

Handbills adorn bulletin boards throughout Singapore with caricatures portraying the legally correct coiffure: not one strand over the forehead, ear, or below the collar. Underneath runs a caption in bold black letters: "Longhairs will be served last." And they mean it. A British friend with modishly long hair applied for a visa renewal only to see his passport go to the very bottom of the list whenever the dour-faced bureaucrat, who typed him as a hippy, spied someone else entering the office.

Some overlanders who had to enter Singapore to connect with onward transportation went to extraordinary lengths to maintain their long hair. One traveler managed to pass himself off as an "American Sikh," darkening his face and wrapping a turban around his locks. Some Australians who started their venture with a flight or boat direct to Singapore wore wigs. But most of us succumbed to haircuts. Those travelers who landed at the airport with "unacceptably" long hair had a choice of flying right out or visiting scissors-happy barbers who delighted in "Sluggo-cuts."

Hitchhiking with two Singaporean citizens, I held my breath during customs. I wanted no problems here, for our flight was scheduled to leave in a few days. We were given the most rigorous search for drugs this side of the United States. But being in the presence of middle-aged, well-groomed locals no doubt helped us gain entrance.

The blare of traffic and construction jackhammers assaulted our ears, and the fumes of Singapore's thousands of autos made our throats rasp and our eyes red. The warmth of Malaysia was just a memory as locals here ranged from curt to downright nasty. Even the shopkeepers who sold duty-free goods, the country's mainstay for foreign exchange and prosperity, were sour and impolite whether or not in the process of bargaining. A typical salesman's response:

"If you just here look, not buy, den go." Accustomed to wandering around easygoing bazaars, this came as a rude shock.

That mainland China has managed to harness the energies of such a hard-driving culture to meet the demands of their society's needs must be seen as a formidable achievement. On the other hand, the industrious work ethos of the Chinese that we witnessed in Singapore and elsewhere is no doubt a vital factor in the economic success story of the People's Republic.

Tourists flock by the busload to Tiger Balm Gardens. Tiger Balm Gardens is a ridiculous recreation of Taoist purgatory in which monsters, in garish laminated plastic, dine on or dismember unrepentant sinners. This homage to bad taste is a beneficent donation to Singapore by the Orient's foremost fourflushers, the brothers Aw Hoon Haw and Aw Poon Par. These wealthy medicine men have bamboozled millions of Asians with their highly hyped "Tiger Balm," a pungent mentholated salve sold throughout the Orient as a cure for virtually any ailment. How fitting that such charlatans should locate their preposterous exhibit in Singapore, for Tiger Balm Gardens is the embodiment of that frenetic city—itself an earthly, animated purgatory.

BALI, INDONESIA

Paradise Found, Paradise Lost

Weary from months of travel, we looked forward to a month's rest on fabled Bali. As our plane landed on the runway of Djakarta's international airport, I saw an endless urban sprawl. In fact, once on the ground, it seemed to take forever to reach the heart of that dingy, destitute capital city of over four million inhabitants. Given our aversion to major Oriental metropoli, which varied principally in quantity of misery, we booked seats on the first available train south.

People and paddy fields, paddy fields and people, people, people. For ten solid hours, we glimpsed images from our train's window which brought statistics to life. Java is hopelessly overpopulated— sixteen hundred people per square mile. And I had found the States crowded at times with its density a mere sixty! A recent conference of demographers projected that Java's population will double in thirty-five years. The poverty was already unspeakable. What will happen? I was still mulling over the grim realities when the train pulled into Jogjakarta, the island's cultural center.

"Jogja" holds a special charm for overlanders. We, like many travelers who plan to use the city simply as a stepping-stone to Bali, found ourselves caught up in Jogja's seemingly dichotomous languid flow of life and creative exuberance.

A city of half a million, Jogja nonetheless retains the look and feel of an extended rural hamlet. Few buildings are higher than one story, and with automobiles still a rare commodity, "betjaks" (three-wheeled rickshaws) rule the dirt roads. In Jogja, the ringing of bicycle bells supersedes the honking of horns, though the town may impart the sense of a country village, there is nothing provincial about its hundreds of gifted artists.

Long before the coming of Islam, Jogjakarta served as the political, religious, and cultural capital of a vibrant Hindu Java. A legacy of its spiritual side stands in the impressive ruins of temples like Borobudor and Preambanan. But even though the Javanese faith shifted from Hindi scriptures to the tenets of the Koran and the seat of political power was moved elsewhere, the artistic flame of Jogjakarta's golden age still burns brightly. Today, as in the past, a preponderance of Java's finest artists hail from Jogjakarta. And of all the extraordinary crafts here, none is more renowned than the Jogja batik.

Enraptured, we watched an artist demonstrate the making of a batik in the time-honored way. Having outlined a design in charcoal over light cotton fabric, he meticulously retraced the pattern in hot liquid paraffin, using a needlelike implement called a "tjanting." The wax will preserve the design when the fabric is thrown into boiling vats of dye. Repeating this process for each hue desired, the craftsman will produce either the traditional tricolored batick or one of the tourist-oriented modernistic multi-tones. In purchasing a beautiful tailor-made batik shirt for two dollars, I felt as if I were wearing a work of art.

Wandering about the town's back lanes one night, we were attracted by the happy squeals of children. Their laughter emanated from an open-air arena of benches, where a crowd had gathered to enjoy "wayang kulit," a performance of shadow puppetry. Peering backstage, we spied a solo puppeteer manipulating buffalo-skin marionettes, accompanying their actions with an enthusiastic narrative. To the beat of drum and flute, silhouettes of sliver-thin legendary beasts, deities,and spirits grappled and danced. Their shadowy images were illuminated against a diaphanous curtain by a tiny oil lamp. The puppets represented not the spiritualism of Islam, but the mythology of its predecessor, again reminding us that Moslem Java had been the seat of a powerful Hindu dynasty.

Once considered invincible, the long-reigning Madjapahit monarchy collapsed in 1515 under the onslaught of an army of Islamic zealots. Driven to the very tip of Java, the Hindu priests and princes braved the treacherous waters of the slender Strait of Bali, ferrying to the sanctuary of a serendipitous isle. Their royal cortege of refugees included Java's finest musicians, dancers, artists, and architects, who exiled themselves because their religious precepts and creative prowess were inexorably intertwined. They feared that under Islamic rule their beliefs would be stifled. By sinking roots in Bali, their arts would flourish as never before.

The Hindu refugees were hospitably received by docile animists and ancestor-worshipers who had for centuries reaped the fruit of the emerald island's fertile soils. Time forged a unity between the natives and newcomers, tempering the sharp edges of each culture into a harmonious social order that emerged distinctly Balinese.

Why have visitors to Bali made its name synonymous with "paradise"? Its volcanic mountains are magnificent, but can't be compared with Hawaii's; its jungles are luxuriant, though not as splendorous as Malaysia's; its beaches are sublime, yet not really on a par with the white sands of Tahiti. Other tropical islands rival, perhaps even surpass, Bali in overall physical allure. But Bali is endowed with one special ingredient that leaves it wholly without peer: the Balinese themselves.

Perhaps the most appropriate way to introduce Bali is through the following allegory. When Hindus in India suspect death is near, they make haste to Benares. There arrangements are made to have their ashes cast upon the holy Ganges, thus sparing them the miseries of reincarnation. The Balinese, on the other hand, believe themselves to be truly blessed if they should be reborn a Balinese.

No one in Bali cries for the deceased, for those who pass on are seen as en route to yet another life. Their death marks not an end to be mourned; rather, a new beginning—a reason to rejoice!

The Balinese attitude toward death, or more appropriately life, is only one facet of their Hindu-animist philosophy that makes this society unique. For here is a culture which is communal without being tyrannical, threaded by a traditional connective tissue linking life, religion, music, and art. The result: a continuous festive flow of the aesthetic, the spiritual, and the shared.

Balinese life is order: Every Balinese is secure in the knowledge of his preordained role in the cosmic scheme of things and his function within the community. There is nothing on the order of a Western "identity crisis," in which life seems to lack purpose or direction.

Children are inculcated with Balinese cosmology from early on and one rarely sees them expressing jealousy or fighting. Because their behavior is prescribed, they have little reason to quarrel. Lack of "personal freedom"? *For us* that may be true, but anyone who has ever visited Bali would be hard-pressed to condemn the Balinese way of life.

Some who cringe at the social divisions of Hindu India and know Bali only in the abstract are tempted to criticize the Balinese as well for their caste system. But the two cannot be equated. Roughly ten per cent of the Balinese are born Brahmin, the rest of the populace belonging to three castes nearly equal in the hierarchy. Unlike rigid India, caste lines in Bali are blurred and the discriminatory ethos that fetters caste to class is not apparent. Dishwashers and the poorest of peasants may be Brahmin, the most affluent of entrepreneurs lower caste. And in Bali, the monstrous concept of "untouchability" is an utterly alien notion.

Bali may not be an egalitarian society, but it is assuredly a communal one. Every married male participates in the "bandjar," the maintenance unit responsible for the individual, public, and spiritual needs of the village. The bandjar constructs all housing and regularly repairs water supplies, sanitation drains, and temples. It finances a community treasury which loans money to those in need and purchases any necessary equipment for the village. Festivals, cremations, marriages, cockfights, and shadow puppetry are organized by the bandjar. Irrigating the terraced slopes of mountainous Bali also falls within the realm of collective action, as the men harness river water, lay pipes, and dig ditches. Thus, while one's land holding may vary in size, the bounty of a farmer's harvest is enhanced through communal effort. The Balinese note without boasting that no one in the countryside goes hungry—if a man's crops fail, he finds succor in his neighbors.

The Balinese are not obsessed with being something other than what they are. Their philosophy: as long as one is well-fed, is respected in the village for attending to community functions, and pays proper homage to the gods and spirits, what else need one aspire to? The Balinese do not envy the affluent traveler. Indeed, they find it nearly incomprehensible that these foreigners should actually choose to cut themselves adrift from their homes. For the Balinese, to be removed from the order and rhythm of one's society is the cruelest fate conceivable.

The Balinese sense of inner tranquillity is infectious. Basking in their perpetual warmth will touch even the most world-weary cynic. In Bali, there is no hard-sell, no hurry, no worry. Yet the Balinese are not merely marvelously laid-back, for each of them is a constant contributor to a society in which art and life are one.

At the behest of the gods, Balinese life is a continual pageantry of color and creativity. Wonderful wood- and rock-carved dieties and spirits adorning village temples succumb to the ravages of the tropics. As each shrine deteriorates, it must be regularly resculpted by the men of the community. Thus Balinese temples are never-finished works of art.

Wrapped in batik sarongs, Balinese women spend hours daily preparing ornamental arrangements of rice cakes and flowers on woven bamboo mats. No matter that these are immediately gobbled up by scavenging dogs—the gods have already partaken.

When not renewing their temples, fashioning their offerings, or painting or carving for the sheer joy of it, the Balinese immerse themselves in theater, ballet, and music. Some men are members of a gamelan orchestra, for every village has its own symphonic group.

151

Children are weaned on the dance and drama of Hindu myth and legend. Ultimately, each will play a role in at least one of the classical works.

In Bali it is the process of creating, not the final painting or performance, that holds meaning. That's why one may find more of a village assembled at dances and drama rehearsals than at opening night. Having been involved in the production (or having seen it any number of times), the audience feels no gulf between themselves and what is happening on stage. Rather than sitting sedentary as mere spectators, the villagers freely offer opinions to the performers, thus participating in the creative process.

Although the same dances, music, and sculptures are being endlessly recreated, they never bore the Balinese, for they are always different. The same, yet different—how can that be? While each endeavor is rooted in a traditional framework, no attempt is made to exactly duplicate the work. Instead, the artist injects his own interpretation. Flexible Balinese culture thrives upon this inventiveness and thus never goes stale. Yet even with its stamp of originality, Balinese art remains anonymous, belonging to the community, rather than the individual.

Whenever the sacred order of their cosmology has been threatened, the outwardly gentle Balinese have shown themselves to be fierce warriors. Javanese Moslems, who for centuries sought to forcibly convert the Hindu heretics, suffered thousands of casualties as invasion after invasion was repelled. The Dutch colonizers of Indonesia also learned the ferocity of the Balinese. Realizing the impossibility of defeating the heavily armed Dutch, one prominent Balinese prince ordered his subjects, including officers, common soldiers, women, and children, to wear their finest dress and advance relentlessly into the fire of enemy cannon. No Balinese survived, as the wounded died by their own hand, driving kris swords deep into their breasts. Numerous other struggles cost the Dutch many lives despite superior firepower. Ultimately, Dutch might prevailed and the island was colonized. The European presence remained merely physical, for Dutch Christian priests never made so much as a dent in proselytizing among the Balinese. During the Second World War

Japanese troops occupying the island found fabled Bali quite the opposite of Nirvana, losing many a man to brazen local guerrillas.

In 1949 a movement for independence led by the Indonesian George Washington, Sukarno, drove the Dutch out. But Indonesia remained dominated by foreign capital and its economy stagnated under Sukarno's inept fiscal policy. Trying to spur the new nation out of its doldrums, Sukarno swung ideologically further and further to the left, greatly influenced by the Indonesian Communist party. This frightened U.S. corporations which had invested heavily in Indonesia. The CIA subsequently helped instigate a coup led by right-wing army officers which overthrew Sukarno and his leftist advisers (1965).

The direct victims of the coup were the Chinese minority, long loathed throughout Indonesia (as in Malaysia) for their mercantile expertise and commercial dominance. Indonesians discovered that the quickest way to get rid of both debts and these hated alien infidels was to call them "Communists" and chop off their heads. Within just four months, a quarter-million civilians, mostly Chinese, lay dead.

Few Chinese lived in Bali, but from what I can piece together, there was a growing indigenous movement to remove power from the hands of the priests and to equalize land holdings. This was seen by many Balinese as irreparably disrupting the harmonious balance of their society.

Stirred by the example of the other Indonesian "anti-Communist" movements, villagers rounded up those who spoke of change and murdered them under the guise of killing Communists—the all-purpose label for those who advocated another way. The terraced fields of the countryside and the once white beaches ran red with the blood of forty thousand Balinese.

Why did the Balinese leftists not defend themselves? One theory holds that the men, confronted with the full wrath of their religious leaders and fellow villagers, felt some remorse for departing from centuries-old cultural patterns. In Balinese cosmology, one is reborn higher or lower, depending upon one's mortal sins. Many about to be executed, therefore, asked the priests for absolution before a kris slit their throats. This last-minute effort to appease the gods demonstrates the depth of Balinese religious fervor.

One educated Balinese related matter-of-factly to me: "I saw my friend across the paddy and put a bullet in him. We grew up together and went to school together. But he was a part of those who would change things here. To preserve our way of life, I had to kill him and others. I do not like to think of such times."

Even those who do not know the history of Bali are astonished to discover the underlying theme of violent vengeance which permeates so much of Balinese dance and legend. But no Balinese rite can match the "barong-kris" ceremony for dramatic intensity. It depicts a contest of power between the mythical four-legged barong representing the forces of good and the Witch Rangda symbolizing the forces of darkness.

The hairy barong is portrayed by two men who coordinate movements at the costumed front and rear sections of the beast. Hair streaming from its benign demon's face, the barong snaps open and shut its wooden jaws in its never-ending crusade against evil. Its adversary, Witch Rangda, clawing the air with her foot-long finger nails, menaces the creatures of creation. While the Balinese view the barong as a comical protector, Witch Rangda is seen as evil incarnate. Children in the audience shriek with fright at her very appearance.

The Witch Rangda commands a half-dozen Balinese men to turn their daggers upon themselves. Countering her magic, the barong casts a spell which keeps the men safe.

When the human participants enter the arena, tension grips even those spectators who do not know what will follow. The Balinese men, eyes aglaze, wander about in a self-induced trance. From the sidelines, priests and their assistants watch warily to be certain that all are in a deep hypnotic state. Then, as gamelan and gong beat wildly, each man seizes a razor-sharp kris, thrusting it repeatedly into his own abdomen, Adam's apple, even eyeball. Yet so great is their belief that the barong will save them that miraculously, the sword leaves not a scratch.

I have attended the barong-kris twice and on both occasions saw participants literally jump on their blades without even piercing the skin. Anyone who has observed the barong-kris will attest that there is no cheap gimmickry involved – the spectacle is frighteningly real. Only the trance somehow keeps the men from mutilation. Call it the power of the mind, the intervention of the spirits, anything you will . . . I would behold even stranger incidents of possession and self-torture on a later visit to Sri Lanka.

Other traditional dances, such as the Ramayana Ballet, reflect the grace and gentility that one observes daily in the Balinese. Thirteen-year-old girls generally perform the lead of the Ramayana (by sixteen, females are considered no longer delicate enough for the major roles) and each eye and finger movement is a subtle expression of this Hindu legend. To me, the girls' intricate hand motions are more sensously exciting than the flashy footwork of other societies' dance.

Each Balinese ceremony is punctuated by drums, gongs, and of course the gamelan. The latter is an indigenous xylophone played with hammers through the memorization of hundreds of notes synchronized to mesh with the dance. The musicians read no music; father teaches son.

We rented a motorbike and toured the back-country roads, driving along stunning beaches, through lush jungles, and up terraced hillsides with spectacular views of ten-thousand-foot Mount Gunung Agung and Penelokan Volcano. Everywhere we were unfailingly greeted with smiles. Early in the mornings, we laughed at the spectacle of peasants marching herds of waddling ducks in formation down to forage fields. There farmers impaled wooden poles, said to keep the fowl from wandering off. Outside the tourist areas, bronzed bare-breasted young women walked, balancing heavy baskets of vegetables on their heads. (In response to the leering tourists, all coastal women but the eldest now cover their breasts.) Of course, each village had its own stone temple, daily decorated with scarlet hibiscus tributes to the deities.

Approaching an isolated hamlet, we heard laughter and the echo of gongs. A cremation! How lucky we were, the only Westerners here. The dead man would progress to yet another life and the entire village was delighted for him. His body was carried atop a twenty-foot tower, spun round and round by the bearers to confuse any lurking evil spirit. In the process, a telegraph line was severed, shooting sparks into the air. I worried that the tower might catch fire, but the near calamity only accentuated everyone else's mirth. After all, the body was soon to be burned, and if the gods wanted to hurry the process, that was their will.

As the deceased was a Brahmin, his coffin was embellished with the wooden effigy of a huge bull. Food and other "necessities" were heaped upon the pyre to aid the dead man on his journey to another life. A white-robed priest sprinkled holy water over the corpse. Then he signaled and the pyre was put to the torch. Flames licked at the coffin, black smoke billowed, and soon all was ash. The deceased's family would later make a pilgrimage to the sea, where skilled boatmen battling heavy surf would scatter the charcoal remains.

At length we returned to relax once more in Kuta village by the sea. Here overlanders paid less than two dollars for a double room in clean, bamboo-walled losmans, living a life of unsurpassed ease. We would arise with the sun to enjoy a swim, then bake in the tropical warmth until drowsy. Back at the losman, a "dipper bath" would revive us. This "shower" consisted of pouring buckets of cool, cool water over our heads—sheer ecstasy. We usually slept during the heat of the day and followed the nap with a late-afternoon swim. Walking down the beach to avoid the nightly horde of tourists from the luxury hotels who paid three-dollars bus fare to enjoy "The Splendor of Kuta Sunset," we met with fellow overlanders to discuss plans for dinner at one of numerous open-air restaurants. Dining was a social occasion and talk of travel adventures might go on well into the night, unless preempted by a traditional dance or gamelan concert.

The sands swept on for miles and travelers could swim nude on isolated stretches. No hassle from the Balinese—they also swim au naturel. When the sun parched our throats, Balinese girls would come by selling cooling coconut milk. One never worried about leaving valuables on the beach; Balinese acknowledge that stealing is not part of their culture. I wore a sarong at all times, marveling at the comfort of the airy cotton and thinking how foolish pants were in tropical climes. Yet to wear a sarong in macho Australia or even California would guarantee verbal abuse.

Balinese restaurants were quick to learn Western tastes and overlanders, myself included, became gluttons without regret. For a mere dollar we ate "splurge meals" like lobster, veal cordon bleu or wiener schnitzel. Other less-costly favorites were veal scallopini à la torino, spaghetti bolognese, steak and eggs. Dessert might consist of rich chocolate cake, tart apple fritter, or banana pancake smothered in honey. Also available were mildly hallucinogenic mushrooms served on a choice of pizza, omelette, or salad!

Here I regained all the weight I had lost in India, sating myself without remorse. Why not, I thought. After all, our next stop was Australia, where the cost of a mere hamburger would seem exorbitant by comparison. We would toke up at our losman and then troop off to our favorite open-air restaurant, accompanied by friends and a mangy dog who had adopted us in appreciation of the food we dropped.

On our last evening in Bali "our dog" cried. And so did we. As we strolled down the beach for the sunset—a nightly vigil for Balinese and visitors alike—the long line of a religious procession followed on its way to a seaside temple. Women carried on their heads ornate, four-foot-high headdresses of offerings, proudly silhouetted in the shadows of the dying day. Gongs, drums, and exotic gamelans accentuated the pageantry. On the beach, the music stopped and all watched a spectacular blood-red sun sink into the sea, only to be reincarnated—filling the sky with brilliant flames of gold, pink, and orange. Soon it was dark . . . time to leave.

A full moon came up, illuminating a solitary fishing outrigger which seemed to be calling, "Return to Bali." I knew someday we would, but little did I realize in only a year's time.

Perhaps one should never return to a place he has loved and left. Every place changes, but so dramatically in twelve short months? Well, quite possibly I had been so blinded by the delights of Bali that I was oblivious to the impact I and numerous other foreigners were having on the Balinese. Intensive tourism is accomplishing in a decade what Moslem invaders could not do in four hundred years: the erosion of Balinese culture.

Most Balinese have only what they need for subsistence. Some parts of this fertile isle are becoming overpopulated, the young men drifting to the towns in search of work. Bali is dominated politically by a corrupt Javanese military government which has allocated little for schools (I met a high school principal who earned twenty-eight dollars per month) or social services. Some affluent Javanese officials are fueling the wrath of the Balinese toward their powerful Islamic neighbors by buying up lots from peasants for personal resorts and hotels.

Young Balinese men in constant contact with tourists observe the material prosperity of the idling Western visitors. On my first stay in Kuta village, I saw few Balinese men in anything but sarong; a year later, many wore blue jeans. I had never seen a Balinese smoke grass—it is against religious law. Now, quite a few smoke in Kuta. As noted earlier, stealing is not a part of Balinese culture, yet Western valuables are now disappearing with increasing frequency. (Of course, the Balinese still blame Javanese thieves.) The only whores on Bali were from other islands; now there are said to be a few Balinese prostitutes. Attending a cremation, I watched in disbelief as Balinese peddlers hawked souvenirs to busloads of tourists.

Though these changes, which I witnessed only in widely touristed areas, may seem superficial, they are symptomatic of a deeper breakdown. I spoke with Idas (who worked at my losman), Ms. Dayu (the restauranteur), and Ms. Kompiang (who runs a losman), three Balinese friends whose opinions I deeply respected. Yes, they acknowledged, things are changing fast in Kuta, their native village. People are not so ready to lend food, bicycles, etc. to neighbors in need, because they hope to sell any surplus for movie money or Western dress. Less time is being spent in cooperative village work. Young men talk about marrying a Western woman and moving to Australia or the United States for "the good life."

"They don't realize what they would be giving up," I groaned. My Balinese friends understood but could suggest no way to counter this growing sentiment. They instinctively knew that what had started was irreversible. While the Balinese have always fought off threats to their way of life, this new menace was, like the spirits, invisible, an incubus on the psyche. I thought of Denpasar, Bali's only city, where the all-encompassing order of Balinese life has turned into chaos. Then, thinking of the rest of Bali, I shuddered.

Although Idas shared my premonition, he advised me nonetheless, "Go back to the rural villages away from Denpasar, Kuta, Sanur, Ubud, and Mas. There you will still find Bali." True for the present. But Bali is a small island and the government's plan to increase luxury tourism guarantees more road building and greater exposure to Western ways. I know that what is happening in Kuta is contagious . . . I have seen it elsewhere.

Saddened, I walked down to the beach my last evening in Bali and once again saw a fishing canoe gliding tranquilly on silvery waves. As I remembered the boat that had "called me back" and thought wistfully about the delightful culture that makes most of Bali very special still, a cloud drifted by and blotted out the moon, extinguishing the canoe.

Book Two
AFRICA AND BEYOND

AFRICA OVERLAND

AN INTRODUCTION
and
SOME WORDS ON BLACK RACISM

Our transcontinental expedition through the heart of Africa differed from overlanding the Orient in almost every way.

Hotels were few and far between outside African capital cities. Those that did exist we found generally expensive and unpleasant by Asian standards. So, unless invited by missionaries or Peace Corps, we slept in our tent.

Unlike Asia where we enjoyed delightful, low-priced cuisine, savory, nutritious meals were hard to come by in Africa. If you've ever wondered why there are no African restaurants in cosmopolitan centers like New York and London, it is simply because a sub-Saharan "haute cuisine" never evolved. As most Africans can afford only bland dietary staples such as cassava, we could rarely find high-protein meat, poultry, and fish in rural markets. Consequently, travelers had to contend with both a paucity of "chop houses" in the bush and overpiced European restaurants in cities. The unvaried food prepared by local cafés was as hygienically suspect as it was tasteless. In view of such alternatives, Marzi and I stocked up on rice and tinned goods, cooking for ourselves on a little one-burner gasoline stove.

India excepted, trains and buses in Asia were quite satisfactory. But public transport in Africa proved generally uncomfortable and costly relative to the Orient. In some areas, it was nonexistent.

Without the amenities of decent transport, food, and accommodations, or the enticement of man-made wonders (nothing remotely on the order of the Taj south of the Sahara), why travel in black Africa?

I could gush over the diversified natural beauty, teeming game reserves, and fascinating traditional peoples like the Bambuti pygmy, Tambulma, and Masai. I could also emphasize the learning experience derived from personal contact with the citizenry of "emerging" African nations. But what I want to stress in this introduction is the very challenge and adventure of a trans-African journey.

Overlanding Asia is strictly child's play compared to traversing the "Dark Continent." Crossing Africa, a traveler rarely knows from day to day where he will lay his head, if there will be food supplies before his run out, or if he will be stuck without transport for weeks. The turbulent African political scene may well force a complete revision of plans. An overlander must also be prepared to drastically reroute should extreme weather conditions obliterate what passes for the "international highway." Vulnerable in his tent, he must be wary of wild animals and deadly insect carriers. He also must be ever alert to the presence of thieves who, unlike the sneaky but harmless petty rip-off artists of the Orient, may commit bodily assault. Finally, an overlander in Africa needs to be a "psychologist" with the patience and cool of a saint, who can roll with the punches of a haughty bureaucrat's racism.

Nothing comes easy in Africa, but to venture from coast to coast in this vast, untamed continent is an achievement bringing no little satisfaction, a rugged adventure unique in its demands . . . and rewards.

If an overlander learns nothing else in Africa, it is that racism is a two-way street. Brutally exploited as inferiors for decades under the aegis of European colonialism, some postindependence Africans are now responding with distressing contempt toward both white visitors and resident ethnic minorities.

Given the heritage of white bigotry, as well as the temper of the times, black racism is a most delicate subject to broach. One is tempted to skirt the issue. However, prior to writing this book, I decided not to mince words, for the thinly veiled prejudice many overlanders must confront is an integral part of the trans-African experience. To ignore this unfortunate yet pertinent reality is to be dishonest. Furthermore, the racist displays of power we encountered reveal, on a smaller scale, the personal caprice and arrogant ethnocentricity that is draining the lifeblood from present-day Africa.

As the citizen of a country which has long maintained second-class status for blacks, I tried to understand the roots of the racial animosity extended to me in Africa. But to merely comprehend was not enough, for as an overlander, I also had to deal with it.

WEST AFRICA: GHANA, TOGO, DAHOMEY

Cultural Schizophrenia

We left the damp chill of October London, arriving by air eight hours later in steaming Accra. Ghana: the former Gold Coast, infamous slave center, home of the fierce Ashanti who battled European intruders until the turn of the twentieth century.

Touching down in Africa rekindled the apprehension I experienced a few years earlier when I entered the black republic of Haiti to research my doctoral dissertation. Like most American whites, I frequently felt uneasy in the presence of blacks. This was largely attributable to burgeoning black rage emanating from centuries of discrimination. At times I found the verbal bitterness, vented randomly with characteristic ghetto toughness, more than a little threatening. Living in a highly ghettoized society only heightened such fears; it was all too easy to project the intimidating behavior of a few onto the race as a whole. Though I recognized this to be irrational, my gut response sometimes overwhelmed my reason.

*After our visit, dictator Kerekou decreed that Dahomey would henceforth be known as "Benin."

For one uncomfortable around Afro-Americans, I was initially ill at ease in Haiti's predominantly black society. But that island held none of the racial tensions so pervasive in the States. Within a brief period, my extreme consciousness of color evaporated into the soft Caribbean air. Then I returned to the United States, only to be stung by the icy hatred and aloofness, understandable or not, of black university students.

I luckily had begun my Caribbean field work in Haiti, rather than Jamaica, where passions of color run so high. Ghana, likewise, proved a propitious introduction to a continent seething with ethnic tensions, for the Ga, Twee, and Ashanti ranked among the warmest peoples we would encounter in Africa.

Most overlanders start their transcontinental venture in Morocco, moving through the Algerian Sahara to Niger, then skirting the eastern extremity of Nigeria. We had already observed Orthodox Islamic societies in Asia and had heard that Morocco was "touristy." Furthermore, while the sparsely populated desert posed some challenge, we were far more interested in West African cultures. London being the European center for inexpensive flights, we obtained an air ticket to Ghana that cost us less than the expense of many weeks hitching through Europe and crossing the Sahara. By landing in Accra, we were able to explore Ghana, little-visited Togo and Dahomey, Nigeria and Cameroon, before heading east through the heart of the continent.

The oppressive humidity of coastal Accra turned my shirt black after a ten-minute walk with a backpack from the airport to a public transport stand. The welcome shadow of the tin-roofed shelter felt a good twenty degrees cooler. Like a nail to a magnet, I would be irresibly drawn to such patches of shade in sultry West Africa.

A "trotro" (a colorfully painted pickup truck with wooden planks for seats) dropped us at a hostel within walking distance of downtown. That first evening, after tossing for hours bathed in sweat, I followed the example of other travelers, dragging my mattress onto the veranda to catch whatever air movement there was. But this left me vulnerable to the voracious mosquitoes that make this coast one of the primary malarial sectors in Africa. Their drone and insatiable

167

appetite soon sent me scurrying back to that stifling purgatory inside.

Accra was a spacious, modern capital with a friendly populace who always went out of their way to orient us and make us feel welcome. But like most third-world capitals, it had more of a European than an indigenous flavor. There was little reason to spend much time here, for Kumasi, seat of the great Ashanti Empire, lay but eight hours' drive to the north.

The best means of getting to Kumasi was the "shared taxi." Peugeot 404's served as the preeminent form of long-distance public transport in West Africa. These rugged cars, built high off the ground, were second only to vehicles with expensive four-wheel drive for handling the region's rough roads. Only in Ghana, where restrictions on the number of occupants were strictly enforced, were Peugeot taxis comfortable. Elsewhere, packed tightly, in passengers sizzled.

We struck up a conversation with a twenty-one-year-old engineering student, Daniel, who was on his way home for vacation. A soft-spoken youth, he inquired eagerly about soul singers James Brown, Aretha Franklin, and Jamaican raggae king Jimmy Cliff. When I asked about local artists and traditional music, Daniel disclaimed any interest, stating that on Ghanaian campuses, Brown and Cliff were the rage.

Daniel invited us to stay with his family, a household of twelve headed by his oldest brother, a university economist. Welcoming us, the professor immediately offered a refreshing beer and proudly turned on the new TV for us. His house, located in a middle-income suburb, was elevated on pillars for better ventilation. All of the adjacent homes were surrounded by high chain-link fences behind which lurked immense watchdogs. Subsequent discussion with Daniel's neighbors revealed a near-pathological fear of thieves.

One of Daniel's sisters, a ravishing young woman of nineteen, invited us over to sample an African-style meal. Anita and her husband, a young bureaucrat then in Accra, were zealous converts to Jehovah's Witnesses. Having recently given birth to a baby boy, she denounced the many "sinful" local women who bore children out of wedlock. In her mind, legitimization was the real key to Ghana's development.

Anita told us that Ghanaian men will generally marry as many wives as they can afford to maintain (the traditional "bride price" is often still paid to the woman's father). She scorned this as "a remnant of our dark days." In view of Ghana's population pressure (the nation can't feed what it has now and is expected to double before the year 2000), I asked Anita if contraception was becoming widespread.

"Lord, no," she laughed. "If a couple doesn't have a number of kids after a time, neighbors will gossip that something is wrong with the marriage."

Preparing the meal, Anita rhythmically pounded cassava for hours with a huge wooden pestle and mortar. We would see this sight frequently throughout West and Central Africa, where cassava is the subsistence, and sometimes only, food. I picked up the heavy three-foot pestle to pound for a while, only to tire after ten minutes, my hands raw. The lithe Anita laughed, returning to beat the starch for the next two hours with the insistent throbbing of a drum.

Meanwhile, his record player blaring James Brown, Daniel and I discussed student life. According to Daniel, there had been little political activity on Ghanaian campuses since the 1966 fall of Nkrumah, the students being fearful of military retaliation. All criticism of the government was guarded, for it was said that spies were everywhere.

To insure good grades, Daniel revealed, he usually visited the local "juju" priest prior to exams.

"Does the priest really help?" I asked.

"Yes! He has The Power. I pay him something or bring him a chicken and he gives me a charm for good juju. I have always done well."

At last the cassava was ready. Called "fufu" here, it had the consistency of cornmeal mush and by itself tasted awfully bland. To the fufu Anita added "soup," scattered traces of stew meat in a hot red chili sauce. We followed the example of our hosts, dipping the fingers of our right hand into the communal bowl.

169

I wish I could report that fufu is tasty, but we personally did not care for it. Fufu always reminded me of globs of spiced glue. We did eat it elsewhere, when no other foods were available, but generally avoided it. Starchy cassava has very little nutritional value and most Africans can rarely (if ever) afford to add any meat to the "soup." Hence so much protein deficiency in this part of the world.

Early the next morning, Daniel and the professor showed us around the teeming Kumasi market. From some distance, the atmosphere reeked of smoked fish and, within the market itself, this putrid stench became almost unbearable. The food section operated under the most unhygienic conditions. Fetid vegetables sat in an earthy muck still oozing from the morning rains; rotting meat and fish festered under the blistering sun.

The greatest shock of all was the prices. Meats were absolutely prohibitive, vegetables and fruits U.S. cost or higher. All foods but cassava seemed out of the range of most Ghanaians. The scarcity of more nourishing fare was disturbing. Those who could afford the meager display of vegetables snapped them up in short order. The few truly affluent Ghanaians paid exorbitant prices for imported goods.

The professor traced this sorry state back to the British colonial era when cocoa plantations were established. Cocoa soon became the Gold Coast's leading export and today Ghana grows one-third of the world's supply. Local farmers were neither taught nor given the incentive to grow anything else. This pattern has persisted with a tremendous quantity of foodstuffs imported and the economy teetering unhealthily on world demand. Presently under a program called "Operation Feed Yourself," government agronomists are said to be encouraging peasants to grow crops other than cassava.

Nevertheless, our economist host noted sardonically, "This is nothing more than a lot of talk. Without adequate funding for agrarian education, fertilizer, and credits, to say nothing of concomitant family planning, the scheme has no substance. But it's a nice name. Starting with Nkrumah, Ghanaians have heard sloganeering of self-sufficiency, yet the only real change since independence has been more mouths to feed."

Dr. Kwame Nkrumah is currently being canonized in some quarters as postcolonial Africa's greatest leader. I asked the professor his opinion of the controversial first prime minister of independent Ghana.

"Nkrumah bandied about a lot of socialist and Pan-African rhetoric. As to his real achievements—well—there remains some question. I can tell you for certain that while Nkrumah became a very wealthy man, his fiscal policy plunged the country deeply into debt. Nkrumah's supporters claim that the debt was necessary for socialist projects yet to be realized when he was overthrown. But as an economist, I must be critical of some of his government's showy but worthless expenditures, extensive graft, and overall mismanagement. At the time of Nkrumah's ouster, our treasury was so insolvent that no roads or bridges could be constructed for three years."

"How effective have been the military regimes that succeeded Nkrumah?"

The professor laughed caustically and looked around. "I dare not elaborate, but I can say that the absurd level of official corruption did not end with Nkrumah. Finances remain deeply in the red, and given our rate of population growth, we are more dependent than ever on food imports."

We caught a bus to the Ashanti Cultural Center, on the grounds of Kumasi's modern university. Amid a fine collection of artifacts, a student related the blood-soaked history of the Ashanti, warriors unvanquished by British troops until the early twentieth century.

During the nineteenth century the Ashanti empire grew to encompass much of southern Ghana. Its expansion was based upon the capture of weaker tribespeople who were then sold to European coastal slavers. The white flesh merchants paid the Ashanti with rifles, enabling them to round up more slaves and expand their empire. Today the Ashanti, some of whom still dress traditionally in kente cloth, walk proudly, aware of their warrior past. While most remain peasant cultivators, a few rank among Ghana's leading educators and lawyers.

Everyone in Daniel's household treated us royally and, as in Accra, we were impressed with the warmth extended by Kumasi's

171

residents. Bidding Daniel and his family good-bye, we booked seats on a bus bound south to Cape Coast where the foreboding Elmina Castle, a "medieval" slaving compound, still stands. Built by the Portuguese (1492), seized by the Dutch (1637), the fortress was ultimately purchased by the British (1872). For centuries, thousands of slaves were incarcerated behind these grim gray walls, awaiting passage to the New World.

We were guided through the dank dungeons along with a tour group of American blacks. Some stared daggers at Marzi and me while a guide recited the history of European slavers' savagery. He neglected to mention the role of the Ashanti. As the tour was about to end, a heavily made-up Afro-American woman scowled at us, "Now, don't you feel guilty?"

Startled, I thought for a minute, replying, "I wasn't around at the time."

In many parts of West Africa, I observed affluent black visitors from the States. They had come with great expectations, seeking their "cultural roots." Yet on innumerable occasions, I overheard them complaining of slow service, filth, smells, heat. The black Americans wanted all the comforts of home, an affirmation of great postindependence progress, plus a floorshow of traditional culture. What they experienced was poverty, staggering bureaucratic red tape, and official corruption in a society so basically different that in no way could they relate to it . . . or feel at home.

Afro-Americans sporting dashikis and kente cloth. Socially mobile Ghanaians wearing the latest Western styles. Afro-Americans demanding traditional entertainment, then quickly growing bored. Ghanaians swinging in discothèques to recorded James Bown and tinny local imitators of U.S. electronic soul music.

The black tourists found the surface similarities of their African brethren most disturbing. They had flown all this way to seek out the "genuine article," not some mimicry of their own fashion and music. Most exasperating of all for these visitors was what remained truly African. The skin color may be the same, as well as the taste in music and dress, but in pace and attitude, the hard-driving black

172

American and the easygoing West African moved to the beat of a decidedly different drum.

A Peugeot took us from Accra down the palm-speckled coast to Lomé, Togo. Muggy and mosquito-ridden, Lomé is nonetheless a colorful town fronted by dazzling beaches.

A former French-colonial capital, Lomé still has a number of "colons" in residence, and hence many shops well-stocked with imported Gallic delicacies. In former British African capitals, one is usually reduced to a diet of tasteless tinned meats. But in the French areas, a budget traveler may dine well at reasonable prices. In all our travels around the globe, we noted that for the French, life was devoid of meaning without Parisian-prepared cuisine. Though this was nice for us, I was aware that such delicacies, imported in quantity, hardly improve a poor country's balance of payments.

Lomé also boasted a couple of Lebanese restaurants, reflecting the substantial number of Middle Eastern shopkeepers who thrive here and in other West African towns. The Lebanese are to this part of the world what the Chinese are to Southeast Asia. Their commercial acumen is a source of envy and loathing.

Lomé's market is one of the liveliest in all Africa. Here amid the din of crowing roosters and bleating goats, Mina and Ewe tribes-women, wearing the most wildly colored dresses, miraculously balanced enormous bundles of produce and bolts of fabric atop their heads. These women boisterously hawked their wares to throngs of haggling shoppers. Unlike most African cultures, where the women are strictly subordinate, some female Mina merchants have gained tremendous economic leverage. With the profits of their "petty capitalism," scrupulously salted away for years, some have invested in fleets of Peugeot taxis and become entreprenuers of the first rank. Indeed, the last mayor of Lomé was a woman, most unusual on this continent unless the woman is related by blood to the national strongman.

Kathy, a Peace Corps volunteer serving as a secretary in the administrative office, put us up in her pleasant five-room villa. I had visited Peace Corps in the Caribbean who lived in the same sort of simple abodes as the locals. In West Africa I was astounded by the luxurious accommodations of many volunteers. Like Kathy, most even had servants!

I later heard a Peace Corps director in the Central African Republic rationalize that as "fonctionnaires" in the eyes of African bureaucrats, volunteers had to be properly housed or they would not be respected.

"Doesn't the hiring of houseboys and cooks perpetuate an image of the white master that should have died with colonialism?" I asked. "One would think the keeping of servants inimical to the ideals of the Peace Corps."

His programmed reply: "Africans need the employment."

The majority of Peace Corps people we met in French West Africa were doing something next to useless: teaching English in largely illiterate French-speaking nations where just about any other skill would have proven more helpful. For most of these young Americans, living the lives of fonctionnaires, the amenities were more than comfortable. In Togo, for instance, though some volunteers had a rougher existence in small villages, most enjoyed conditions similar to Kathy's. Male "volunteers" reaped the benefits of relaxed Mina and Kabre sexual mores, some boasting that they took many a comely lover. Furthermore, the southern Togolese were very friendly, easygoing people, delightful to work with. No wonder so many volunteers here extended their tour from two to three years.

We set out to visit the little-acculturated Tambulma people in Togo's remote northeast. As in Ghana, the lush, tropical bush along the coast changed first to savanna grasslands, and later to barren desolation as we traveled north. In the town of Kande, we overnighted with a Peace Corps teacher named Jerry. He revealed that conditions were no longer so pleasant in these parts because of antiwhite propaganda. Togo's present strongman, Eyadema, hails from the Kabre tribe, which dominates the north, his bastion of support against the rival southern Mina and Ewe. Eyadema had initiated an indoctrination campaign among his own people, blam-

174

ing every conceivable African failure, past or present, on the white man. Even history textbooks were ordered rewritten, to whit: Africans and Arabs never engaged in the slave trade, only whites.

Eyadema shrewdly utilized the all-purpose excuse of white villainy to justify his government's lack of substantive progress. While fonctionnaires and military officers lived like kings, most Togolese remained impoverished and ninety per cent were illiterate. We would witness variations on the "white exploitation" theme propagated by do-nothing African governments elsewhere.

Little wonder Jerry had watched his impressionable students turn almost hostile since the introduction of the new texts. But to openly refute such nonsense or similar mass-directed propaganda could have led to Jerry's dismissal. I didn't envy his precarious position.

As there was no public transport into the land of the isolated Tambulma, Jerry arranged a ride part way for us with a French priest. The dun-colored earth grew starker and starker as we penetrated this infertile terrain. The Land Rover jolted along a rut-ridden track until reaching a fork in the road where we parted company with the priest. It was necessary to hike a good nine miles to a town across the Dahomean border in which we hopefully would find some lodging.

Gagging with the dust that a hot wind swirled in our faces, we had walked only about a mile when a weird image loomed over the horizon. Coming closer, we recognized it as a towering mud castle of the Tambulma.

Tribal warfare persisted in this region until the late 1940s. For protection, the Tambulma made their home their castle, layering mud walls two stories high. From rooftop ramparts, sheltered warriors could rain arrows down upon approaching invaders.

An ominous cow-skull fetish adorned the walls of the imposing residence. The only people apparently home were an evil-looking toothless old man, wearing nothing but a loincloth, and the sickly infant he held in his arms. The weathered man's ears, laden with wooden plugs, extended to his shoulders. The baby's belly was distended, his hair red, a victim of kwashiorkor. Satisfied that we

175

meant no harm, the aged man gave a yell and a woman emerged from behind the "castle" with two young boys. She spoke no French, but through sign language we asked if we might see the inside of her home.

The bottom floor served as the old people's residence, with a special portion reserved for fetishes and charms of all kinds. Only the elders knew what magic was hidden here; for all others the fetish area was taboo. Clambering up to the roof, we spied four conical thatch-covered cubicles where the women of the household dwelt. Some Tambulma men took three or four wives, sleeping in a different spouse's room at whim. Along the narrow rooftop parapet, bow and arrows stood at ready, reminding us that warrior days were not so far removed.

We thanked our hosts for allowing us to look around, giving them gifts of tinned foods, and renewed our hike to the Dahomean frontier. Chalky dust filtered into our every pore, and with no trees to offer shade from the scorching sun, the trek seemed interminable. The burden of packs and tent further sapped our strength; worst of all, our canteens were empty.

Finally, we reached the border, demarcated by a tiny wooden police shed. Marzi and I were doubtless the first foreigners to pass through here in months. Tongues hanging out, we endured three tortuous hours in customs before the confused fonctionnaire concluded that our documents were in order.

"Is there any place to get a drink?" we asked anxiously.

"Oui, let's have a beer," the bureaucrat invited. We wandered over to a wooden shack and gratefully guzzled warm brew that brought us back to life.

"We are lucky," the fonctionnaire exclaimed. "The beer truck comes but once a month to Bekombe." He chugged three bottles more. We thanked the official, but strapping on our packs, realized that we had misunderstood.

"The proprietor says you must pay him now."

In Asia, we were frequently treated by locals, but with African bureaucrats, the reverse usually held true. I hid my anger and paid.

176

This fonctionnaire was the prefect, the "big cheese" of the area, and we wanted no trouble from him.

"How do you plan to leave Bekombe?"

"We figure we can catch a southbound lorry at the market."

"There will be no vehicle here for two weeks." Slowly spreading a malicious grin, he added, "I have the only auto in Bekombe. Please let me know if I may be of service."

To our chagrin, the priest who put us up at a small mission station confirmed this. The cleric's own Land Rover had been towed south for repairs. Yes, he nodded, we would have to make some arrangements with the prefect, and that was certain to cost a goodly sum.

We rose early the next morning to visit Bekombe's extraordinary weekly market. The tribespeople who brought their meager produce here from the hinterlands were a sight to behold. Clad solely in loincloths, some of the men and women had dagger-pointed rocks protruding through their chins. A few carried huge stone axes, slung menacingly over their shoulders.

I asked the priest to translate my request to photograph them. The tribespeople assented, but as I raised my super-eight to shoot, the prefect tapped me roughly on the shoulder.

"No photography in Dahomey."

"Pourquoi?"

Groping for an answer, he finally stammered, "Government orders."

I was later informed that a German photographer had published some allegedly "pornographic" pictures of Dahomean women in a European magazine. Somehow the periodical found its way back to the capital, Cotonou, where enraged officials broadcast the story throughout the land. They urged Dahomeans to refuse whites permission to take their picture, alleging that Europeans brand all Africans as "savages." Consequently I observed some Dahomean women in towns south of Bekombe covering their breasts whenever Caucasians approached. The government had made its people ashamed of their own traditional dress. I might add with no small irony that Dahomey, like Togo, had a much ballyhooed "authenticity" movement, officially denigrating European cultural influences while extolling traditional values.

On nonmarket days, Bekombe reverted to a slumberous hamlet consisting of a wooden store, mission, and immigration office. Unenthusiastic at the prospect of remaining here for two weeks, we approached the prefect with proper humility. He hemmed and hawed, moaning about the high cost of gasoline. But "oui," for only fifteen times the normal Peugeot fare, he would arrange to have his Land Rover transport us fifty kilometers south to the next town. We haggled in vain, forlornly accepting a "compromise" settlement of ten times the norm. Naturally, while on the road, we passed a lorry bound for Bekombe.

Dropped at the town of Natitingou, we found people had really swallowed the governmental line about photos. They pointed at our camera cases, made fists, and spat. While we waited for the local bus, two French volunteers stopped in a Renault, introduced themselves, and invited us to spend a few days at their station twenty-two kilometers deep in the bush. Super! These young French women lived among some of the least acculturated peoples in the region—the Sambla (cousins of the Tambulma), Poole, and Dande.

Beatrix was a dedicated nutritionist, Françoise a nurse. They had witnessed some rather bizarre incidents during their two years of volunteer work in this isolated region. Most of the local peoples are "fetishers." The witch doctors, held in awe by the believers, do a thriving business. Beatrix once saw a fetish priest tell a villager he was going to die. The young man keeled over with fatal coronary arrest that very day, literally scared to death. Françoise also linked some of the more serious illnesses she treated to local witch-doctors. A tribesman with a run of bad luck may visit his fetish priest to determine who has put a hex on him. To break the spell, the tribesman may be advised to resort to an age-old practice in these parts—poisoning.

One heinous rite Françoise described as common practice among the non-Moslem tribes was "female circumcision" (clitorectomy). Teenage girls chewed narcotic herbs to deaden the senses, as they were forbidden to express any sign of pain during the operation. It was not unusual for a young woman to die from infections spread through the fetish priest's use of an unsterile knife.

We accompanied Beatrix on her rounds to nearby villages. The pervasive malnutrition in this harsh land which seemed to bear only scrub bush and thorns was truly appalling—so many kwashiorkor kids. Beatrix distributed soy mix for protein. She no longer parceled out dry milk because local women had only made it into cheese for sale in the Natitingou market. But even the soy may not have reached the children, since the male head of the household always got first choice of whatever was available. Beatrix remarked that her two-year effort at nutrition education had barely penetrated such cultural barriers.

Françoise too had professional problems. Sick tribespeople invariably consulted the fetish priest first, resorting to the nurse only when the symptoms became severe. Due to a lack of hygiene, parasitical diseases were the most common malady. The villagers, more often than not, ignored Françoise's suggestions, for they could not see any correlation between better sanitation and good health.

When the volunteers' stuffy director came by for a visit, Beatrix prevailed upon him to drive us to Parakou, where we could catch the train south. Near the railhead, he stopped to join a "colon" family for lunch at a wooded swimming hole. They were archetypical white settlers, self-exiles from a European society where they had been utter failures. In Africa such colonists have spawned a mutant version of the hierarchy which they found closed to them at "home." Racist to the core, they were as aloof and joyless as their Parisian cousins. I couldn't help but think that the designation "colon," in an English rather than French sense, was most appropriate.

The family related that three days earlier, a southbound train crashed into the northern express. What made this utterly astounding is that the two trains could have collided at all, as there is only one track from Parakou to Cotonou! The "colons" laughed at "African ineptitude," but to us this was no joke, for without a private car, the train was the only transport south.

On the road just outside Parakou, we marveled at the sight of Fulani cattle herders. These proud nomads seasonally drove their cows as far as six hundred miles from Volta and northern Togo and Dahomey to the urban markets of the coast. The Fulani, an ethnic mix of black and Arab, amazed me with the control they wielded over their stock. A mere whistle and the cows would turn left or right.

Second class on the train was cheap enough (in third class, passengers sat on wooden benches or the floor). The seats were comfortable, but to insure air circulation, the windowpanes had been removed. Dust poured in, soon caking us in clay. I emphathized with the passengers of nineteenth-century smoke-belching locomotives.

The local people seemed to carry their every possession with them. Goods being generally cheaper here than further south, Dahomeans purchased more and more at each stop. Vendors hawking from outside platforms did brisk business, passing through the car windows squealing goats, yams, vegetables, even a horse's head. A movable feast.

Abomey, now somnolent, was once the animated center of the great Fon Empire. From the late sixteenth century on, European seafaring captains in the flesh trade did so much business that the Dahomean shoreline became better known as the "Slave Coast." The more powerful Dahomean tribes fought each other for rights to dominate heavily populated regions "ripe" for slaving. Ultimately, the Fon controlled the area. Its king, rich from slaves, invited Europeans to establish trade centers and fortresses along the coast. But with fewer slave ships calling in the early nineteenth century, the Fon Empire fell into economic depression and was easy prey for a Yoruba (a Nigerian tribe) takeover.

In 1818 the brilliant Fon King Ghezo threw off the Yoruba yoke, once again making Dahomey powerful. With the British outlawing of the slave trade, Ghezo insightfully revamped the economy around agriculture. He ordered coconut and oil palms planted in coastal areas for cash crops and had manioc cultivated inland for subsistence. Palm oil today has become the primary export of this re-source-poor country.

Abomey's museum exhibits Fon relics from the days of empire: colorful tapestries depicting military triumphs, expert bronze works, and Voodoo paraphernalia. Belief in Voodoo spirits and ghosts remains strong in the south (the north being predominantly ani-mist). While the Voodoo shrines we visited in the vicinity of Abomey had gruesome paintings of decapitations on the walls, these were merely symbolic of the powerful magic invoked within. Indeed, Voodoo is not the bloodthirsty cult Hollywood has projected. The only bloodshed may be the ritual sacrifice of a chicken or goat. There are, to be sure, magical charms, but not some movie-maker's fantasy of sticking pins in dolls. "Possession," however, is very real to voodooists. In Haiti, I watched a woman "entered" by Dambulla, the snake god, writhe furiously on the floor for hours. That was no sham; in her mind she was possessed.

Ironically, Voodoo is "purer" in Haiti than Dahomey. Haitian slaves, stolen away from their Dahomean homeland, drove their French masters out early. With little European clerical intervention over the course of the next century, traditional Voodoo remained deeply rooted. But in Dahomey, the mission influence has been considerable. Saints like John the Baptist play a larger role among the gods and spirits of Voodoo than they do in Haiti. Nevertheless, Voodoo is the Dahomean religious mainstay, and at night we could hear a haunting drumming from its shrines.

Dahomey's most widely promoted attraction is Granvil, a village of platformed huts erected on stilts high atop a vast lake. A short drive from the capital and thus a tourist trap of sorts, Granvil is nonetheless unique. It was initially built within the lake to deter enemy invasion. Crops are cultivated on the adjacent shore, a good half-hour's canoe ride from the huts.

Granvil's muck-filled lake still serves as the communal toilet, drinking well, garbage disposal, and laundry. Proposals to construct decent sanitation facilities have been rejected by the village. Its inhabitants fear that any modern-looking devices might diminish

Granvil's allure for cash-carrying visitors. The government, which garners the lion's share of tourist revenues, has done nothing to alter this misconception. Therefore, most Granvillians continue to suffer debilitating parasitical infections.

We found the capital, Cotonou, neither as scenic nor as charming as Togo's Lomé. Here one was never far removed from misery. Even in the taxis, we noticed drivers with sizable chunks of their nose or mouth eaten away by leprosy. Hungry children lay beside rows of tin-roofed wooden shanties, too weak to brush swarming flies from their eyes. In striking contrast to these fetid slums stood an opulent three-million-dollar presidential palace and a number of ostentatious villas.

On our last night in Cotonou, we dined with a Peace Corps construction worker and his friend, a resident French engineer. The volunteer noted, "Eighty-five per cent of Dahomean revenues are allocated for administrative and military salaries. That doesn't leave much for development."

The "colon" sardonically took exception to this. "Really John, there's not much to waste in a country whose chief export is palm oil. Even President Kerekou is not yet a millionaire." He looked at us, remarking cynically, "You think this regime squanders its money? Just wait till you get to oil-rich Nigeria!"

Marzi and I would reserve judgment until we could see for ourselves. Since we had experienced difficulties in merely securing a visa for Nigeria, we anticipated further hassles. On the other hand, we were really looking forward to visiting neighboring northwest Cameroon, reputed to be the most traditional region of West Africa.

WEST AFRICA:
NIGERIA AND CAMEROON

A Case of Inverted Bigotry

At first we thought it would be necessary to fly over Nigeria. The minister in charge of visas at London's Nigerian Embassy provided our first encounter with blatantly racist African bureaucrats. We explained that we had been traveling in Asia and were, at the time, living in Amsterdam. "Don't you know," she growled, "that you must get a visa in your own country?" Nonetheless, she gave cause for some hope by handing us lengthy forms to fill out.

"Do you have proof of your professions and sufficient funds? We want to be certain only worthy visitors come to Nigeria." We showed her further identification and money. "And where is your ticket out?"

For overlanders, a requisite ticket from any point on the continent back to Europe will usually satisfy African immigration officials. We had purchased air tickets at a specially reduced fare from Nairobi to London. The bureaucrat glared at the tickets. "This is Nairobi-London, not Lagos-London. Have your ticket rewritten!"

"But we are not exiting from Lagos—we are going overland to East Africa."

She ripped our application forms into tiny shreds. "Don't waste my time. We Nigerians only accept suitable foreigners!"

Oh well, we would get the visa in Ghana, or so we thought. At the embassy in Accra, we surrendered our passports and were told to return in three days. When we stopped to pick them up, the secretary informed us that we must first be interviewed by the consul. Arriving punctually for the appointment, we cooled our heels for two hours outside the official's open office door, watching him leaf through magazines, glancing occasionally at us.

Finally, we were ushered in to speak with the heavyset Hausa swathed in lavish robes, a tiny fez perched atop his balding head. He lectured us rapid-fire on what sort of foreigners were welcome in Nigeria. Examining our credentials and financial resources in mock astonishment, he acknowledged that, yes indeed, we were "properly qualified." But it would take a month for him to cable Lagos for approval. A month! He was doubtlessly angling for a "dash" to "expedite the process," but at this point, we had neither the experience nor the confidence to bribe such a highly placed bureaucrat.

Similarly refused in Lomé, Marzi and I sought the good offices of the American consul. "Contingent upon their whim, the Nigerians treat a lot of people this way. They have oil and are flexing their muscles."

The consul addressed a note to the Nigerian Embassy, stating that he would be happy to furnish any information desired on our behalf. We promptly delivered the note, once again patiently explaining why we had not flown back from Europe to secure our visas in the States. This time it looked as if the American consul's statement would prove the clincher—or so we thought. "All right, now get a letter from your embassy attesting that you are American citizens." Apparently our passports were inadequate identification!

Presenting the voucher, we were finally issued visas—for all of eight days. Ridiculous! Nigeria is as big as France and Italy combined. We would have to shoot straight through. But at least we were spared the cost of an air ticket.

A Swiss administrator for a European pharmaceutical company's Lagos-based subsidiary offered us a ride to the capital. He accelerated the usual border formalities by slipping the immigration official a ten-"naira" note.

"The dash is a way of life here. You simply cannot do business without it. Nor can you live comfortably without all sorts of administrative problems cropping up that can only be satisfied with such gratuities. I find it necessary—yes expected—to dash almost every bureaucrat I deal with. Some colleagues excuse the dash as an 'African tip.' I say the dash is destroying Nigeria. This country is the eighth leading oil producer, yet you see malnutrition, a lack of sanitation, insufficient schools and educators, and poorly 'kept'—if that's the word for it—roads. As a health professional, I find the scarcity of medical facilities in the countryside appalling for a nation getting so much oil revenue. The military is presently allotted a third of the 'legal' budget. The rest of the proceeds run straight from the pipeline into officials' pockets."

I asked him about Nigeria's recent international stand against family planning.

"Absurd in the most populous nation on this overpopulated continent. They listen to Chinese propaganda about 'birth control as genocide.' But China itself practices intensive family planning and is very rich agriculturally. Nigeria has sixty million people, twice the number of any other sub-Saharan nation. Its population is going to double by the end of the century and the quantity of food already being imported is not even covered by the foreign exchange earned from petrol. But the military government either doesn't realize that its people can't eat oil, or it doesn't care. The regime produces a lot for show, but little of lasting value. In downtown Lagos, you'll see a convention center constructed at enormous cost for an upcoming international black arts fair—nonsensical in a country where so many children have kwashiorkor. Nigerian peasants are warm, wonderful people. What a pity they are saddled with such corrupt leaders."

We entered the outskirts of Lagos, driving for a good hour through the sprawling metropolis to the center. Most of the city was composed of tin-roofed timber shacks, occasionally interspersed

185

with imposing colonial mansions. A few modern skyscrapers rose high above the largely one-story central business district.

It took a courageous individual to brave the unregulated traffic, but the Swiss driver had a lot of practice. We weaved in and out of a multitude of honking, muffler-less vehicles. I was thankful not to be behind the wheel amid this sheer chaos. The din was unrelenting, the exhaust fumes asphyxiating in Lagos's heavy humidity; there were no air currents to blow the gaseous vapors out to sea.

Nigeria has been wracked by tribal tensions. The Yoruba dominate in the southwest, the Ibo in the southeast, the Moslem Hausa in the north. The Ibo are popularly characterized as educated, progressive go-getters, the Hausa as "backward," the Yoruba somewhere in between. There is no love lost among these bitter ethnic rivals.

In 1966 a Hausa majority government was overthrown by a clique of young Ibo officers, the top Hausa officials murdered. Shortly thereafter, a counter-coup brought to power Yakubu Gowon, a military representative of a minor tribe. (It was hoped that a leader from outside the competing tribes would bring stability.) But in reprisal for the bloodshed of the initial coup, vengeful Hausa butchered thousands of Ibo working in the north, causing a massive movement of Ibo refugees to flee to their eastern homelands.

The Ibo leadership, lambasting the Gowon government for taking no action to end the massacres in the north, demanded regional autonomy. When negotiations broke down, the east, calling itself Biafra, seceded. The tragedy of the thirty-month civil war that followed, the widespread starvation and misery in its wake, are well known. Combined forces of Yoruba and Hausa succeeded in reunifying the country only at a fearful toll of human life.

We asked the manager of the Lagos YMCA, a highly educated Ibo who fought for Biafra, what had happened to his people since their defeat.

"While there were instances of discrimination immediately following the war, we have actually been rather well treated."

"Isn't that surprising, given the intensity and duration of the struggle?"

"Not when you take tribal feelings into account. Our military

186

might was smashed and we no longer posed a threat, but the Hausa and Yoruba feared each other's potential dominance. We are the best-educated people in Nigeria, also the merchant class. So both sides are playing up to us, hoping to count the Ibo as allies if the two come to a head. That's why when you pass through Iboland, you will see little trace of the war. Both Yoruba and Hausa pumped in funds for reconstruction—not so much in the best interests of the nation or out of compassion for their rebellious countrymen—but basically to win us over. Fear of tribal dominance remains the moving force in Nigerian politics."

That evening a documentary film on India was screened at the Y before an audience of Nigeria's educated student elite. The film was well made, a slick portrayal of the subcontinent's "advances" under former Prime Minister Gandhi. Yet it wasn't the outrageous dishonesty of the film (no poverty, boundless luxuries, attractive Brahmins at an ice-skating rink), but the dress and religious ritual of the Indians that made the Nigerians howl derisively with laughter.

Throughout black-ruled Africa, one hears condemnation of white racism. "Fascist, racist South Africa" is broadcast over the media everywhere. But intolerance toward other peoples' cultures is pervasive. The praise for prophets of "Pan-Africanism" (Nkrumah and company), indeed the very notion of African unity, becomes ludicrous within the contemporary context. Africans we met rarely identified themselves as Ghanaians, Zairois, Nigerians, or Kenyans. They saw themselves as Ashanti, Lokele, Yoruba, Kikuyu. At the Lagos Y, those were highly educated, affluent young Nigerians, not illiterate peasants, ridiculing another culture. A telling experience.

Regrettably, we had to rush through this huge country before our visas expired. Express buses shuttled between the major towns and we rode east in comfort into what was once Biafra. The highway from Lagos was paved, but so filled with chuck holes that the ride would have been smoother on dirt. The buses ran only during the day, as highwaymen terrorized the roads by night. A favorite tactic of thugs was to slam on their brakes just ahead of a vehicle on one of the numerous single-lane bridges and hold up the occupants of the trailing car at knife- or gunpoint.

Alongside nearly every narrow bridge was the rusting shell of a wreck. The government allows these hulks to rot by the roadside in hopes of tempering local drivers' recklessness and excessive speed. Judging from the profusion of accidents and the still-suicidal antics of Nigerian motorists, the deterrent has proven ineffective. Such driving, seen throughout the third world, often symbolized for me a manic attempt to "catch up" with the fast-paced industrialized world.

In Enugu, a three-block line of impatient Ibo kids queued excitedly for a Saturday matinee at the local bijou. Wondering what filmfare occasioned such a crowd, I sidled up to examine the posters under the wooden marquee. A Johnny Weismuller Tarzan epic! Nineteen-thirties Hollywood was rarely more racist in its portrayal of Africans. A curious choice of films for this eager audience.

For the experience, we decided to take a colorfully painted "mammy wagon" (similar to a Ghanaian "trotto") rather than a Peugeot taxi to the Cameroonian border. Passengers were crammed in almost beyond molecular capacity. I watched helplessly as a naked baby, squatting on his mother's lap, urinated all over her—and my backpack as well. The woman, wiping herself off with a rag, uttered no apology. A middle-aged man seated next to her laughed at my displeasure. But justice triumphed—his enjoyment was cut short when that little boy's reservoir burst all over his lap.

"Good aim, son," I commended.

Due to the mammy wagon's frequent breakdowns, the border was closed when we finally arrived. Fortunately, an amicable Nigerian policeman permitted us to pitch our tent in front of his station and even arranged for transport to pick us up in the morning.

Our taxi to the border, with one passenger more than the legal limit of eight, was stopped by an armed man in uniform. He ordered the driver to surrender his papers, stating that he would be under arrest unless a "fine" was paid on the spot. The driver had no choice but to comply. Later the Nigerian passengers snickered over the dash extracted. They unanimously concurred that the "policeman" was really a scheming civilian engaged in "highway robbery."

Cameroon is unique in West Africa. In this fusion of former French and British colonies, both languages of the imperial powers are the official national tongues. Led by the elected President Ahijo, Cameroon was the first nonmilitary state we had entered since arriving in Africa.

But "civilian rule" did not prevent roadblock halts every twenty-five miles. There, our passports and the identity cards of all fellow Cameroonian passengers were checked and rechecked by authoritarian military officials. There were actually more power-wielding soldiers here than in the neighboring military dictatorships!

The road from the Cameroonian seashore up to the northeast offered our first real glimpse of African rain forest. For a few memorable hours we rode through splendorous tropical overgrowth, rich with jungle foliage, hissing with the rush of swollen streams.

At Bamenda, the district capital, we stretched our legs while our driver relaxed over a beer. A wood placard adjacent to the pub announced:

> Traditional Doctor
> Papa Joseph Shu
> Remember I Treat
> Madness, Fainting
> Convulsion, Eyestrain
> Rheumatism, Piles
> One-Side Headache
> Come One, Come All

Driving north, we watched the vegetation thin once more into parched grasslands. Passengers were faced with a miserable choice: to either close the car windows and suffocate from the heat or leave them, open and choke on the dust. We regretfully opted for the latter and, by the time we reached Banso, were speckled with an ocher powder from head to foot. Villagers in the market roared at our appearance, one inquiring in an exuberant pidgin, "You white blackman or black whiteman?!"

We had chosen to depart from the most direct route east to visit Banso, which reportedly adhered to traditionalist West African ways. While beneath the surface this may have held true, the people appeared to be more a hybrid of European and African cultures. They wore European dress and many attended Christian churches, though the influence of juju priests remained considerable. Nonetheless, the Fon (village chief) still ruled with substantial power (he maintains jurisdiction over noncapital or nonpolitical offenses) and we arranged an audience with him.

Entering the Fon's courtyard, we were warmly greeted by a smiling fez-crowned potentate enveloped in a long, flowing white robe. He pounded a carved staff, commanding an attendant to bring us some beer. At frequent intervals, one of his subjects would approach, deferentially bow, clap three times, and relate his grievance through cupped hands. The Fon, scratching his head with all the wisdom of a Solomon, would then make a judgment, definitively settling the issue. Occasionally the chief consulted his imperial court of three old rogues, happily intoxicated with palm wine, who howled with mirth at every plaintiff. Their colorful round-necked "bubus" (togas) were as eye-catching as any traditional regalia we had yet seen. One even wore a spotted leopard-skin cap over his royal brow.

The Fon engaged in cheerful banter with us, asking finally where we lodged. When told the cheapest hotel in Banso, he looked appalled. After whispering with his bemused court, the Fon barked out a command. A caged rooster was delivered post-haste to our feet. The Fon, believing us to be destitute (why else would whites stay in an African hotel?), had taken pity on us. He ordered our innkeeper to prepare us a feast.

The elderly proprietress accepted her chore without question, obviously pleased to carry out the bidding of the Fon. After months of canned corned beef (much of it Cameroonian, the vilest bully beef conceivable—dog food is tastier), sardines, or fufu, we looked forward to this exotic delicacy and we fairly drooled when it was served. Alas, this was one fowl for which we should have filed our teeth. It was so tough, I envisioned its slaughterer brandishing her hatchet in front of the terrified creature just prior to the kill.

On Cameroonian Peugeots, I always tried to arrange our backpacks so that the goats with whom they invariably shared the roof luggage rack were not in a position to defecate on them. We transferred to several of these taxis, the only long-distance transport in the northwest, on our way back down to the port city of Douala, always finding them packed to suffocation. Their drivers were mini-entrepreneurs who tried to cheat us at every turn. One even demanded that all passengers roll up their windows in the stifling midday heat so that he could hose down his vehicle. As in most parts of the third world, gasoline was never purchased until the transport was full—another source of painful delay in these cramped ovens. Oh for the "comfort" of Indian trains!

Arriving in Douala to catch the eastbound train to the capital, Yaoundé, we found we were wrong to type all Cameroonian taxi drivers as avaricious. Exhausted after the hard day's drive, Marzi inadvertently left her purse in the Peugeot while collecting the backpacks I handed down from the roof. By the time she realized what had happened, we had already walked to the railway station. Just when we had written off a considerable sum of Cameroonian francs plus an invaluable address book, the driver, having guessed our destination, pulled into the station to return the purse. In West Africa, where poverty is agonizingly real and travelers are constantly ripped-off, this act of integrity was most appreciated—jarring our perspectives back into focus.

Having suffered our fill of Peugeots, we solicited a ride in Yaoundé from a young New Orleans couple in exchange for sharing expenses. It was utterly amazing that Kendall and Melissa, complaining about everything, had gotten as far as they had. After all, crossing the Sahara, even in a jeep, is said to be difficult. In contrast to overlanders in Asia, Kendall and Melissa were typical of many travelers we met in Africa—eager to boast that they had made the trip, but showing little interest in African culture or politics.

Only twenty miles from the Central African border, we came to a halt behind a truck stopped on the crest of a hill. When Kendall impatiently blew his horn, the driver was so startled he must not have properly engaged his clutch, for the lorry rolled backward into our jeep. Although damage to his grille was minimal, Kendall was livid. He asked to see the Cameroonian's insurance papers, inanely demanding that the accident be reported to a gendarme.

"Now wait a minute, Kendall, these countries don't function like the States—you don't just call the AAA and a cop," I advised.

Kendall replied that it wasn't my car that was damaged, and if I didn't like it, I could get out and walk.

Melissa tearfully reminded Kendall that he had no Cameroonian insurance, only international.

To this Marzi added vehemently, "Come on, Kendall, we're only twenty miles from the border. This road is so desolate, there might be no police by for days. Besides, Cameroonian insurance is mandatory here and you could get into trouble without it."

But Kendall remained intransigent. Meanwhile, the bewildered truck driver tried to pull away, but his engine refused to cooperate. As night fell, a uniformed Cameroonian, who identified himself as the district prefect, drove up. He ordered that we sleep at a nearby mission, promising to examine the damages the following day, for he was too tired to investigate the matter at that hour.

The next morning, the prefect asked to see Kendall's Cameroonian insurance. Informed that Kendall had none, the prefect ordered him to flag down a westbound Peugeot and journey two days back to the district capital to secure the "proper" insurance. Otherwise, he could not drive further within Cameroon—not even the scant twenty miles to the border.

After several months in Africa, we realized that bribery was, regrettably, a way of life on the continent. But when Kendall discreetly offered a "cadeau" to this official, it was refused. What luck—the first honest bureaucrat we had run across!

Later Marzi overheard the prefect discussing a major festival with traditional dancing to be held a day's drive north, celebrating the opening of a railhead. Though it meant going out of our way, it sounded like an event not to be missed. So we climbed atop the roof of a government truck conveying local people to the "fete."

The railway, linking Ngaoundéré in the remote northeast with the coast, had recently been completed with the help of millions of

192

dollars in foreign aid. In a country where the roads are difficult to maintain due to extreme weather, the railway promised to give a crucial financial boost to the national economy. To celebrate, traditional dancers were trucked in from all over this ethnically diverse nation. It promised to be quite a spectacle.

But at the entrance to the fairgrounds, a soldier stopped Marzi, demanding to see her photography permit.

"What permit?" I inquired.

He responded by snatching Marzi's camera, snarling that authorization to take pictures could be obtained only in Yaoundé. Since she was bringing in a camera "illegally," he was obliged to confiscate it!

Marzi was on the verge of tears. She had long looked forward to using the Olympus, with its fine telephoto lens, to photograph the East African game parks. The cost of another quality camera in Africa was prohibitive, and we certainly had no intention of losing the Olympus.

I first tried to reason with the fonctionnaire, relating how we came to hear of the festival and knew nothing about a necessary permit. I promised we would not enter the fairgrounds, if only we could have the camera back. But he obstinately refused, repeating that in neglecting to secure authorization, Marzi had broken the law. He clearly planned to keep the camera for himself.

All the irrational racial conditioning which I had tried so hard to overcome for the past decade rose from my gut. I was tired of being fucked-over by vengeful, greedy bureaucrats. Somehow I refrained from spewing expletives as I argued furiously, aware that such words would guarantee the loss of the camera and could well put us in jail. The virulence of my thoughts later shamed me—this was something I believed no longer a part of me. Reverse racism was no excuse for such feelings. I would find much cause to introspect . . .

But I'm not saying that a sense of outrage, untouched either by prejudice or guilt, was unwarranted. After all, the bureaucrat was using his authority to steal Marzi's camera. Soon a uniformed official pushed through the crowd that had gathered with amusement to watch the verbal fireworks. I composed myself, explaining to the senior officer all that had transpired. The two soldiers exchanged some words in a local dialect, the discussion growing ever more heated. Finally, the superior officer pulled the camera from his subordinate's clutches, returning it to a thankful Marzi. He slapped our humiliated antagonist full across the face and gruffly bade us enter the fairgrounds.

The festivities made all the troubles we had encountered seem well worth it. Dancers from the northwest, wearing immense, evocatively carved wooden masks representing demons or animals, stamped the ground in rhythm to a turbulent drumming. Warriors from the south, adorned in elaborately plumed headdresses, moved to an incessant beat, thrusting their spears menacingly. Turbaned Moslem nomads from the northeast paraded on horseback, swinging curved scimitars in cutthroat motion. The Moslem women, an attractive fusion of Negroid and Arabic features, emitted shrill cries through vibrating tongues à la *Battle of Algiers*. Sweeping pageantry; traditional Africa brought briefly to life!

With the celebration over, all public transport was so crowded that we decided to hitch to the border. A sporty Toyota containing three nattily attired African businessmen picked us up. The driver gave no indication there would be any charge. I should have known better.

In a wilderness of blowing dust and little else, the driver stopped the car, demanding twice the Peugeot rate. When I protested, he suggested that we could always walk. We had no food, no water, had seen nary a village nor shade tree for miles, and any oncoming public vehicle would have no room for us. I had little choice but to agree to his price, saying we would pay at the border, where I could get some Cameroonian francs.

At the frontier town of Garoua Boulai, I unloaded our rucksacks and paid the driver only the normal Peugeot fare. When he and his angry companions leaped threateningly fom the car, a muscular young Cameroonian intervened. I explained hastily that I thought the price quoted, double the usual levy, was meant for the two of us. The young man ordered the cursing driver and his cronies on their way.

194

I bought André a beer, explaining in full what had happened en route and the camera incident at Ngaoundéré. He replied apologetically that some Cameroonians, bitter after years of colonialist privilege and exploitation, saw all whites as rich and now open to be conned whenever possible. He agreed that the wrongs of the colonial past were no excuse for such behavior.

André was a university-educated public-health official. By serving villages dotting this isolated wasteland, he was helping to bring better sanitation to the region. With his high level of education, André might have chosen to live in greater comfort around Yaoundé or Douala, but his dedication to Cameroonian development led him to work at this remote frontier post.

With André's aid, we breezed through Cameroonian customs. To the east lay the Central African Republic, the Ubangi River, and the land of our greatest African adventure, the Congo.

CENTRAL AFRICAN REPUBLIC

A Ubangi Napoleon

Although leaving Cameroon had been a breeze, we were jolted back to the exasperating realities of African border crossings at Central African customs. The bureaucrat in charge of Immigration, we were told, was drinking beer with buddies back in Cameroonian Garoua Boulai. A minibus to Bangui, the Central African capital, waited for the backlog of Africans also requiring visa validation. Geared to a different clock, the Africans were not irked in the least by the delay. Nothing they could do about it—after all, government administrators have the power to come and go as they choose.

At sundown the immigration captain staggered in, so intoxicated that if a match were struck near his beard he would have exploded. "Blanc merde," he cursed when I softly pointed out that he had mistakenly stamped my Cameroonian visa. Fortunately, he was too inebriated to vent his anger further and I proceeded to board our "Boeing 707."

"Air France," "Jumbo Jet 747," "Boeing 707"—the boldly painted names on dilapidated Central African Republic buses could scarcely have been less appropriate. While the C.A.R.'s road to Bangui is not bad by African standards, our minibus had to coast backward even on minor slopes to summon sufficient power to reach the crest. On each and every hill, we would hold our breath and strain forward, hoping such body English would give an added measure of strength to the struggling bus.

In the town of Bouar, halfway to Bangui, the driver replaced his burned-out sparkplugs. He also delivered all his jerry cans of gasoline, purchased in Cameroon where it is cheaper, to the bus-owner's residence. Though this surprised me, I wrongly assumed that there must be petrol stations between Bouar and Bangui.

With the change of plugs, the vintage bus surged along at the breakneck speed of thirty miles per hour. It was now daylight and I could make out the bleakness of the sun-baked terrain. The Texas-sized C.A.R. is a sparsely populated country of less than a million and a half inhabitants. Most of its early settlers migrated here solely to escape slavers—for given any alternative, few would have chosen to live in such an inhospitable environment. Central African villages were as destitute as any I had seen.

Near midday the bus started sputtering, gradually grinding to a halt by a roadside hamlet. We had run out of gas.

Furious, I asked the driver why he had dropped off all the jerry cans.

"Patron want."

"Then why didn't you fill up in Bouar?"

"No money."

"And the bus fares?"

"Patron take."

"Now what?"

"Lend me francs, I hitch back to Bouar, get petrol."

A trucker had stopped at this village for palm wine. Yes, he would take our driver to Bouar—for a price. Since I had seen no other vehicles heading toward Bangui, we had no choice but to lend our money and stick with the bus.

Our stomachs growled as we waited. When Marzi and I boarded "Boeing 707," we expected to arrive the next morning in Bangui.

197

Not bothering, therefore, to replenish our supplies, we had not eaten for twenty-four hours. I scoured the village—no rice, no tinned foods, only cassava. Women worked the meager fields, as usual the beasts of burden. Men snored on prayer rugs in the shade of their straw huts. Hundreds of flies buzzed around the excrement-strewn hovels, where children, bellies bloated with kwashiorkor, wandered aimlessly in their bare feet. The parasites that entered through the soles of their feet further sapped what little strength they had.

At sunset our driver returned, sloshing a half-filled jerry can which he maintained would get us to Bangui. I was skeptical that he had spent all our money on gas. His breath confirmed this.

The driver halted every fifteen minutes to relieve himself, complaining of abdominal cramps and diarrhea. I treated him with some tetracycline, effecting an immediate "cure." White man's magic! I thereafter was known as "Monsieur le Docteur." The driver's energies and appetite were so restored that he nearly ran us off the road, swerving to hit that delicacy of delicacies, the bush rat.

"Boeing 707" crawled to the outskirts of the capital, then died. A taxi waited beyond a roadblock. It was necessary to obtain a special form here to enter the city; this held even for residents. Security! Bangui is like a heavily guarded island, a country within a country, an entity unto itself.

The town marked the most startling contrast between city and countryside of any municipality we had visited. I was anticipating the typical urban jumble of tin-roofed merchants' stalls, interspersed by a scant remnant of "European" shops. After all, Bangui, like Timbuktu, is virtually in the middle of nowhere. I found instead a spankingly modern French ville whose residents were almost exclusively white. With the exception of well-to-do government officials and students, Africans lived primarily on the periphery.

We pitched our tent at Foyer Protestant and wandered into one of the two air-conditioned, largely vacant high-rise hotels overlooking the Ubangi River. On the opposite shore rose the legendary jungles of the Congo.

A comical fanfare of trumpets and cymbals shattered an idyllic Ubangi sunset. We raced over to view the commotion. A red carpet was rolled out, upon which marched a spiffy honor guard, followed by the bulky, uniformed figure of Jean-Bedel Bokassa, C.A.R.'s "Emperor for Life." Every inch of his ample chest was covered with medals—a strutting neo-Napoleon, bigger than life in blackface.

Terror, on the order of Haiti's Papa Doc Duvalier, has distinguished Bokassa's reign. Whatever opposition remained alive was hardly insane enough to show itself. Bokassa, nonetheless, has prepared for the inevitable, purchasing some seventeen chateaux in France.

Bangui's white residents, largely untaxed, have kept their privileged status of colonial days, reaping the benefits of Bokassa's strong-armed "stability." The dictator also has gained the unflagging support of American diplomacy, thanks to his staunchly pro-United States stand in the international political arena. As a reward, the United States has sent considerable aid, most of which winds up in the pockets of Bokassa and his cohorts.

In December of 1977 Bokassa spent twenty million dollars, or one-third of the national budget, on his coronation as self-proclaimed emperor. His royal crown and scepter alone cost five million dollars. On the thesis that an emperor must have an empire, Bokassa renamed his country the Central African Empire.

Under Bokassa's iron rule, overall conditions in this near-destitute "empire" have either deteriorated or stagnated. The inadequate road network is crumbling, export cotton and coffee have fallen greatly in output, ninety per cent of the people remain illiterate, and only ten per cent operate within the money economy. Governmental revenues from lucrative diamond mining are siphoned primarily into Bangui's luxury hotels, bureaucrats' villas, and a television station broadcasting to all of forty sets!

Overlanders informed us that no public transport existed through Zaire. This was disturbing news, for we envisioned riding on the roofs of trucks, unable to stop when and where we chose. Unless we caught a ride in a fellow traveler's vehicle, Marzi and I would miss some of Africa's most spectacular scenery.

By a stroke of good fortune, we met two former Peace Corps

volunteers who planned to drive their camper to Nairobi and were looking for someone to share expenses. Although they did not intend to leave for a fortnight, we decided the wait would be well worth it. We arranged to meet them at Bangassou, two hundred miles to the east, where Peace Corps stationed in the C.A.R were gathering for a Christmas party.

I felt quite safe camping at Foyer Protestant. A night watchman, armed with bow and arrows, guarded the mission grounds. Nevertheless, we arose early one morning to the glare of light pouring into the tent. The fabric had been razored while we slept!

Stolen were fifty dollars' worth of C.A.R. francs, reading glasses, a Swiss army knife, and most distressingly, Marzi's treasured camera and lenses. Still worse, since we would have to camp almost nightly in rainy Zaire, our once water- and bug-tight tent was now a sieve.

I tore out the rear exit, finding the adjacent tents slit as well. Then a ray of sunlight shone upon something black against the garden's green. Marzi's camera and lenses! The minister in charge of Foyer Protestant later explained why the thief had forsaken such valuable booty.

"A camera can easily be traced in a place as small as Bangui— particularly in the possession of an African. Of course, burglars are cautious—Bokassa's initial penalty for theft is amputation of the right ear. For the second offense, the victim loses his left. On the third conviction, he disappears. Even with such horrific consequences, the situation here is so desperate that robbery has actually increased."

In a way, I suppose we were lucky. If the thief had cut a few inches to the right, he might well have slashed Marzi's face. As it was, we lost fifty dollars, an easily replaceable knife, and glasses needed only for reading. I managed to patch the tent with radiator duct tape. This miraculously held up under some driving tropical rainstorms, providing adequate shelter the remainder of the trip.

Before setting out to join our Peace Corps friends, we journeyed to the southern river village, Mongoumba, where Bokassa was commemorating a political anniversary. Dancers from all over the country assembled for the festivities. Light-skinned Moslems from the far north danced a slow, stately step, tossing crimson shawls back and forth across their shoulders in time to a distinctive cadence. Frenetic black southerners writhed to a booming of drums, heads tossing, breasts bobbing, eyes afire. A witch doctor cloaked in a tusked elephant fetish costume scattered fearful followers, charging this way and that into a terrified crowd.

Most intriguing of all, pygmies–miniature adults clad only in "G-strings"–danced a simple stomp in a collective circle. One relatively acculturated pygmy entered wearing shorts, only to have them brutishly torn off by a huge Bantu official. All in the spirit of "authenticity."

While most of the fete's women danced bare-breasted, wearing only grass skirts, a number of spectators were decked out in dresses with picture prints of Bokassa and his wife stamped on their derrières. No one found it the least bit insulting to sit on the likeness of the "President à Vie."

At the roadblock where permits were checked for those entering or leaving Bangui, the officer in charge helped us to catch a truck to Bangassou, "because you are American and our president loves America." He ordered the first freight camion to take us on. A Russian teacher sat in the cab as another passenger, while we rode on the roof.

At the first rest stop, Vladimir offered to share his lunch with us. Fluent in both French and English, he had been teaching in a Bouar lycee for over a year and was now posted in a remote town near the Sudanese border. He was astounded to hear our critique of American foreign policy in Indochina. We, in turn, were even more astonished to discover the Russian's carefully articulated distaste for the Soviet invasion of Czechoslovakia.

Vladimir's experiences in Africa had convinced him that the building of "socialist man" in these parts was an evolutionary task which he probably would not live long enough to see. "There are no ideological shortcuts through cultural barriers," he commented.

We lodged overnight at the cottage of a Russian couple teaching in a village. They offered a bed and meal, but were otherwise aloof. Vladimir, so loquacious when alone with us, was clearly reluctant to broach any subject of controversy in their company. We too refrained, not wishing to get him into any difficulty. But once we hit the road, he initiated a political discussion without hesitation, dispensing freely his slightly cynical perspectives on the state of the world.

In Bangassou, Vladimir introduced us to Heinrich, a West German agronomist. Heinrich had been working for three years in a program sponsored by his government to aid the Central African peasantry. He revealed that while enthusiastic when he first came, he was now merely going through the motions.

"Most of the local people have little incentive to grow cash crops. In the extended Bantu family, relatives will move in and share the wealth of those who accumulate a surplus of anything. When French plantations exploited African labor, whole villages of men were employed, so this was not so much of a factor. But with the 'colons' gone, when someone works hard on his small plot and achieves a higher yield than his neighbors, he is obliged to distribute the harvest among his less ambitious kinsmen. So nobody bothers to cultivate beyond a bare subsistence."

I remembered university courses glorifying the "collective social security blanket" of the African extended family. Its debilitating effect on national development was never discussed.

This incentive-robbing cultural pattern was described to me by both locals and foreign volunteers in other African countries. They claimed that it led to bureaucratic nepotism: government workers adding their relatives to the payrolls in order to keep their kinsmen from living off them. The extended family is one of the major factors in today's overstuffed African bureaucracies—a crippling expense for societies so short of financial resources.

What a paradox! The extended family, long the salvation of desperate peasants, may undermine the future of developing societies whose populations and needs are growing in the modern world.

We met our Peace Corps companions and learned that they had decided to stay an extra week to celebrate New Year's Eve with their friends in Bangassou. That was certainly their prerogative, but what a drag being tied to somebody else's schedule! In Asia we set our own pace and chose our own company. But to see what we wanted in a land without reliable public transport, we had to sacrifice some measure of independence.

After a long week, we were finally given the word. The Peace Corps party was breaking up; our ride would depart the next morning. Anxious for a preview, we joined a contingent of volunteers for an afternoon outing, canoeing across the sluggish Ubangi to the Zaire frontier post. Our exploration of that comatose hamlet proved uneventful and we returned to load the car, unaware that the brief excursion would deal a near fatal blow to our transcontinental expedition.

THE CONGO (ZAIRE)

Enter, The Heart of Darkness

Dawn broke sharply over the muddy Ubangi and we gazed at the dense tangle of vegetation on the opposite shore. Despite the wilting humidity, our adrenalin flowed, for we were soon to enter that infamous "heart of darkness," the Congo (known now as Zaire). In this land of impenetrable jungles, mountain gorillas, and pygmies, we would find our most challenging overland experience.

Richard and Jan, the former Peace Corps volunteers with whom we were traveling, drove their VW van to the waterfront while I contacted the local headman to arrange ferry transport. He sent a messenger to the Zairois side and soon the fern-covered banks reverberated to a throbbing of drums, calling villagers together to operate the ferry.

The river service, under the auspices of the Zairois government, was supposed to be free. To save gas, the villagers laboriously paddled the empty barge across to our landing. They stopped short of the makeshift dock and weighed anchor. We sat staring at the moored ferry until the portly chief waddled over, explaining, "The

204

government has not paid us for five months." By now veteran African travelers, we immediately understood the source of the delay.

"Baksheesh," "dash," "cadeau," and here "matabiche," it's all the same. There were no other ferries; it was either pay or stay. The only question was how small a bribe we could get away with. Bartering, we finally reached an agreement: five dollars for the chief and cigarettes for the crew.

On the opposite bank, a burly customs official announced that both immigration and customs had just closed for lunch. He "suggested" we pass the time drinking beer. From experience I knew what that meant—the drinks were on us. Better to remain in his good graces or we might never get through.

A good hour past his scheduled reopening, the immigration officer returned. He was a lean, tough-looking bureaucrat who, the previous day, had stopped our contingent of Peace Corps visiting the Zairois shore and chatted with the volunteers in Lingala, the local tongue. We were simply told that he had asked what we were doing there and thought nothing more of it.

Now he stood scowling at us. "You said you were teachers in Bangassou." To this we hastily replied, "Our friends answered for themselves; they didn't mean us. We could not understand what you were asking, because we don't speak Lingala."

The official stamped his feet, fuming, "You lied! You will not enter Zaire!"

Having ventured two hundred miles out of our way on bad roads and waited two weeks for this ride, we now faced the distressing prospect of buying a three-hundred-dollar air ticket to bypass the most fascinating country in Africa. Crushed, we apologized profusely, paying lip service to the big man's authority. He clearly enjoyed watching us grovel.

While the bureaucrat berated our "dishonesty," I recalled the experience of Bill, an American traveler, who waited two days to enter Zaire across the border from Bangui. The local immigration captain, on an anti-"blanc" vendetta, refused to open the gates, accusing the American of being an "enemy agent." Bill responded by acting out the fantasy of every overlander: he inked the immigration seal and stamped his own passport! The infuriated official retaliated, picking up a brick and heaving it through the windshield of Bill's jeep. Before he could be arrested, Bill leaped into his battered vehicle and fled back to Bangui.

At length, our immigration captain ended his tirade and validated our visas. Then the customs chief, whom we had earlier treated to a half case of beer, rummaged through our luggage, expectantly holding up a pack of laminated playing cards.

"Go on, take them," I replied, happy it had not cost us more. Satisfied with his new treasure, he searched no further.

Hearing our engine turn over, the immigration officer reemerged, warning, "No pictures of pygmies or roads in the People's Republic of Zaire!" Roads? We had heard that they were bad, but so terrible that photography was verboten? Soon we would understand.

He also read a decree stating that no camping or cooking was allowed in Zaire and that it was illegal to stay with missionaries. Furthermore, all currency exchanges were restricted to banks. But there were no hotels, restaurants, or banks within a good week's journey! If the military caught us camping, we would really be in trouble.

The coup de grâce came with the issuance of a currency voucher. Banks and hotels were to officially stamp this form after all transactions as proof that we had spent a requisite forty dollars a day. We were informed in no uncertain terms that the voucher would be thoroughly scrutinized when we left Zaire.

"Forty dollars a day!" Marzi muttered. "That's more than we spend in a week. Even if we had that kind of money, without hotels and restaurants we'll be hard-pressed to spend more than one dollar. This is absurd!"

Due to the delayed start, we made camp that night disquietingly close to the border. Backing the VW as deep into the bush as possible, we pitched the tent behind it. But apparently we could still be seen from the road, for a curious Bantu hunter sidled up to gape. We returned the compliment, admiring his monkey-fur cap, its tail dangling down his back.

Noting that the Bantu carried some still-bloody meat wrapped in leaves tied with a vine, Richard bargained in Lingala for our supper. I started a fire and we roasted the stringy meat on a skewer. It tasted a bit like liver, yet was rather gamy.

"What sort of bush animal is this?" Marzi asked Richard.

"Grass-cutter, Africa's largest rodent."

My appetite dissolved momentarily, but I forced myself to take another bite.

"Not bad, compared to Cameroonian corned beef," I admitted grudgingly.

Marzi grimaced.

There was no twilight; the sun quickly disappeared, leaving a moonless sky. The jungle exuded a wall of eerie noise. My imagination ran wild and I conjured up, in the darkness, images of man-eating beasts, drunken military, Simba guerrillas, dread "Leopard Men," and other nameless horrors. Ears straining with every sound, I thought I might remain on guard until daybreak. But the night was endless. Exhausted, I fell asleep to the cacophony of crickets.

About midnight a blood-curdling scream pierced the rain forest. Followed by another. The shrill sounds compared favorably with Fay Wray's performance in *King Kong*. A woman being tortured? The nearby village being raided?

I ripped out of the tent, banging on the VW where Richard and Jan slept. "What the hell was that?"

Richard laughed. "I should have warned you. That 'call' is made by a little nocturnal tree rodent called a hyrax. He's just looking for a mate."

Still trembling, Marzi and I retreated to our tent.

We had driven less than an hour the next day when we were stopped by a wooden barrier whose sign read: "Arrêt pour Immigrasi."

"Again? Shit!" the four of us said simultaneously. To our relief, the soldier who greeted us was polite, merely requesting that we fill out a form. In five minutes we were finished, surely a record.

"This is too good to be true," whispered Marzi. Indeed, it was.

"You will take my brother, M'tuku, down to Bondo," the bureaucrat beamed. The VW was already overburdened with four passengers, our gear, and heavy wooden planks on the roof to help us navigate some treacherous roads. Nevertheless, we had no choice but to take on brother M'tuku.

"How are the roads?" we asked the fonctionnaire.

"Good, this is the dry season. But remember, no photos. Recently our soldiers caught two Germans filming the highway and made them cut grass on their hands and knees for three days."

"How many days to Bondo?"

"Oh, maybe three."

At least three days to drive ninety-five miles on "good roads!" Sounded as bad as we had heard. Actually, it was worse. Marked in bright red on the Michelin map as Zaire's "international highway," the road was a scarred dirt track with holes big enough to swallow an elephant.

Every kilometer, we performed this exhausting scenario. Climb up to the roof of the van and hand down the four cumbrous ten-foot boards. Figure out how best to align this makeshift wooden bridge. This could be tricky—especially if the ruts extended beyond the boards. Then, painstakingly guide the vehicle over without its slipping into the hole. The dripping humidity made this the most taxing physical labor I have ever undertaken. M'tuku participated fully and we began to appreciate his company.

On short stretches where the track was relatively unbroken, we would admire the Dark Continent's densest rain forests. Hollywood has popularized the myth that Africa is nothing but jungle. In reality, most of the continent is desert or savanna grassland. But Zaire, the equatorial heart, boasts the thickest tropical foilage imaginable. The VW plodded through an endless tunnel whose tangled leaves emitted so little light that I often thought I was wearing tinted sunglasses. Immense, creeper-matted trees, glistening with the wetness that seeped everywhere, contributed to an overwhelming sense of being dwarfed. When not on the lookout for holes, I relished being enveloped by this indomitable, primeval wilderness.

While multicolored butterflies were delightful to watch, other flying insects proved aggravating. Congolese mosquitoes were so voracious that our ankles and wrists soon swelled into continuous scarlet welts. Cutter's repellent, so effective elsewhere, did nothing to deter the swarms that descended upon us. As a precaution, we doubled our dose of malarial prophylactics.

Sweat bees were even more obnoxious. Though these tiny insects, attracted to human perspiration, do not bite, they make life miserable by swarming into your eyes and mouth. Each time we got out to deal with a rut (which was every fifteen minutes), they assaulted us with a vengeance. One could go mad! Yet I noticed that they hardly bothered M'tuku or any of the local folks. Perhaps they possessed some adaptive immunity.

Finally it happened. The VW slipped off the boards into a water-filled trench so wide and deep that we were unable to push it out. A group of eight Bantu bow-and-arrow hunters happened by and M'tuku spoke to them in a dialect different from Lingala. The hunters, although excruciatingly thin, joined in to help. After hours of sustained work, we managed to move the VW to a smooth track.

We thanked the hunters, compensated them, and asked to take their photo. They acquiesced, but M'tuku pleaded that we refrain, maintaining that a photograph of such malnourished tribesmen would create a negative image of Zaire abroad. He did laugh uproariously when I nervously photographed the road.

M'tuku's company proved a real stroke of luck. Other travelers reported trouble with villagers in this area, who chucked stones at their vehicles. Indeed, as we drove alongside conical thatch-and-wattle hamlets, locals would start to shake their fists at us. But seeing us with a uniformed black man, their glares quickly turned to grins.

African peasants were, for the most part, hospitable to overlanders. This atypical enmity toward whites in Zaire was unquestionably government instilled. President Mobutu, via radio, had told these country folk that white travelers were spies of foreign governments. How else could they afford to travel? Furthermore, when the Muhammad Ali–George Frazier heavyweight championship was held in Kinshasa (the bout was widely billed as "President Mobutu's gift to the people of Zaire"), the radio transmitter broke down during the fight and rural people were unable to hear the broadcast. Mobutu, "The Infallible," pinned the blame on white travelers' sabotage. Ever since, overlanders have encountered hostility here.

Stopping at a village to buy pineapples, we were approached by a local woman carrying a monkey wrapped around her waist, its head cradled against her breast. "Oh, look!" Marzi said, thinking it was a pet. Then I noticed its dazed expression. The monkey had been freshly clubbed, the woman hoping to sell it to us for supper. Many hamlets we drove past displayed monkeys skewered on stakes. These were peddled to the resolute truckers who dared ply these roads but once a fortnight.

It had taken four days to travel the ninety-five miles to Bondo. We seldom shifted out of first gear. Driving so slowly did pose an advantage—we saw, in detail, every scenic kilometer. Of course, we probably could have walked it faster.

We said good-bye to M'tuku at Bondo. He had been a congenial companion and a great aid. Now we felt alone ... and vulnerable.

A missionary we met in the market place, ingeniously plugging a leak in his radiator with goat manure, informed us that the road from Bondo to Kisangani was better, though not by much! Apparently, the priest had not been north for some time, for the road to Kisangani was a super highway by comparison. We only had to "make bridges" every fourth kilometer and were able to take a good measure of the track in second gear!

On one occasion, a chimp burst through the forest, clowned a bit in front of the VW, then dashed on his way. Later we spied a tribesman monkey-hunting with a curious looking crossbow, whose wooden stock he had shaped like a rifle. His arrowheads were dipped in a deadly toxin which, within minutes, traveled the bloodstream to the heart. No wonder the chimp was in such a hurry.

The closer we came to Kisangani, the friendlier were the peasants. While their villages differed little in construction, ritualized culture varied tremendously in this nation of two hundred tribes. The most striking feature common to the Zairois peasantry was malnutrition. We saw many children with swollen abdomens and reddish hair, the classic symptoms of kwashiorkor. Local cultivators had no incentive to grow a much-needed surplus of nutritious foods. And given the sorry state of the roads, it would have been impossible to deliver perishables to major village markets before they spoiled.

Belgium ranks ignominiously with Portugal as the colonizer who did the least for the indigenous peoples. At independence, the Congo had fewer than thirty native university graduates. No wonder, here and elsewhere in Africa, military strongmen have filled the leadership breach resulting from a lack of trained civilian administrative personnel. Zaire's President Joseph Mobutu is archetypical.

Expelled from a Catholic secondary school for disciplinary reasons, Mobutu rose ruthlessly through the army ranks during the civil turmoil of independent Congo's first five years. Now ruler of black Africa's potentially richest nation (Zaire has an abundance of copper, diamonds, and palm oil), he is one of the world's wealthiest men. Most of Zaire's revenue is squandered on posh chateaux and resorts for Mobutu and his powerful supporters. Little development of any kind has taken place outside the capital, Kinshasa. Despite Zaire's lucrative income from mineral resources, its treasury is reportedly near bankruptcy.

Mobutu has tried to deify himself among his citizenry. Statues and posters of him appear everywhere and he has proclaimed himself the "new messiah." Travelers who watched the national news over television in the capital told us it was preceded by an image of clouds parting to reveal the stern portrait of His Eminence. Accompaniment was provided by harps playing heavenly background music.

Norman Mailer once said, "Like a snake around a stick, the name Mobutu is intertwined with the revolutionary ideal." For all Mobutu's rhetoric, there are few social programs which benefit the nation at large. Yet much of the American press (Mobutu is pro-United States) has long rationalized his dictatorial reign with the logic that such a huge, tribally diverse nation needs a strongman for cohesion.

One of the few major "reforms" Mobutu has wrought are name changes. To emphasize "African authenticity," it is illegal for anyone to retain his Christian name. The "Congo," referring originally to a powerful African kingdom which ruled the western region prior to the European intrusion, was rechristened "Zaire" by Mobutu simply because the Belgians had adopted its original name. Later, to the strongman's chagrin, scholars disclosed that "Zaire" was really a label Portuguese explorers hung on the western sector of the Congo. But God makes no mistakes and neither does Joe Mobutu—history books are rewritten and "Zaire" is "African."

Priests at Buta, three days south of Bondo, put us up with understandable hesitation. By governmental edict, they were forbidden to house travelers. Mobutu, evidently retaliating for his ouster from parochial school, has come down particularly hard on Catholic missionaries, who make up the vast majority of clergy in the country. A few weeks prior at Buta, representatives of Mobutu's party smashed all images of Jesus and Mary, proclaiming that their man was the one and only messiah. Catholic preaching has since been outlawed throughout Zaire.

By the time I left the country, I would greatly alter my preconceived notion of missionaries. I formerly thought of them as zealots who undercut viable indigenous cultures and beliefs with their own brand of mumbo-jumbo, and as perpetuators of white colonial privilege and the status quo. While I am certain this held true in the past, I met some missionaries clearly devoted to the well-being of their parishioners.

In Zaire, Mobutu has failed to provide much in the way of schooling or rural medical centers. Therefore missionaries continue to function as the only teachers, vocational trainers, and medical personnel over wide areas. In the absence of locally trained professionals, the missionaries provide a service necessary for national development and individual well-being. True, some are self-serving egotists, seeing themselves as bringing "enlightenment to the heathen." But most missionaries we met appeared to be dedicated people who stayed on to aid their parishioners despite Mobutu's persecution campaign. Some had lived in the Congo for twenty or thirty years, staying through even the brutality of the Simba revolt when all whites were marked for death. Many we spoke to felt

212

certain that Mobutu would soon exile them, leaving most of the countryside without doctors or teachers.

We had seen from our car the thick, dark columns of safari ants crossing the road by the thousands, devouring all vegetation in their line of march. Stopping at a village to patch a tire, I inadvertently stepped in their way. It felt as though red-hot coals were being applied to my leg as the ants crawled up my body. No time for modesty, I yanked off my pants in the middle of the hamlet, slapping these vile, biting creatures from my skin. The villagers thought this hilarious, and when the fleeting pain left, I laughed with them. From then on, I looked *very* carefully where I stepped.

Something had gone wrong with the VW. We were running on only three cylinders and kept fingers crossed that the van would reach Kisangani for repairs. (There were no mechanics or automotive parts between Bangassou and Kisangani.) As the car limped along, we passed one gutted plantation after another. These formerly productive farms had earlier been destroyed by the Simbas. Belgian planters who escaped with their lives abandoned their homes for Europe. Now the once magnificent manors house local African fonctionnaires who have let them deteriorate further. Yet the real tragedy lies in the fact that little of this fertile land is under cultivation. With the exception of a few acres share-cropped by poor peasants (virtual serfs), chiefly to the benefit of their powerful overlords, the estates have been largely reclaimed by the jungle.

The VW wheezed, coughed, and finally died just as we reached a campsite along a tributary of the Congo (now "Zaire") River on the outskirts of Kisangani. We pitched our tent, wrongly anticipating a short stay. A "British Scientific Expeditionary Force," invited by Mobutu, camped nearby. These men had been studying the varied flora and fauna of the river. Most found their research fascinating, but were sick of paying matabiche as well as having to scrape and bow before governmental strongmen.

We heeded our fellow campers' warnings and kept a close watch on our tent. The local gendarmes offered no protection against thieves who stole from "blancs" and the British had already lost a good deal of their supplies. Having had our tent razored less than a month before, we were particularly wary. Any unusual sound in the night (and there were many) tended to make us uneasy.

The scientists told us that we had just missed the departure of some irate Canadian surveyors. Hired by the government to map Zaire from the air, they barely escaped with their lives. Their plane had been fired upon by ill-disciplined soldiers who thought the Canadians were rebels.

Richard and Jan put their van in the hands of Philo, a Cypriot mechanic. He was so openly prejudiced in relating to his African assistants, I was amazed his shop had not yet been "nationalized." It appeared that Philo knew whose palm to grease. But we later learned that the Greek was a mercenary, one of many Mobutu kept around for his personal protection and subsequent adventures in Angola.

After a week of the mechanic's tinkering, the VW was nearer death than when we brought it in. Richard concluded that only a skilled mechanic, equipped with every conceivable spare part, should consider bringing his own car into Africa.

The repairs gave us plenty of time to explore Kisangani, the once elegant Belgian town of Stanleyville. On most of its regal houses the paint peeled and jungle rot had set in. Only a handful of whites, predominantly of Greek or Portuguese extraction, stayed on here. In 1964 Simba forces (whose "ideology" was simply one of plunder and the murder of all whites) seized Stanleyville. When it became evident that the captive European citizenry would soon be massacred, Belgian paratroopers made a lightning raid on the town. Forty whites were murdered before the Simbas were driven out. The survivors fled to Europe where they were joined later by shopkeepers whose businesses Mobutu had "nationalized"—that is to say, turned over to his supporters. Most of these stores, run by those without any previous business experience, are now devoid of merchandise, collecting ghostly cobwebs.

The few stores still operating displayed imported goods from South Africa. Despite all the Pan-African rhetoric of embargo, we found South African products for sale in half the countries we visited. Apparently profits were more important than principles.

We wandered over to the nearly deserted red brick post office to mail a letter. An owlish clerk told us that if we wanted stamps, we would have to go to Kinshasa, a mere eight hundred miles' distance. Incredulous, we found a vendor outside selling them. I returned to the clerk, angrily flinging the letter across his desk. I should have known better; the envelope arrived in the States eight months later, minus the contents.

Tsopo Bridge connected our camping area with the town. It was from here that Simbas had thrown scores of educated Africans (due to their "association" with Europeans) to their deaths in the roaring cataract below. The bridge is now largely used for automobile traffic, but also has a cordoned-off sector for pedestrians.

Crossing the bridge one afternoon, I was startled to see three Europeans at the far end, an unusual sight as there were few whites in town. Gazing at them as I walked, I failed to notice a gaping hole on the wooden footbridge ahead. Marzi shrieked as one of my legs slipped through! The other leg caught on the wood and I staggered to my feet.

It had all happened so suddenly. The full impact did not hit home until I reached the other side and looked down at the water cascading over sharp rocks a lifetime below. Only then did I start shaking. If my other leg hadn't caught . . .

Coming so close to death made me pause to introspect. Accidents could happen crossing streets back home. How grateful I was for that stroke of fate that sent us to Istanbul. It was crucial to see the world *now*—to do my living *now*—later it might not be possible. Every minute seemed precious.

Marzi and I wearied of being stuck in Kisangani. The car was in its second week of repairs with little progress reported. Richard cynically spoke of selling the van for scrap, before he went broke. Of course, we could always fly to the Rwanda border, but that would be expensive, and we wouldn't see anything. Besides, Air Zaire was said to be a big joke. Mobutu has squandered millions of dollars for the DC-10 and 747 which daily fly nearly empty to Europe. Once service was cancelled abruptly when the president commandeered one jet to Paris and his wife the other to Brussels. Domestic schedules, too, were so erratic that a distraught traveler dubbed the flight system "Air Maybe"!

In town, we met the Flemish administrator of a local brewery who offered us a ride to the Rwanda border on one of his trucks. As much as we wanted to leave, this would mean that we could not stop when and where we wanted. A few more uneventful days elapsed. Just as we were ready to take the truck, two travelers drove up in a Land Rover. We volunteered to share expenses if they would take us east. Eddie, the vehicle's owner, was amenable, so long as we did not mind cramming the four of us in the front seat (the rear section held the gear).

Mathematician Eddie, who looked like Woody Allen, disclosed that he had left Britain for Rhodesia to escape "Socialism." Balding Paul, resembling Fred Mertz of "I Love Lucy" fame, presented himself as an archeologist born in Austria who was now a citizen of Australia. Somehow his profession did not jibe with his character; he whined about everything.

These were the people with whom we would share the next five hundred miles of twenty-miles-per-hour driving?! To really see the rest of this extraordinary country, we had no alternative.

The "Paul and Eddie Show" began straight off. Paul was reading the map when we came to a fork in the road. "Which way, Paul?" Eddie asked.

"Straight."

"Right or Left?"

"Straight."

"Right or left, you bloody bastard?"

"I told you, straight!" And so they carried on, quarreling like two miserable spouses.

Fortunately, Eddie was a first-rate mechanic. He also had the foresight to carry from the United Kingdom a compendium of spare parts. We felt every jolt and jar in his ancient Land Rover but had confidence that its high clearance and four-wheel drive would get us through these wretched roads.

The matted jungle grew thicker still, and we entered the vast Ituri forest, home of the Congolese pygmy. Thought to be the original inhabitants of this region, the pygmies (or "Bambuti," as they call themselves) had mixed even less with the Bantu than the dancers we had observed in the Central African Republic. It was often difficult to tell which pygmy males were adults, as their facial features resembled those of adolescents. Except for pendulous breasts, so out of proportion to the rest of their bodies, the straight-hipped females also looked like teenage boys.

We watched many of the little people, clad only in a brief loincloth which partially covered their genitals, stalking game with bows and arrows. While most timidly disappeared into the forest at the sight of our vehicle, one fearless hunter peered with curiosity into the parked car. He spied a pair of old, unelasticized underwear I had hung near the window to dry. Noting his admiration for the briefs, I traded them to him for his bow and monkey-fur quiver of arrows. Somewhere today in the depths of the jungle there is a pygmy cursing me while running around in unelasticized "Fruit of the Loom."

The pygmy have long had a symbiotic relationship with their taller Bantu neighbors, exchanging bush meat for cultivated foods and metal arrowheads. Each pygmy has a Bantu "Master," passed on from generation to generation. Until recently, this could hardly be called slavery as the pygmy vanished into the forest at will and often seemed to derive greater benefit from the relationship than did the Bantu.

Along the roadside we unexpectedly passed a number of Bambuti leaf huts shaped like an inverted "U." Mobutu's present policy of coercively resettling the pygmy into a sedentary life of farming adjacent to their bigger neighbors threatens to destroy the Bambuti.

The pygmy have been traditionally hunters and gatherers. The Ituri, so inhospitable to outsiders, is their friend and provider. They have neither the desire nor the know-how to farm. Furthermore, their forced static state has been exploited by the Bantu, who as "Masters" are able to place greater demands upon their now more accessible vassals.

Eschewing cultivation, many pygmy have turned to regularly stealing crops from the Bantu. Although they have always pilfered from peasant cultivators, some Bambuti, no longer hunting, now raid the Bantu gardens more frequently. Those caught pay a fearful penalty.

The Bambuti have also been devastated by disease resulting from greater contact with the outside world. They are particularly susceptible to respiratory illnesses like the common cold, which can be deadly for them. In the isolation of the wilderness, such maladies are not so prevalent.

There is tragic irony in Mobutu's forced settlement of the pygmy. The originator of African "authenticity" policies that have spread through the continent, Mobutu is destroying the culture of one of the few truly traditional peoples left in Zaire.

We reached the country's eastern extremity, climbing south into the Ruwenzoris, the legendary "Mountains of the Moon." A signpost acknowledged that we were now directly on the equator. Hopping out of the jeep to photograph the green-sloped mountains, our teeth chattered in the cold and we quickly dug into our packs to don sweaters and jackets. Imagine freezing on the equator!

The curving track threading the Ruwenzoris was only wide enough for one vehicle. Fortunately, we had little worry of a collision, having seen not one lorry or car outside the sleepy towns for the past week.

Soon we were descending into savannas for the first time since entering Zaire. Virunga, our initial game reserve, once among the most famous in Africa, loomed ahead. Because the Zairois government charged exorbitant sums to drive off the main track, allowed no camping in the heavily patrolled park, and offered accommodations only in an expensive lodge, we decided to do most of our game watching in Kenya and Tanzania.

Nevertheless, who can explain the excitement of seeing their first bull elephant, dwarfing everything else in his realm? Or their first pool of hippos, surfacing and submerging like immense chunks of floating liver? The all-too-brief exploration of Virunga only whet my appetite for upcoming visits to bountiful game reserves like Serengeti, Ngorongoro, and Amboseli.

We rose again to a pleasantly cool altitude, overnighting in the

218

former resort town of Goma. Nyiragongo, one of the world's largest active volcanos, lay a few miles outside the town and all four of us had earlier planned to climb it. But the rough roads had taken longer than Eddie anticipated. Anxious to make up time, he and Paul lost their taste for the ascent. Marzi and I informed Eddie that we had not contracted to go any particular distance with him. If he wished to move on, we could take a beer truck to the Rwandan border. We were not about to miss out on sights we had come so far to see. An irate Eddie cursed and kicked the ground, but waited while we climbed the volcano, too tight-fisted to forgo our financial contributions.

It took a full day to hike up the steep, forested trail to the summit overlooking the volcanic crater. Although the path was clearly marked, we were required by governmental decree to hire a guide for "protection," as well as a bearer to lug our negligible overnight gear. Noticing that our guide carried grenades on his belt, I asked, "What are those for?"

"To scare off elephants."

"He's got to be joking," I said to Marzi and we laughed. Although I was skeptical that any elephants lived in this mountainous region, I knew anti-Mobutu guerrillas lurked in these forests. (A few months later a band of rebels kidnapped three students studying chimpanzees with naturalist Jane Goodall across the Tanzanian border.)

While the trail was well-made, the ascent was steep and we were soon pacing ourselves carefully. Hiking since 6 A.M., it was not until late afternoon that we reached a spartan hut erected to lodge overnighters. Fatigued and trying to adjust to the thinner air at this altitude, we still had to scramble up loose shale to a vantage point above the crater. It was bitterly cold, the winds howled, and we were happy to have been forewarned to bring our warmest clothing. Putting on two sweaters each, we cautiously made our way to the top.

Peering into the crater, we saw nothing but mist. Agony—all this way for nothing! Shivering against the chill wind, I asked, "Does it ever clear?"

"Sometimes at six-thirty," replied the guide hopefully.

"Yeah, just like clockwork," I muttered under my breath.

I wanted to return to the warmth of the hut, but Marzi convinced me to stay. My mustache felt frozen solid to my lip. What a change from the steaming lowlands.

Six-thirty on the dot, the mist miraculously evaporated, revealing a fiery lake of brilliant vermilion. Lava leaped and spat as far as the eye could see. After three minutes, the crater was again enshrouded. But those 180 seconds had made the taxing climb more than worthwhile. It was now pitch dark, and since the guide had forgotten his flashlight, we had to slide blindly down sharp shale most of the way to the hut.

The next day I felt a steady pricking beneath the nail of my little toe, which was considerably swollen. A chigger had crawled under the nail, laid its eggs, and died.

While for the next few weeks the pain slowed me down somewhat, I largely disregarded it. Given our previous experiences, I was reluctant to trust country doctors. But without proper care,. infections fester in the tropics, and by the time we reached Nairobi, gangrene had set in. There, only heavy doses of antibiotics saved my foot (though I lost the septic tip of the little toe).

Our "guide and protector" was eager to get home, marching briskly a couple of hundred yards ahead. Suddenly the jungle's silence was shattered by an explosion and we realized the guide had thrown a grenade. Envisioning stampeding elephants or rebel guerrillas, I ran as fast as I could on the inflamed foot. We soon caught up with the guide, who stood leaning against a tree.

"Elephant," he smirked.

Maybe, but more likely he wanted to hurry us up. At any rate, I ignored the pain as we quickened our descent to the base camp.

Reunited with Paul and Eddie, we drove south into the Kivu region, home of the mountain gorilla. Only here and in western Uganda can one find this rare primate in its natural habitat. Eddie and Paul, unwilling to pay the eighteen-dollar fee for the reserve's six guides, remained at a mission. Angry that we again held him up yet reluctant to lose our continued financial assistance, Eddie refused to drive us to the national park's office in Bukavu.

So we walked the three miles into town. But my foot slowed us and we reached the office too late to catch the government jeep to the gorillas' reserve. Also, the park's superintendent told us that no other tourists were expected to fly in from Kinshasa that week and that to send a mere two visitors would not justify the expense of hiring trackers. When he saw our disappointment, the superintendent surprised us by offering to drive us there himself. Such a pleasant change from the other Zairois bureaucrats. He, in fact, remained in the park the entire day in order to personally escort us back to town!

At the gate to the reserve, the superintendent asked a villager to guide us to the party already in search of the gorillas. Leading us through the thickest bush I have ever seen, the tracker hacked a path with his machete. The massive vines he severed landed atop swampy pools, and we tight-roped across the fallen plants, literally walking on water.

The gorilla troupe of twenty members was difficult to find, for these six-foot, five-hundred-pound primates are really very shy and not nearly as ferocious as they look. We first discovered two of the apes munching bamboo shoots and thistles. Our guide whispered that they also enjoyed fruits, tree bark, and needles. For these big creatures, such a sumptuous meal could last as long as two hours.

Gorillas are among the largest and surely the least understood of animals. They really do beat their breasts like a tom-tom, but this is merely intended to intimidate. During the course of the afternoon we saw quite a few members of this particular troupe. Some hammed it up for us, posing and swinging their huge frames from tree to tree when they felt confident we meant no harm. But after awhile, they would once again grow wary and vanish into the depths of the jungle.

Our encounter with the mountain gorillas was one of the highlights of our African experience. What a sensation to stand below a quarter-ton of black fur swinging overhead from tree to tree!

It proved just as difficult to leave Zaire as to enter. Not that we were unprepared: fellow travelers had warned us about the immigration captain at the Bukavu border and his standard matabiche of twenty to twenty-five dollars per person. True to form, the bureaucrat first berated us for losing our currency voucher (as did all overlanders, considering the forty-dollar-per-day demand and an irresistible black-market rate of two to one). Then he lectured us on crimes perpetrated by white visitors in Zaire. Finally, he began his celebrated currency count, tallying and listing by country all our money. When he saw four hundred Spanish pesetas Paul had kept as a souvenir, his eyes lit up.

"I don't see Spanish money on the governmental approved list. Don't you know it is illegal to bring currency from a Fascist country into Zaire? I am forced to confiscate it." He put the pesetas in his desk and, without looking up, added contemptuously, "You are free to go."

Obviously, he had thought four hundred pesetas to be some extravagant sum, not the mere eight dollars it was worth. We were ecstatic. But to our disbelief, Paul started to protest. Thankfully, Marzi silenced him with a swift kick.

So we left this wild and wondrous country, paying a matabiche of only two dollars apiece. Aside from stops, it had taken us three grueling weeks to cover seven hundred miles on some of the world's worst roads. But what an adventure! The most splendid scenery in all Africa, pygmies, gorillas, and snowcapped "Mountains of the Moon." To say nothing of our sense of accomplishment at having successfully overlanded the invincible Congo.

EAST AFRICA: RWANDA, TANZANIA, KENYA, UGANDA

On Safari!

East of Rwanda's rugged Ruwenzori Mountains stretch the grass-lands of Kenya and Tanzania, where some of the most magnificent wild creatures on earth roam free. Serengeti, Ngorongoro Crater, Kilimanjaro's Amboseli, Masai Mara, the vast game reserves whose very names quicken an adventurer's pulse.

The bucolic charm of Rwanda and its southern neighbor Burundi's pastoral mountains belie a horror story little known to the world whose impact is still shaking these tiny former Tutsi kingdoms. Some four hundred years ago the towering Tutsi, light-skinned cattle herders with Arabic features, invaded these highlands from the north. They forced the Hutu inhabitants, a squat, dark people, into serfdom. In exchange for Tutsi "protection," the Hutu were tithed a share of their harvests and forced to provide personal services upon demand. This subjugation continued until Rwanda's independence from Belgium in 1962, despite the fact that the Hutu outnumbered the Tutsi by six to one (1,500,000 to 250,000).

Tutsi dominance had been psychologically eroding for decades, due in part to the missionaries' influential preaching of "Christian equality." In the late 1940s postwar democratic ideals reverberated throughout the colonial world and lent fuel to the Hutu fires while the cash crop of coffee provided economic independence for some.

Doomed to majority rule by the Hutu, many Tutsi fled after independence, regrouping to organize a military campaign aimed at seizing political power. But their 1963 invasion was quashed, and the aroused Hutu wreaked a fearful vengeance. Westerners know the "WaTutsi," regal warriors standing well over six foot, from a host of Hollywood epics (notably *King Solomon's Mines*). But for the Hutu, the Tutsi's graceful stature was symbolic of centuries of dominance. In the massacre of 20,000 Tutsi that followed the ill-fated invasion, many were literally chopped "down to size," their long legs brutally hacked off by "pangas." The killing was indiscriminate, causing 200,000 Tutsi to flee south to Burundi.

There, in 1975, the tables were tragically reversed. A force of Hutu invading Burundi was similarly repulsed, instigating a blood bath. Anywhere from 100,000 to 200,000 Hutu civilians were butchered by the enraged Tutsi military. Much of this slaughter took place right in the capital, Bujumbura. For "political reasons," foreign diplomats who would later have to deal with the Tutsi dictatorship remained silent in the face of the savagery they had witnessed. This also held true for the numerous clerics of the Catholic Church who feared expulsion, should they protest. Due to the diplomatic cover-up and Bujumbura's geographical isolation, few newsmen covered or even knew of the massacre. Thus the outside world was kept in the dark concerning one of the goriest outrages of the decade, if not the century.

We met a Belgian volunteer in Kigali, the Rwandan capital, who had been teaching in Bujumbura at the time. "They came to the lycee at dusk and lined up my Hutu students. The poor fellows were so accustomed to following Tutsi orders that they didn't try to escape, even when they knew what was coming. The Tutsi commandant walked down the single file of Hutu, slitting each throat in turn with his panga. Some of his soldiers, maddened by the sight of

Hutu blood, broke ranks and began licking at the spurting jugulars of the decapitated corpses. The Tutsi held me back against a wall. I could do nothing."

Barely repressing tears he added, "Now I come up here to work with the Hutu and see the insanity from the other end.

"You know, after the massacre, neither your embassy nor mine uttered the slightest protest. I suppose that's the price of courting political favor.

"I hear all this propaganda about South African racism and African unity from Zaire and Tanzania. Yet during the mass murders, Mobutu sent troops and Nyerere military aid to the Tutsi. White racism may be a 'cause célèbre' south of the Sahara, but tribal genocide and subordination remain largely swept under the rug."

The "Mountains of the Moon" scarcely seemed an appropriate setting for such barbarities. Rwandan roads were passable, an enormous improvement over those in Zaire. At times our Land Rover climbed at what seemed a ninty-degree angle, as we rose from Lake Kivu to an altitude of nearly twelve thousand feet. It was so invigorating to breathe the crisp air of the highlands after that dripping Congolese humidity. For the first time in Africa, we slept in our sleeping bags, rather than on top of them.

We lodged one night at a mission whose stately parishioners were among the few thirty thousand Tutsi who had not fled into neighboring lands. "They live in constant fear," the priest revealed. "They expect another Hutu vendetta at any time. Most of these people plan to join kinsmen in Tanzania and Burundi after saving a little money. To see these giants so intimidated is quite ironic when you remember how long they have ruled this land."

Within two days we neared the Tanzanian border. Rwanda is one of the most densely populated, resource-poor countries in Africa, as the appearance of village children, Hutu and Tutsi alike, attests. Overgrazing of spindly cattle has destroyed much good farmland, a problem not uncommon in the underdeveloped world. Communist China is trying to aid with developmental projects such as road improvement, but the Rwandan government has geared most of its

225

meager resources toward the military, out of fear of yet another Tutsi invasion. Given such priorities and an ever-growing populace, the future of this so-called "little Switzerland" looks grim.

We were amazed to find the Rwandan immigration shed on the Tanzanian border abandoned. However my pleasure at the thought of avoiding customs was shortlived as an Oriental head peeped out of a rock crevice some thirty yards away. The Chinese screeched something unintelligible from that distance, then waved his arms spasmodically. It was only when he covered his ears that we suddenly understood. Running full-tilt to the shelter of the rock, we arrived seconds before dynamite scattered debris in and around the customs shed.

The Mao-jacketed engineer screamed at a uniformed Rwandan in French, "Why didn't you set up the road barriers?" The African stood still without replying. Fortunately, our Land Rover, bathed in an additional coat of dust, was otherwise undamaged. The immigration official was so unnerved by the dressing down he received from the Chinese that he just waved us through without the requisite stamp and inevitable delay. Some trade-off for nearly being blown to bits!

The subtropical green of the Ruwenzoris was dramatically transformed, first into an arid brown Tanzanian plateau, then into thornbush plainsland as we descended. The sole thread of continuity was the poverty. Tanzania is damned by one of the most infertile terrains south of the Sahel. Most of its inhabitants are dependent upon scanty subsistence harvests.

A former German colony which became a British protectorate (Tanganyika) after World War I, Tanzania was largely ignored by the English colonial administration, which concentrated its developmental efforts in the fertile "white highlands" of Kenya. Thus, at independence, illiteracy remained high, the road network woefully inadequate, the drought-plagued soils unirrigated, and the life expectancy tragically short.

Tanzania, however, has been blessed with the one incorruptible leader of post-independence, sub-Saharan Africa, Julius Nyerere.

With so few resources to work with, Nyerere, a man of tremendous personal integrity, is doing his best. His "ujamaa scheme," an African version of the Chinese agrarian commune, has improved the yields of some villages. But collectivization has met with violent resistance in a few hamlets where private ownership of plots has been traditional. Nonetheless, the socialist Nyerere is convinced that the ujamaa village is Tanzania's only hope for significant rural development. He notes that small subsistence plots hardly provide sufficient food for the country's soaring population, let alone allow for the cultivation of export cash crops for foreign exchange. The ultimate success or failure of ujamaa villages may provide insight into not only Tanzania's development, but the future of black Africa.

We encountered tsetse flies—those dread bearers of sleeeping sickness—for the first time in the forlorn dust bowl of western Tanzania. Only one in a million carries that terrifying disease, so the slim possibility of contracting it didn't worry us much. It was the tsetse's vicious bite, like a searing injection that both itched and ached afterward, that was nearly unbearable. Tsetse flies are huge, as big as horseflies, and we were among the few victims they could find in this inhospitable, sparsely populated region. They flocked to us in swarms, as if they hadn't dined in days. Whenever the vehicle slowed, the tsetses buzzed upon us through open windows (too insufferably hot to close). Only speeds above twenty-five miles per hour, not always possible given the rutted roads, brought relief.

Near the entrance to the famed Serengeti wildlife reserve, we parted without regret from Paul and Eddie. We left them quarreling and complaining to the bitter end and hitched up with a Swiss couple in their truck. The Unimog, built by Mercedes-Benz, was ideal for game viewing. With four-wheel traction, we could take the liberty of driving well off the track. We followed thundering herds of horned buffalo, reputed to be the most dangerous animal in Africa because they will charge unprovoked, and surprisingly fluid-striding giraffes. Following heatedly on the heels of an ostrich duo, we marveled at the speed of these colossal, awkward-looking birds.

But there was no question as to the grace of the streamlined "tommies" (Thompson's gazelles) who appeared to float slow-motion, bounding across that endless savanna.

Perched atop the Unimog's sun roof, Marzi and I looked out upon a 360-degree spectacle of zebra and wildebeest, thousands of them, sweeping across the Serengeti. Nowhere else in Africa is wildlife so abundant as in the Serengeti. We were even lucky enough to spy an exquisitely spotted leopard, partially hidden amid the branches of an acacia tree. No zoo or American reserve for transplanted African animals can match the sensation of seeing such magnificent creatures in their natural habitat.

Our safari continued from Nairobi, where we rented a Renault with another couple. Driving to Tsavo, Kenya's "elephant park," we gazed at formidable tuskers accompanying attendant mothers with their Dumbo-eared youngsters. I was grateful to be in Kenya at a time when it was still possible to observe this majestic procession, for ivory poachers are fast annihilating these mammoth creatures.

There remain but ten thousand elephants in Kenya today and they are being killed off at the staggering rate of one thousand a year. For better than a decade, Kenya's largest ivory poaching operations were headed by none other than Prime Minister Kenyatta's wife, Mama Ngina. Kenyatta's oldest daughter also got a cut of the lucrative profits.

While vultures pick at enormous carcasses rotting on Kenyan plains, illegal ivory tusks are shipped off to Hong Kong for carving. As long as poaching continues to be dominated by those with political connections, the extinction of the great East African herds seems inevitable.

Pitching our tent for the night, we could hear the roaring of lions, the bloodcurdling "cough" of leopards, the howl of hyenas ... and at times, the pathetic screams of their prey. It was hard to believe we were here, camping in the midst of this splendid savagery. Slowly the excitement of the day's game watching turned to fatigue, and I drifted into a deep sleep.

An ominous thrashing in the bush startled us awake. Something was moving just outside our tent and, judging from the sound, something big. I nervously poked my head out, catching the moon-lit silhouette of a bull elephant, rubbing himself ecstatically against a solitary tree.

Marzi whispered my own worst fear, "Maybe he won't see us and step on the tent! We're so low to the ground. Elephants aren't supposed to have very good vision."

I tried to calm us both with a bad joke, "He'll probably piss and flood us out," but as that seeming absurdity was a real possibility, it only increased our fears.

For what seemed like forever, we waited. Finally our thick-skinned friend decided he had scratched himself enough and ambled off. But if that was a night to remember, the following morning in Amboseli Reserve proved even more remarkable.

Set against the spectacular backdrop of silvery, snow-capped Mount Kilimanjaro lies Kenya's renowned game park, Amboseli. Here we hired a Masai guide to help us track that most elusive and colorful cat, the cheetah. A youthful Masai, armed solely with spear and shield, must kill a lion to earn tribal status as a "moran" (warrior). The fearlessness of our guide, a full-fledged moran, would serve us well.

En route to the cheetahs' stamping grounds, we stopped the car a few feet from a royally maned lion for photographs. The big cat, typically, lay stretched out on one of those great granite outcrop-pings called "kopjes." Since lionesses do most of the hunting, the males seem fundamentally preoccupied with lazing in the sun.

Ready to leave, I turned the ignition key of the Renault. Nothing! The battery cable which we had tightened repeatedly since leaving Nairobi had once more come loose. The Masai glared expec-tantly at the four of us, none of whom volunteered to get out of the car to secure the cable. Not wishing to remain in the car a day or more until the lion was hungry enough to move on, our guide eased himself out the door. Gingerly lifting the hood, he hand-tightened the cable, returned stealthily, and leaped catlike back inside the car. The lion did not so much as twitch.

With great relief, we renewed our search for the cheetah. After a two-hour hunt, the Masai saw one stalking the grasslands, advancing in our direction. The curious cat circled the car, letting us observe at close range his small head, trim trunk, and sinewy legs—a body built for speed. Cheetahs have been clocked at sixty miles per hour, the fastest animals on earth. Watching the muscles ripple in his shiny, spotted coat, we sadly realized that the cat's very beauty had brought his species close to extinction. The cheetah's sumptuous pelt is a magnetic lure for poachers.

Driving south, we crossed once again into Tanzania, heading for famed Ngorongoro. East of the Serengeti, this ancient volcanic crater is home to the greatest concentration of wildlife in Africa. Here we photographed numerous rhino, albeit with great caution lest they view our car as a threat and charge. These giants, prime targets of poachers merely for their horns, may soon perish. Rhinoceros horn, composed of tightly tufted hair rather than bone, is shipped off to Hong Kong, where the Chinese consider it an aphrodisiac and buy it, powdered, at one hundred dollars an ounce.

We chanced upon one tawny lioness who stretched her taut body close to the ground, allowing her male companion to loll over her. Then to our amazement, they proceeded to mate! No foreplay, the act lasted but a few seconds. We interpreted the female's parting howl as a groan of disappointment.

"The male is saving himself." Our guide laughed. "Lions mate an average of eighteen times a day in season."

Eighteen times! No wonder they say, "Strong like a lion."

We later saw two splotchy brown hyenas run down a young wildebeest, tear its throat, and begin gorging themselves, ripping at the soft underbelly. They easily drove away two pilfer-minded jackals, but retreated themselves at the appearance of a pair of lionesses.

This seemed a curious turnabout to me, for I had thought that hyenas were basically scavengers and lions solely hunters. Our guide corrected this misconception, remarking that lions scavenge more of their food than do the largely predatory hyenas. Lions can be notorious scavengers, running wherever telltale vultures are sighted. In fact, even leopards drag their preys onto the branches of thorny acacia trees to protect their dinners from the "King of Beasts."

A scant hundred yards away from the feeding lionesses, we discovered a wildebeest giving birth. The mother gently lapped up the afterbirth while her fawn struggled first to stand, then minutes later to walk. In order to survive he would soon have to learn to move swiftly. Within these game reserves, there is plenty for all, and life goes on. Unlike man, the predators take only what they need.

Already there has been some speculation that, given East Africa's projected population growth over the next quarter-century, the game reserves may have to be transformed into farmlands to meet the region's food requirements. Obviously, human needs must be considered, but it would be tragic if these wondrous creatures were destroyed in the process.

Returning to Nairobi, we blew a tire on an isolated stretch of road close to a Masai village. Once the most feared warriors of East Africa, this tribe has largely refused to adopt Western ways. Most still herd cattle and subsist on a dietary staple of milk mixed with blood drawn fresh daily from the pricked jugulars of cows. A colorful people, Masai men still wear lobe-extending earrings and long "shuka" robes with one buttock exposed. The tall, lithe women don elaborately beaded, multitiered necklaces which hang over their bare breasts. The distinctive red cast of their hair is achieved through a mixture of ocher mud and cow manure.

A group of Masai women heard the blowout. They came running and unabashedly started removing our things from the car. We pulled these from their grasp and locked all the doors to safeguard our gear.

It can be more than a trifle disconcerting to have a young Masai woman persistently peddling a necklace, taut breasts pressed ardently against you while you are trying to pry off a hubcap. It can be even more distressing to change a tire in southern Kenya's parched heat as hundreds of flies swarm around the dung-anointed head of a Masai maiden dangling her souvenir over your shoulder.

When I asked the Masais' permission to photograph them in their village, they demanded money, having previously received handouts from countless tourists. I bargained with a fierce, spear-bearing "moran" who had just joined us, using my limited Swahili and demonstrative sign language. We came to a surprisingly quick agreement: thirty cents to film the entire village . . . or so I thought.

We took our pictures and paid our three shillings. When the moran spat venomously, thrusting his open palm under my chin, I realized there had been some misunderstanding. He soon made it clear that he expected three hundred shillings! Some mighty affluent tourists must have showered their money in these parts. I turned my back and strode double-time to the car, expecting at every step to be impaled on his lance.

Later, we encountered several groups of Masai women leaping in unison along the roadside, bouncing their breasts up and down to attract oncoming vehicles. They hawked their trinkets, and when that failed, begged with outstretched hands. With the Masai population increasing and their herds and grazing lands shrinking due to the encroachment of private farms, this once-proud tribe is paying a grievous penalty for refusing acculturation.

Arriving in modern, mile-high Nairobi, I was surprised to find its commercial sector largely in the hands of Indian merchants. "Asians," as they are called here, were originally brought to East Africa as indentured labor by the British. Clannish, hard-working entrepreneurs, often openly derisive of the unhurried African way of life, the Asians are hated and envied by the agrarian-oriented native peoples.

Since independence, the Indian has become the political "whipping boy" of East African politicians seeking to increase their popularity. Idi Amin, dictator of Uganda, threw the Asians out of his country in one fell swoop; Kenyan politicians have been a bit more subtle.

One Sikh shopkeeper explained his situation, a plight shared with many others. "You can understand why most of us retain our British citizenship. If we became Kenyan nationals and were later expelled, where would we go? Back to an India without hope?

"The Kenyan Parliament now requires all noncitizens to procure special work permits. But when my clerks and sales personnel applied, they were refused. I was forced to fill their positions with Africans.

"In the past few years, I have seen more and more Indian merchants denied business licenses. Their stores have been expropriated and awarded to Africans who coveted them. My father came over from Amritsar to work on the railroad. He saved every shilling and built this shop from scratch. Because my family and I have invested a lifetime of work into this business, I took a gamble and applied for Kenyan citizenship. I filed the requisite forms, yet the papers have remained unprocessed over the course of a year. Last month I received notice that my shop is to be nationalized. I've appealed, but it's hopeless—a Kikuyu with influence wants the business."

"Africanization" of Indian enterprises is proving economically disastrous. Most of the blacks taking over have little mercantile experience or education. Their reluctance to reinvest profits back into their stores is often attributed to pressure from the extended family to share in the wealth. Business failures run high.

As noted, licenses for the more lucrative establishments go to cronies of powerful politicians or to wealthy Africans who have rewarded the appropriate official. So the stated goal of expropriation, "the advancement of needy Africans," is all too often an excuse for rich blacks to get richer.

The Asians are not the only minority who have faced discrimination. Under Kenyan Prime Minister Jomo Kenyatta, most of the country's ranking politicians were Kikuyu. As the majority tribe of Kenya, only the Kikuyu substantially benefited since Kenyatta came to power following 1963 independence. Bitter Luo and Wakamba students we met at Nairobi University cited case after case of governmental favoritism toward the Kikuyu and decried the wholesale neglect of their people's needs.

Kenyatta, the George Washington of his country, miraculously managed to keep Kenya's seventy-odd tribes from warring with each other. But just before this book went to press, the eighty-year-old Kenyatta died.

When we were in Nairobi, nearly every resident we queried, regardless of tribe or color, predicted violent political upheaval within a year of the venerable "Mzee's" death. The Luo and Wakamba had pledged to even scores, the traditionalist Masai and Samburu were tired of being treated like savages and having their grazing lands deeded away to wealthy Kikuyu, and even the Kikuyu themselves were divided into feuding factions.

Kenya, the richest colony in Africa, attained its independence with great hopes. Kenyatta, revered throughout sub-Saharan Africa, was already a wealthy man, a statesman seen as being above tribal favoritism and corruption. His reputation had grown ever more tainted over the years and, with it, his nation's early promise of prosperity and democracy.

The Kenyan bureaucracy's overall state of operational paralysis, pervasive graft, and tribal bias kept Kenyatta's most ambitious programs from transcending rhetoric. One-third of the country's children have never seen the inside of a classroom. Public health schemes have been woefully inadequate. The social and economic prognosis is bleak for the country which was to have been Africa's showcase for development. And beneath the surface, political tensions seethe as an anxious populace awaits the uncertainty of post-Kenyatta Kenya.

Recuperating from my foot infection in a comfortable Nairobi hospital, I had time to reflect upon our journey. Tanzania excepted, all nations on our route shared the following: staggering corruption, high illiteracy, tribal antagonisms, and catastrophic population growth. Some of the countries were actually in worse economic straits than during the colonial era; others had made little progress since independence.

This assessment is intended as neither a glorification of, nor an apology for, the reign of Europeans in black Africa. The exploitation and degradation of the African (as manifest today in South Africa) is unquestioned, and the legacies of colonialism still tear at the fabric of present-day sub-Saharan societies.

But the tyrannies of the colonial past have all too often been used as an excuse for current problems. Time and again we saw the caricature of "the villainous white master" paraded out to disguise or minimize the excesses, brutality, and ineptitudes of contemporary African leaders. These strongmen, so quick to cry "Racism," have themselves revived old tribal hatreds in order to consolidate their power. While "white-supremacist" Rhodesia and South Africa are understandably a continuous target for criticism, blatant tribal discrimination and even the near-genocidal atrocities of Rwanda and Nigeria have been ignored.

Almost all the countries we visited billed themselves as "Socialist, Democratic, One-Party States." Ruled by despots who tolerate no opposition, they are socialist and democratic only in name. Domination by a white minority has been exchanged for exploitation by a privileged black elite. The spector of kwashiorkor kids wandering past the opulent villas of the African nouveau riche is riveted in our memory.

While overlanding Africa had been a challenging, eye-opening experience, Marzi and I longed to revisit the rich cultures of the Orient. We discovered that for a mere hundred dollars we could sail deck-class on an Indian ship all the way from Mombasa to Bombay. Though the week's passage promised to be as agonizing as third-class Indian trains, we were amenable, as long as no financially viable alternative existed.

Then a brainstorm! Why not take a "small risk" and venture to Uganda? With the black-market rate there hovering around four times the official exchange, we might find an airline which would accept local currency in payment for a ticket.

Hitching to downtown Nairobi from City Park campground, we were picked up by a Ugandan businessman in an air-conditioned Citroën. A mere coincidence of timing? With utmost discretion, I asked his opinion of his country's mercurial President Amin and was amazed at his candor.

"Idi—I know him well. A very clever chap, but sometimes a bit mad, I believe."

Marzi asked the Ugandan, who had introduced himself as Henry, how safe his country was for tourists.

Henry roared with laughter. "The newspapers exaggerate everything. Look, why don't you come with me to visit Kampala and find out for yourselves. The capital is a very pleasant place and you will be perfectly safe with a man of my influence."

The winds of fate were blowing. But we hesitated, making excuses. Too dangerous—and besides, our ship would soon set sail.

"If you change your mind, I'll be at the New Stanley Hotel."

For the next few days Marzi and I discussed the attendant risks. Though the American Embassy discouraged visiting Uganda, citing the capriciousness of Idi Amin and the dangers of his unruly soldiers, we had met several overlanders who had ventured through the country without incident. Indeed, travel in repressive dictatorships was hardly new to us. Of course, these were rationalizations— the temptation of that air ticket undermined our common sense.

I called Henry, accepting his offer.

He replied almost flippantly, "Fine. I would just ask you not to bring any literature that might even remotely be viewed as subversive. You know, some of our guardians are just a wee bit zealous."

We brought no written material whatsoever.

Major Kenyan highways are superb. In that luxurious Citroën, we traveled a greater distance in one day than we had covered in three weeks on Zairois roads.

Our host boasted that he had many profitable ventures, the most lucrative of which was flying contraband into Zaire.

"Yes," he remarked, "I send Mobutu and friends a cut."

Henry looked forward to investing in resource-rich, soon-to-be-independent Angola: "A gold mine for a sharp operator like me. Mobutu and I already have plans." *

Henry clearly relished impressing us. But I grew increasingly skeptical of his tales, until we watched him peel off two hundred dollars in crisp bills to bribe a Kenyan customs inspector who obviously knew him well. On the Ugandan side, Henry got away more cheaply, passing out bundles of gaudy clothing to his pals guarding the border.

We were curious, yet afraid to ask the reason for the bribes. Before dropping us at a hotel, Henry beckoned conspiratorially: "Have a look under my seat." There we saw reams and reams of the more stable Kenyan currency. We had entered one of the world's most repressive dictatorships in the company of a smuggler!

* To Mobutu's chagrin, his plans for economic and political influence in Angola were dashed when a mercenary army led by his brother-in-law was defeated in bloody civil strife. Today Angola is not only a socialist state but also a staging ground for anti-Mobutu rebels.

The rolling green hills of Uganda are considerably more attractive than Kenya's grasslands. This fertile country should be self-sufficient in foodstuffs and rich in cash crops. But under the leadership of a megalomaniac for the last seven years, its economy has come apart at the seams. In Kampala, there were shortages of nearly everything.

The Western press avidly prints Amin's outrageous antics. Sending England a planeload of bananas to help "a rapidly underdeveloping country" out of its economic doldrums; jealously accusing his former lover and Foreign Minister, the statuesque Princess of Toro, of "fornicating with a white man" in an Orly-Airport toilet; organizing a contingent of English businessmen to parade his enthroned 260-pound bulk on their shoulders; cabling Nixon to wish him a "speedy recovery from Watergate." Such inanities and Amin's ex-post-facto dreams (Arab military victories, Nixon's resignation, etc.) make great copy.

But to educated Ugandans, the corpulent "Big Daddy" is far from amusing. An estimated one hundred thousand Africans have been murdered during his reign of terror. Most of the murders were tribally inspired, directed toward ethnic groups who had supported Amin's ousted predecessor and chief rival-in-exile, Milton Obote. Anyone thought to be a threat to Amin's leadership has been ruthlessly eliminated. Disappearance of prominent citizens, some of whom were reportedly fed to crocodiles, has become commonplace. Amin (who once praised Hitler's genocide of the Jews) is fond of explaining his victims' absences in the following terms: "Zionists and imperialists have confused them and they have run away."

To maintain his power, Amin has spent three-quarters of Uganda's budget on a prolific expansion of the military. Amin's army is the best paid in black Africa—and the least disciplined. Drunken soldiers do what they want, without fear of prosecution. They wear a license to kill on their hip.

Yet Amin is tremendously popular with the Ugandan masses. They are highly amused by his baiting of the white, imperial powers. Most of all, they revel in his ouster of the Asians. When the country's five thousand Indians were expelled, seventy-five per cent of Kampala's businesses closed down and forty thousand blacks who had worked for the Asians lost their jobs. Hospitals formerly staffed with skilled Oriental personnel were forced to operate below capacity. "Africanization" of thirty-five hundred firms led to price gouging, chaotic mismanagement, and bankruptcy. Despite the ensuing economic catastrophe, Amin has successfully fed off the prejudices of the Africans, who loathed their Asian shopkeepers. To most black Ugandans, the tyrant is a folk hero.

Seeing no other whites on the streets of Kampala, I wondered if we had made a terrible, if not fatal, mistake to come here. Then I found an international airline whose sales clerk said she would accept Ugandan shillings; she would even introduce me to a gentleman who would change our money at the "unofficial" rate! He would bribe the appropriate official to circumvent a law obliging foreigners to purchase all air tickets with "solid" currencies.

This was all too easy. Was it a trap? I wondered, my fears growing. I sorely regretted bringing Marzi along, envisioning us languishing forever in some nightmarish Ugandan prison ... or worse. The murders of an American journalist, university professor, and Peace Corps volunteer at the hands of Amin's sadistic troops lingered in my mind. "Small risk" indeed!

But the transaction went off without a hitch. The moneychanger, to our amazement, was an obese Indian.

"How have you managed to stay in Uganda?" I asked stupidly.

"Baksheesh!" he grunted.

Carefully counting our money, the Indian was virtually salivating. I could hardly blame him. Ugandan shillings were worthless outside the country and his status here was tenuous, to say the least.

The tickets enabled us to fly back to the States, with stopovers in Egypt and Sri Lanka, as well as numerous points in Southeast Asia and the South Pacific, for less than the price of a direct flight home.

Our bus approached Entebbe Airport, later the scene of Israel's courageous commando raid. My only remaining qualm: Was the ticket truly valid? On board a 727, the roar of our jet bound for Cairo answered that question definitively.

EGYPT TO CEYLON

Pharaohs and Firewalkers

Entering Cairo, Africa's largest metropolis, we wondered if we had mistakenly landed in the depths of Asia. Winding alleyways, slender minarets, mysteriously shrouded figures, hubble-bubble smokers, teeming bazaars, baksheeshers—were we not back in the Orient?

While sub-Saharan cities seem modern on the surface, centuries-old Cairo reflects its ancient history. The rich Egyptian culture has imparted a national character neither torn by tribal fragmentation nor confused by a Western loss of identity. It seemed almost as if the arid atmosphere preserving the great monuments of pharonic civilization has also maintained for Egyptains a unique sense of themselves.

Predictably, a society so deeply tied to the past has had difficulty adapting to the exigencies of the twentieth century. Cairo's streets, built originally for camel caravans, are now thronged with muffler-less motor vehicles. Unlike the bargaining of the bazaars, we found no "give" in Cairoene traffic; unlike the mathematical order of

Islamic architecture, there is nothing but anarchy. The guidelines of custom have no applicability to the streets.

Traffic signals are meaningless in the jostling for position that characterizes contemporary urban life here. Cairoene drivers, demanding recognition by constantly blasting their horns, are rivaled for insanity only by their Tehranian brethren. I could hardly doubt the shopkeeper who remarked with typical, sharply honed Egyptian irony, "Pedestrian deaths are the only certain check on our city's growth."

Cairo, its blighted slums overflowing with rural refugees, has clearly been unable to cope with urban sprawl. Egypt's population has quadrupled since the turn of the century, with Cairo the recipient of a massive exodus from the countryside. Though nearly all (ninety-seven percent) the people of this desert land reside along the Nile, that fertile strip can only provide for so many. "Fellaheen" (peasants), whose inherited family plots have been too often divided to yield a viable subsistence, believe the city is paved with gold and flock to Cairo. But the capital can meet neither the employment demand nor the housing needs of its burgeoning numbers. And no end to this calamitous migration can be expected, for every year the population of Egypt increases by a million.

Since relations between the United States and Egypt at that time were not particularly cordial, Marzi and I had qualms about coming here (not the least of which was being Jewish). Nonetheless, we wanted to see the country's antiquities and to hear, first-hand, Egyptian opinions of the volatile Middle East situation. Not wishing to be refused visas, we became "closet Jews," claiming we were Protestant when asked our religion on the application form.

Much to our surprise, the Egyptians we met were remarkably hospitable. We would be asked our nationality on the streets and then deluged with invitations from merchants and students for tea or even meals. This buoyant welcome, which we certainly had not experienced in black Africa, came as a bit of a shock. So did the political perspectives of our hosts. Whether we questioned a fair cross section of the public is debatable, but those who discussed the Middle East crisis expressed a sincere longing for peace.

Malmoud, a middle-aged gem dealer, best articulated what we

generally heard. "The Palestinians' problems are not our battle—let them settle their own grievances. But our territory has been stolen and we want it back. Otherwise, we have no reason to fight Israel.

"This continual state of war has drained our treasury, taken our best young men, and misplaced energies better devoted to national development. Look at our economic problems—what a waste of money and manpower."

In the next breath, however, Malmoud spouted scornfully, "Don't forget, the Zionists are imperialists. How do I know? They have proven it by colonizing our lands. When they decide they want more territory, they will attack us. Because the Israeli expansionists can never be trusted, we must make some sacrifices to remain militarily on guard."

These widely held sentiments were daily reinforced in the media, which seemed to trace all the world's woes to "Zionist conspiracies." Probing deeper, we found most of our hosts differentiated little between Zionism and Judaism. Critiques of Zionism were all too often thinly veiled anti-Semitic diatribes. Egyptians have been fed so long an image of the "conniving, greedy Jew" that the stereotype has become rooted in the national psyche.

The Heartbreak Kid, Elaine May's satirical film on American middle-class Jewry, was the smash hit of Cairoene cinema. Curious to see the audience response, we braved the long line of a sell-out crowd. What we saw was most distressing. Because they had no exposure to the subtleties depicted, local moviegoers grasped only the broad farce which reified their prejudices.

International problems dissolved in the cobbled wilderness of old Cairo's "Mouskie" and we joyously lost ourselves in the bustling bazaar's tangled passageways. This "souk" is built around the venerable al-Azhar Mosque and the oldest functioning university (built 970 A.D.) in the world. Its architecture represents the flowering of Egypt's second great, though less appreciated than the Pharaonic, civilization. While Europe sank into the vacuity of the Dark Ages, Egypt flourished. Today that period's impressive high-walled building are inhabited by thousands of indigent families from the countryside, their numbers swelling daily.

A seemingly directionless tide of men clad in loose-fitting galabia robes, and women encased in layers of black cloth, surged through the Mouskie's narrow lanes. In the crush, water vendors plied their trade, miraculously spilling not a drop. Haunched human bearers, sweat dripping from their foreheads, shouldered cumbersome sacks of goods. While jugglers and magicians entertained.

Here our senses were overwhelmed by the odoriferous pastiche of spices, sewage, and tobacco-hash and the unremitting commotion of banging coppersmiths, beggars, and hawkers. This tableau of medieval Middle East was breached only by the occasional motorbike or VW beetle.

At Giza, on the outskirts of the city, we were thrust even further back in time. Viewed from a distance, each of the three pyramids resembled a massive triangular stone. Closer up, however, we gazed upon row after row of bricks, set like so many steps soaring to their pointed pinnacles. What genius and staggering effort went into their construction! Archeologists are still undecided as to just how the pyramids' planners achieved such architectural precision, to say nothing of the formidable undertaking itself, in that premechanized age. The guardian of these five-thousand-year-old tombs was an even more imposing sight, the Great Sphinx. We were astounded to learn that this gargantuan head of man and body of lion was sculpted, except for the paws, from a single piece of rock.

It is lamentable that these "Wonders of the World" are situated just outside the city. Nothing seemed more out of place than the nightclubs, discos, and belly-dancing joints that cluttered the boulevard leading to the pyramids. Even worse, visitors had to suffer an army of shrieking touts and peddlers who lay in wait around the monuments. Luckily, we met a young Egyptian archeology student, who, hoping to practice her English, volunteered to show us around. Her vigorous tongue-lashings kept even the most determined hawkers from dogging our footsteps. I must confess, however, to momentarily succumbing to tourist instincts, mounting a saddled camel. True to his nasty reputation, the beast nearly tied his neck in a knot while trying to chomp off my foot.

From desolate cliffsides bordering the Nile at Luxor, the heart of Pharaonic civilization has been unearthed. To reach this "Valley of the Kings," one must journey four hundred miles south through the desert by rail.

Beyond the towering twin stone Colossi of Memnon lie the crypts of King Tut, Ramses, and sixty other Pharaohs, cut into rock gorges engulfed by desert sands. Mummy cases, frescoes, hieroglyphics, and those antiquities which have not been shunted off to museums or stolen have remained remarkably intact, thanks to the aridity of the region.

We explored the valley on mules, trusting these sure-footed animals to transport us safely up and down steep escarpments. At times the scorching sun seemed to be sucking the very marrow from my bones. What a relief to enter the coolness of the tombs!

From look-outs high above the valley floor, we surveyed the terrain. A green ribbon of farmland outlined the muddy brown of the Nile on either side ... and beyond, nothing but sand. To the south lay Aswan, site of the immense dam built to reclaim arable soils from desert. Financed largely by the USSR, the Aswan Dam has helped to irrigate a million additional acres and provided a much needed source of hydroelectric power.

But nature has played a terrible trick on man's best-laid plans. The Nile contained, it no longer flooded sufficiently to deposit the rich nutrients needed to renew the soils. Expensive fertilizer, which few fellaheen can either afford or know how to use, is now an essential substitute. Indeed, the newly restored lands, not nearly as fecund as other areas, have even greater need for chemical nutrients and costly irrigation facilities.

Compounding these problems, the loss of silt from the now-dammed Nile has killed the once-vital sardine fishing industry. Most disastrous of all, with the river's currents slowed, schistosomiasis, the debilitating disease derived from snails breeding in languid waters, has become a severe health problem, infecting thousands of peasants.

We ferried across the Nile on one of those picturesque flat-bottomed sailboats called "feluccas" to the ancient capital, Thebes. Here stands the Temple of Karnak, a dizzying labyrinth of hieroglyphically inscribed columns, ruined pylons, and magnificently proportioned obelisks. Over a period of two thousand years, each

243

pharaoh contributed to the shrine some personal stone legacy of his reign; half of ancient Egypt's history can be traced in this awesome maze.

Returning to Cairo by rail reaffirmed this aura of antiquity. We rambled past scenes of camels turning waterwheels, oxen hauling wooden plows, fig-treed oases, and fellaheens' mud-brick villages. Thirty million peasants, three-quarters of all Egyptians, live in such humble hamlets along the Nile. Most of these people farm for a bare subsistence, their villages having neither schools nor medical dispensaries.

Diaddin, a student traveling home to Cairo, noted that the government's attempts to introduce birth control to the fellaheen have met with staunch opposition from conservative local religious leaders. The fellaheens' geometric growth, he added, had already outstripped the increased productivity engendered by the Aswan Dam. Consequently, more and more foodstuffs have had to be imported to fulfill the need.

I asked Diaddin about changes introduced since the 1953 revolution.

"When Nasser threw out the king and broke up the large land holdings, that was certainly a long-overdue reform. Medical and educational personnel were sent to the countryside. Endemic diseases like trachoma were greatly reduced. But now the revolution has turned to stone and our paper-shuffling bureaucracy has become the new privileged class."

"What about your fellow students? Aren't they interested in Egypt's development?"

"Only one university student in twenty is enrolled in the natural sciences or engineering. Most graduating engineers in my class plan to emigrate. The government subsidizes their education, then they leave for a place where they can make more money."

On the outskirts of Cairo, the near-biblical imagery was replaced by the gloom of dilapidated tenements. We bused from the central railway station to the airport, first past squalid squatters' slums, then alongside a heavily guarded modern military installation where millions of dollars have been invested in sophisticated firepower.

Whatever political enmity Egypt held toward the United States was in no way expressed personally to us during our short stay. Nearly everyone we met went out of their way to make us feel welcome. As a Jew fearing for the survival of Israel, my experience here only heightened the absurdity of the Middle East crisis. But then, powerful political figures, not average citizenry, kindle the fires of hatred and make the decisions that lead to conflict.

Upon our landing in Bombay after the long flight from Cairo, the noxious atmosphere confirmed that we were back in India. Shit and charcoal. Greetings from Bombay.

In the dark streets, flickering kerosene lamps betrayed the presence of countless shadowy figures sprawled along refuse-strewn sidewalks. The Indian city.

Yet by the light of day, it was apparent that Bombay differed strikingly from Delhi, Benares, and Calcutta. The flaunting of wealth in this commercial heart of the subcontinent was stupefying in juxtaposition to its cruel poverty. A walk around the luxurious Taj Hotel or the financial district staggers the outsider with incongruities. Seemingly oblivious to the surrounding misery strolled bejeweled women, accompanied by well-heeled husbands in their modish Western best.

Another sight that left us dumbfounded: Bombay Indians queueing in orderly fashion for buses. It was evident that the British Raj had concentrated most of its colonial endeavors here.

I wandered about the seaside Gate of India, across from the opulent Taj, and laughed aloud as peddlers bombarded me with familiar pitches from the past. "Change mun-ee?" "Hashish?" "Want Chinese girl?" "Postcard?" And of course, the inevitable demand, "Baksheesh!" Now I could view with good humor the nonstop pestering, secure in the knowledge that in two days I would be flying out of this madness.

"See mongoose kill cobra?!"

The snake charmer, a paunchy, turbaned old man, kept entreating. Finally, my curiosity got the better of me.

"How much?"

"For you, only twenty rupees."

"Seven rupees."

"O.K., ten rupees, you pay now!"

A dollar! Cobras must come cheap in these parts.

With a cherubic grin, the charmer opened a knotted sack, from which a long, russet-brown rodent scampered, stretched himself, and licked his chops. The furry mongoose knew a call for dinner when he heard one.

The cobra, on the other hand, all too aware of who waited impatiently for him outside, was in no hurry to leave his wicker basket. The snake charmer had to pull the reluctant serpent out by the tail from his straw sanctuary.

Spreading his hood, the cobra struck. The lightning mongoose dodged, bobbed, and weaved. Within thirty seconds, the razor-toothed mongoose grasped his overmatched enemy below the hood and, shaking violently, bit the snake's head off.

The exuberant charmer quickly held up yet another basket, "See mongoose kill fresh cobra?! This mongoose champion cobra-killer!"

"One more cobra and I'll be the basket case," Marzi replied. "But fangs for the memory."

"Better be careful in Ceylon," I retaliated. "They may have a law against that sort of verbal abuse, and if there is, I won't defend you."

The super-charged intensity of the Indian subcontinent dissolves in the placid straits separating the mainland from the resplendent isle of Ceylon. Like Nepal, Sri Lanka (the official, though not popular, name) is remarkably relaxed for a nation straddling the Indian hurly-burly. Even the country's two million Tamils, originally of southern India, appear relatively at ease. This all makes sense, for despite current economic woes, Ceylon's soils are so fertile that there exists little outright starvation. Survival is not yet really an issue here.

Riding the excellent rail and bus network through Sri Lanka, I marveled at the variety of terrain packed into such a concentrated space—only the south island of New Zealand is comparable. Ceylon is pure delight for tourists. Crystal waters calmed by coral reefs abounding with spectacular acquatic life, tropical forests rich with the ruins of great civilizations, alpine-esque hill stations terraced with celebrated Ceylonese teas, and above all, amiable peoples living their fascinating cultures. Fine for the tourist. But as we discovered in discussions with numerous locals, there is big trouble in Eden.

The light-skinned Singhalese, the majority ethnic group on the island, emigrated here by sea from northern India in the fifth century. Their brilliantly engineered construction of artificial lakes for irrigation yielded the bounteous harvest which supported a remarkable Buddhist civilization. Later, they were invaded by fierce Hindu Tamils. Fighting between Singhalese and Tamil left the island vulnerable to colonial conquest, first by the Portuguese, then the Dutch, and finally the British. Ill-feeling between the Singhalese and Tamil, who speak different dialects, persists to this day. The island's political leaders have capitalized upon the old colonial tactic of playing one group against the other to help maintain their own hegemony.

Following 1948 independence, Ceylon's future looked bright. Its rich fields produced sufficient food for all, and planters reaped windfall profits from the postwar demand for tea, rubber, and coconuts. Progressive administrators set up schools throughout the island, and free education was offered from first grade to university. An extensive network of clinics was established, providing medical care without charge. Preventive-health measures (such as malarial spraying and inoculation) doubled life expectancy within a decade.

Yet ironically, while other third-world nations suffer from the neglect of such basic needs, Sri Lanka's economy has been devastated by the high cost of its irrationally implemented social services. A mastodonic civil service, swelling disproportionately to meet the demands of the island's fast-growing populace, seems to trip over itself in administering its own projects. A Singhalese merchant ruefully remarked that, as in India, a half-dozen functionaries might be employed to do the work of one.

With the majority of Sri Lanka's university and high-school graduates unable to find jobs corresponding to their level of educa-

247

tion, the government has opted for the expediency of padding the civil service. But even the bureaucracy can only expand so far, and no real effort has been made to stimulate an economy that will constructively absorb the unemployed. Furthermore, the affluent supporters of Ceylon's ruling parties have been immune to the few legitimate reforms of the last decade. So despite the progressive legislation, little has changed. Although the recently ousted government of Prime Minister Bandaranaike espoused socialist ideals, those pronouncements were largely rhetorical. It remains to be seen whether her more ideologically conservative successors will do any better.

As a Colombo University professor discreetly related to us: "The answer is not the outright elimination of vital social programs, but efficient execution of well-thought-out schemes by competent administrators. Of course, the government must also be willing to sponsor incentives for local development, intensive family planning, and a trimming of the civil service. Our bureaucratic bungling is proof positive that poorly planned welfare states can be every bit as disastrous as the worst excesses of laissez-faire capitalism."

Despite these problems and a growing discontent, I could not help but be impressed that for the first time since Europe I was in a land of high literacy and relatively little malnutrition. The absence of misery made overlanding this variegated isle all the more pleasurable.

Moving inland, we spied bronzed peasants, wearing only a scant cloth between their buttocks, plodding through flooded rice fields in water which at times rose to their hips. Here well-trained elephants do the work of bulldozers—no expensive parts to replace. Climbing into the bracing highlands surrounding Nuwara Eliya, we watched Tamil women carrying a harvest of famous Ceylonese tea by Sherpa-like forehead straps. Then we descended through the ravishing jungles where *The Bridge on the River Kwai* was filmed. Within lay the remains of Sri Lanka's great ancient capitals, Anuradhapura and Polonnaruwa, reclaimed only this century from the dense rain forests.

Most spectacular among Ceylonese ruins was Sigiriya, a fortress one thousand feet high, carved into a black anvil rock perched atop a sheer precipice. This bastion was built fifteen hundred years ago by a power-hungry, paranoid prince, who, having murdered his father and brother, sought a sanctuary safe from reprisal. Like a juggler's ball on a cane, the immense, oblong rock which houses the citadel sits balanced upon its stone pillar. This grotesquely eroded formation looks sufficiently precarious to come crashing down with the first breeze, yet has withstood the test of centuries.

Cautiously placing one foot before the other on steps chiseled into the cliff, we began our dizzying ascent to the top. About the halfway point, we paused to catch our breath, admiring a gallery of well-preserved frescoes sensually depicting the bare-breasted Singhalese concubines of the prince's harem.

Approaching the summit of the anvil, we were besieged by a ferocious swarm of hornets. The higher we climbed, the more aggressive they became. Imagine the horror of being savagely attacked while clinging to hand- and footholds some nine hundred feet above the ground. Stung twice each, we readily concurred that to go any further would be insane. When we returned to the base, we were informed that only the week before an Englishman had been stung to death. Consequently, the government tourist board was "considering" closing off the upper reaches. How nice to have been forewarned! We learned later in Bangkok that after two subsequent near-fatalities, the government finally decided to cordon off the area.

This harrowing experience only served to worsen digestive problems I had been suffering since Egypt. Mindful that my lack of trust in African country doctors had nearly cost me a foot, I sought out the closest physician, whose dispensary was located two-hours' bus ride from Sigiriya. In his wooden shack of an office, the swarthy, turban-clad Tamil pumped me for more than an hour concerning my medical history and present symptoms.

"At least he's thorough," Marzi whispered.

Three times within the course of the consultation, I informed him that I had been treating myself unsuccessfully with tetracycline. His inquiry concluded, the doctor wrote out a prescription which his wife filled on the spot.

Examining the pink pills, I asked, "What are these?"

"Tetracycline."

"But I already told you I've been taking this antibiotic for a week, and it's not helping."

"Just take four tablets a day, drink coffee instead of tea, and you'll be cured."

"But coffee is a diuretic," I protested.

"Nonsense, it will calm your innards while it stimulates your mind."

After this, I dropped all medication and was well within a week.

Journeying back to the coast to snorkel at the coral gardens of Hikkaduwa, we observed a ritual of penance being performed along the seashore. To invoke the aid of the gods in ridding his daughter of polio, a young Tamil drove steel skewers through the skin of his back and upper arms. He followed this by impaling a long needle between his cheeks. We then watched in anguish as he extended his tongue and proceeded to twist, twist, twist a six-inch skewer until it penetrated the other side.

At this, one Western spectator became violently ill; others found it more than they could bear and left. But the human porcupine was not quite finished. Strapping on a pair of spiked shoes, he wandered trancelike up and down the beach. A priest, at long last, removed the skewers and needles, leaving neither a trace of incision nor a spot of blood.

Another repentant Tamil lay flat on a table while the priest inserted into the flesh of his back circular iron meathooks which were secured by ropes to a tree. The self-hypnotized youth didn't bat an eye or move a muscle. Then observers gasped as the priest's assistants pushed the table away. Held only by that butcher's truss, the Tamil was given a push by the priest, swinging back and forth, the ropes moaning in the breeze. Finally, the table was returned, the hooks removed. Not a mark! If I had not seen this with my own eyes, I would not have believed it.

Attention shifted next to a lengthy bed of sizzling coals where glassy-eyed men strode barefoot over the red-hot embers. We examined their feet afterward—no sign of burn.

I later discussed the ritualized self-torture with a young, London-trained Singhalese physician. "I have been studying such phenomena for the past two years with a research team at Colombo Medical School. One thing we have noted is that most skewers are placed in areas with relatively few nerve endings. That is not to say there is no pain. These chaps believe to the point that they are able to build up a formidable threshold of tolerance. This, though, certainly doesn't explain how they endure that spike through the tongue—plenty of nerve endings there. The auto-suggestion of self-hypnosis? The powers of the mind controlling physiology? ... To date, we simply have no definitive answers.

"As for the fire walkers, the soles of their feet are extremely tough, and it is conceivable that the perspiration induced by their trance insulates the skin. These are possible contributory factors coupled, doubtlessly, with their mental state. And of course"—he laughed—"they move very fast."

I had heard that Hikkaduwa was a bastion of Ceylonese Devil Dancing and asked the priest in charge of the penance proceedings if this ceremony of exorcism would be performed in the near future. He disclosed that an ailing importer had summoned him to administer the rite the following evening. Impressed with the genuine interest we had expressed, the holy man invited us along.

The expense for a Devil Dance is so great these days that only the affluent can afford the sacred ceremony. The sick man greeted us warmly at the door of his rather opulent home, introduced us to his family, and bade us sit down on the veranda. Next to us was the merchant's personal physician.

"Will this dance really cure him?" I asked the doctor, skeptical despite all I had seen the previous evening.

"Because his abdominal problems may be largely, if not wholly, psychosomatic, I raised no protest. It can only help."

The priest and his assistants danced till dawn, wearing a sequence of grotesque fang-toothed masks designed to frighten malevolent spirits from the sick man's body. Shadows of the masquerade were outlined in hideous detail against the torch-lit courtyard wall, an aura of evil incarnate. At intervals, the nightmarish atmosphere was accentuated when the holy man threw powder into a fire, causing

251

flames to shoot skyward. Then we looked on with incredulity, watching the priest lather his coffee-color chest with blazing wooden stakes, demonstrating his power over the spirits.

At daybreak, the "possessed" merchant crawled into a miniature bamboo hut rigged up inside the house by the priest's assistants especially for this occasion. Here the diabolical spirits would be, once and for all, exorcised. Bursting from the realm of the bewitched, our host greeted his family with a nod of assurance, and beaming beatifically, thanked us all for coming.

We ran into his doctor a few days later on the streets of Colombo. "How is the patient faring?" I inquired.

"He has no more symptomatic discomforts," replied the physician with a wink.

For all the scenic natural wonders and "unearthly" phenomena witnessed, among my most stirring recollections of Sri Lanka are the island's striking women. Singhalese mocha to Tamil mahogany, their delicately sculpted faces, jet-black hair, and sari-clad bodies sear the male psyche. Yet the passion these women induce is tempered by a realization that they are sexually unattainable. So the response is not quite from the groin; rather, it is an acknowledgment of ethereal beauty—of a delicate tapestry that inexorably draws one, only to materialize always beyond reach.

I recognize this illusive quality in the Orient itself. It pulls a Westerner from lands where all is direct and "rational" into a web of intricacy and mystery impossible to fully grasp. That is the key to its allure, engulfment by the infinite.

We moved on through Southeast Asia, Bali being a fitting last stop in the Orient. From there we flew through time to the homelands of highland New Guinea's Stone Age warriors.

PAPUA NEW GUINEA

"The Last Unknown":
A Visit with the Wigmen

It is a bank as we know it: modern, sterile, air-conditioned. But patrons who wander in, presenting their savings books, are of another era. Their faces are adorned with feathers, paint, and a bone through the nasal septum; their bodies are covered solely with fiber G-strings and a few leaves—"ass grass" in the local vernacular. The bank is situated in the wild highlands of Papua New Guinea (P.N.G.), an untamed land aptly dubbed by historian Gavin Souter "The Last Unknown."

For me, exploration of New Guinea meant fulfillment of a boyhood dream. How many *National Geographics* and films had I devoured depicting this lost world which, along with the Amazon jungles, remains the last stronghold of primitive man. Both regions are experiencing greater and greater contact with "Western civilization" and undergoing rapid cultural breakdown. I was determined to see New Guinea before it was too late.

A British volunteer, enjoying his R & R on Bali, had invited us to visit him. As an agronomist posted to a remote region of P.N.G., he worked with some of the fiercest warrior clans on this dragon-shaped island, the wigmen of Tari. Our journey into the interior proved unique among our travels—an encounter with Stone Age cultures suspended in time.

P.N.G. shares the world's third largest island with Irian Jaya, a former Dutch colony annexed by Indonesia in 1963. The southern half of the country was awarded to Australia by Great Britain in 1906; the northern half became an Australian trust territory after World War I when the League of Nations took it away from Germany. Colonially administered in a relatively benign fashion, P.N.G. was accorded independence in September 1975.

Much of P.N.G.'s inner reaches had been little explored until recently due to its topography of impenetrable jungles, raging rivers, and rugged mountains. Over the centuries, such natural barriers in an area larger than the state of California have insulated native clans from each other. This isolation was reinforced by perpetual warfare directed against intruders. As a result, seven hundred distinct linguistic groupings and an extraordinary variety of primitive cultures have evolved.

Many highlanders have had but fifteen to twenty-five years' contact with the outside world. Some have never seen a car, only an airplane. Pilots have flown over villages near the Indonesian border whose inhabitants have yet to meet a white man. Even in areas where there has been extensive exposure to Westerners, sporadic uprisings of interclan warfare persist and cannibalism is still practiced.

No roads connect Port Moresby, the modern capital, to P.N.G.'s interior. Except for one major artery which runs from the coastal town of Lae into the highlands, P.N.G.'s "highways" are the skies.

So we flew from Moresby into the suffocating humidity of Lae, making further travel arrangements at the marketplace with a native truck driver. For a few dollars, he agreed to take us to the central highlands' frontier settlement, Mount Hagen, a two-day journey.

After my ear became attuned to the singsong "pidgin," a short-hand English which serves as the lingua franca in this land of so many dialects, communications posed little problem. Pidgin reminded me of patois variants spoken in the Caribbean and West Africa, albeit with a considerable difference in inflection and colloquialisms. It was a most colorful tongue, as evidenced by the following exchanges overheard in the market:

Toothless elderly crone offering praise to a young woman ("mary") nursing her baby: "You gat numba-won pickaninny."

Tribesman asking if I would take his picture: "You kissim picsa?"

Sign above shop: "No gat wok."

New Guinean pidgin is nothing if not direct. Our driver, so soft-spoken and polite, startled us by quietly cursing at a slow pedestrian, "Fuckin' bastid." These and other choice expletives, rarely tinged with genuine animosity, are an integral part of everyday pidgin exchange.

As we meandered up the highway, the trucker sought to cut his gasoline expenses by serving as a commuter transport. Tribespeople bound for distant markets clung to shaky wooden benches lining the back of the pickup and took the jostling in high spirits. We also stopped periodically for the driver and passengers to buy great quantities of betel, as the value of the nut escalated the further inland we traveled. The New Guineans chewed this mild narcotic incessantly, spitting streams of its red juice onto the dusty road.

The narrow track rose steeply with sharp switchbacks which the driver navigated at breakneck speed. When I finally realized that he knew every foot of the road intimately, I relaxed and began to appreciate how dramatically the scenery had shifted since we left the jungled lowlands.

The hair-raising climb to Daulo Pass (8,150 feet) was spectacular. We paused at various points for the truck to cool off, gazing out over sheer limestone cliffs to tree-carpeted valley floors. Waterfalls thundered over precipices to swell streams into tumultuous rivers hundreds of feet below. High above rose the snow-covered peak of P.N.G.'s highest mountain, Mount Wilhelm (15,600 feet). Invigorating alpine air, a welcome relief from the steamy humidity of the coast, accentuated the beauty of the majestic highlands.

The topography and climate were not the only changes. Indigenous people, who had sported basically European apparel on the coast, dressed more and more traditionally as we ventured further inland. For the men, shirts and shorts were replaced by bark girdles from which dangled fiber penis sheaths; their buttocks were festooned with "ass-grass." Around Chimbu the warriors carried spears, clubs, bows, and arrows. As intertribal warfare rages here from time to time, a chilling thought crossed my mind: were these warriors armed for protection, or were they en route to a raid?

Along the roadside we passed women bare to the waist in grass skirts, harvesting their gardens or tending pigs. Whenever a hog roamed onto the road, our driver made certain to come to a dead stop—for to hit a pig is to risk being speared in retaliation.

As the tribespeoples' only domestic animal, the pig plays a role of paramount importance in highland cultures. A man's wealth is measured by how many pigs he owns. The purchase of a healthy young wife may cost a warrior from one to two dozen hogs. Blood feuds are often settled through compensation of a negotiated number of swine.

At one point, I thought I saw a tribeswoman nursing a piglet. Wondering if my imagination were not getting the better of me, I asked the driver.

"Sometime sow die, so lik lik (little) pig suck mary who gat pickaninny. Sapos he no gat suck—den he die an him Mastuh gat poor."

Later I learned that a pig is so significant for highlanders that a lactating woman may nurse her baby and a sow-less piglet equally.

A stolen pig is the catalyst for many of the bloody clashes which still occur in the highlands. "Payback," revenge murder for past homicides, has been customary for evening scores. A victim's kinsmen are obliged to avenge his death by killing anyone belonging to the guilty clan.

Given that highland warriors have a heritage of hostility toward intruders, one must respect the missionaries, administrators, and patrol officers who braved this region and laid the groundwork for pacification of the more warlike clans. While the trucker stopped to fill his radiator with water from the well of a mission, a veteran cleric recited to us the tale of Father Ross, whose pioneering efforts here are legendary.

256

"The good Father was accompanied on one of his treks into unmapped territory by a clergyman from the coast. Whenever a spear-bearing tribesman approached them, Ross' pious mate would thrust his crucifix toward the warrior. Ross' curiosity got the better of him, leading him to ask, 'What on earth are you doing?'

" 'On the coast, we show them the cross so that they know who we are.'

"Pulling a .38 from his hip, Father Ross shot back, 'Well, up here we show 'em this!' "

As the truck continued its ascent, we passed through a region infamous for the bizarre malady which afflicts the local tribespeople. "Kuru," a terminal illness in which the victim loses control of his facial muscles and appears to laugh to death, has long been the subject of scientific investigation. More than a decade ago, researchers concluded that kuru results from the traditional eating of the brains of dead ancestors. The authorities and missionaries made substantial efforts to educate the people as to the cause, and the incidence of kuru diminished over the next few years. But there has been a recent resurgence of the "laughing disease." Either the scientists were wrong, or old ways die hard.

Mount Hagen, a modern frontier town, stands amid P.N.G.'s towering central highlands. Its wide, paved streets are lined with modern shops, pubs, and restaurants, patronized primarily by Australian administrators and foreign technicians. But the New Guineans who wander into town to do their marketing or exchange gossip contrast strikingly with the town's contemporary architecture.

It is cool in this mountainous region and, lacking clothes, many of the tribespeople smear pig fat on their bodies to insulate themselves from the chill. A few warriors who had saved enough money from the sale of coffee beans to buy a transistor radio, sauntered about the main street in their finest ass-grass, ears glued to country and western classics. "C & W," the popular mainstay of Australian airwaves, has been enthusiastically adopted as the local favorite. It is strange indeed to see a fearsome tribesman humming the latest melodies of an Aussie "Johnny Cash."

Kurt, a jocular Australian administrator who had put us up, invited us to accompany him on a visit to an outlying village.

257

There, an elderly woman startled me, thrusting cupped hands toward my groin.

"That's just her way of greeting you." Kurt laughed. "About fifteen years ago, natives welcomed each other by stroking the genitals of the opposite sex. Not a bad custom, to my mind. Too bad the missionaries horned in. All that's left is this friendly gesture."

We glanced into one of the thatched huts. The interior was blackened with the soot of daily cooking fires and reeked of rancid pork grease. Kurt informed us, "This hut houses a family of six and two pigs. Everyone, including the pigs, sleeps huddled together to ward off the cold. 'Marys' in this clan become so attached to their animals that when a creature is to be clubbed to death, the woman who raised it is mercifully sent away."

Two village teenagers wearing European shorts asked for a ride to Mount Hagen's cinema. When told that I was from the States, one exclaimed, "You American? You know John Wayne?! You and he 'one-talks'?"

Kurt explained that while kung fu epics were catching up in popularity, John Wayne "oaters" remain the cinematic staple. The Hollywood cowboy star being revered in these parts, it is assumed that fellow Americans are "one-talks" (i.e., "kinsmen") and personally acquainted with him.

Returning to Hagen's market, we encountered a tour group of Australians. There were few travelers in P.N.G. and those that came usually paid outrageous fees to be squired around by Talco, a private company with a seeming monopoly. Only through Talco could one arrange a visit with the internationally famous Asaro "Mud Men," whose village is situated about halfway between Lae and Hagen. It seems that whenever New Guinea is in the news, *Time* and *Newsweek* run photos of these grotesquely masked warriors. Even Queen Elizabeth stopped to pose with them. But Kurt revealed that their celebrated costumes of clay had less to do with tradition than with their newly discovered flare for show biz.

"Those Asaros are mighty shrewd. They invented that 'Mud Men' get-up several years ago to cash in on the budding tourist market.

They're now about the richest tribespeople in the highlands. But you know, they simply can't decide what to buy with all that money, so their cash remains buried somewhere."

"Aren't they afraid of being attacked for their loot?"

"Naw, warriors here raid only for payback, pigs, or women."

On Self-Government Day (a year prior to P.N.G.'s full independence) celebrating highlanders anxiously anticipated a visit from Queen Elizabeth. Many tribesmen had seen the official portrait of the Queen wrapped in her impressive royal robes, some even hanging it in their huts. Expectations high, they dressed in their finest feathers and paint to greet Her Majesty.

What a disappointment! The Queen flew in, dressed not in those famous regal robes but rather in a sensible pants suit. Although the P.N.G. legislature has since adopted the Queen as their symbolic sovereign, in the hearts and minds of unimpressed highlanders, she is just "another woman."

The onrush of progress can certainly burst illusions. Flush with governmental rhetoric on the benefits of home rule, tribesmen descended upon the airstrips in all their finery on Self-Government Day. They were breathlessly awaiting the appearance of their benefactor, "Mr. Self-Government," in the flesh. Imagine the massive trauma when all they found was the usual array of missionaries!

We lingered on the market's periphery until the tour group departed, then entered, asking permission to take some photos. One sturdy warrior who assented stood with his hand out after I snapped. At first I thought he wanted money. When he demanded, "Give-um picsa!" it occurred to me that one of the tourists must have distributed Polaroid prints.

"No gat," I stammered in my best pidgin. "Dis picsa fellow long me no wok quick quick." I left him so disappointed and disbelieving, I'm lucky not to have been speared for "holding out" on him.

Because there were no roads leading to the land of the wigmen, we had to fly from Mount Hagen. Though we felt considerable turbulence in the low-flying Cessna, this was more than compensated for by the panorama of sweeping ridges and valleys observable flying at a mere seven to ten thousand feet.

There are hundreds of weekly flights to the interior in four- or six-seater aircraft, conveying administrators, missionaries, or supplies. New Guinea boasts some of the finest bush pilots on the globe, for it takes real expertise to cope with the unpredictable up- and down-drafts generated by the country's sharply discontiguous chains of mountains and valleys, especially at the altitudes these small craft fly. Only a skilled professional could handle the tricky descents for safe landings on some of the minuscule airstrips carved out of dense rain forests. Many of these pilots, throwbacks to pioneering aviators, carry pistols in their cockpits just in case they are greeted with a hail of arrows.

As we touched down, I had to pinch myself to remember that what I was seeing was no movie. Gathered around the airstrip at the tiny administrative station of Tari to watch the "silver bird" land were muscled, stately warriors, whose greased bodies glistened in the sun. Their heads were crowned with the distinguishing mark of the Huli tribesmen: enormous wigs composed of woven hair which had been collected since puberty. Some headpieces were lavishly decorated with the brilliant vermilion and turquoise plumage of the "bird of paradise." A few wigs had a macabre touch of the twentieth century with glued labels from tobacco pouches or tinned fish.

We had arrived on a market day when Huli clans from all over the valley assembled to barter and swap stories. Their hairpieces were embellished with the region's gold and white flowers. The men had painted their faces in imaginative patterns with lustrous blue, red, and yellow dyes. Several had passed the quill of a cassowary bird through their nose for further beautification.

My agronomist host, Chris, noted: "These chaps are real dandies. Give them the social occasion of a market day or any other excuse and they'll go to great lengths to impress fellow warriors with their appearance. I know some who spend at least an hour daily, like a fashion model, primping, preening, and painting before their reflection in the river."

In contrast, Huli women wore no adornment of any kind. Prematurely aged from the rigors of their labors and continuous child-bearing, these indefatigable women carted heavy loads of produce for miles in hand-made string "bilums." These they slung over their backs, supporting them by straps straining their foreheads. Infants were often carried in the very same bag, squashed in with the yams and vegetables.

Much of the produce brought into the market consisted of the indigenous variety of sweet potato. "Kow-kow" is the Huli staple, eaten in enormous quantities three times daily. It is basically a starch with little food value other than calories, which helps explain the high rate of post-weaning infant mortality. With the exception of rare pig feasts when they gorge themselves, the Huli get next to nothing in the way of animal protein. Chris's most vital endeavor was to develop for the Huli a more nutritious variety of sweet potato.

The thatch-and-wattle huts of the wigmen are strictly segregated by sex. Huli males believe that they will be contaminated by "menstrual pollution" if they have any contact whatsoever with a female during her period. Women are said to be possessed by spirits and thus particularly dangerous when emitting the "evil fluids" that rob a man of his health. As one tribesman explained to us, "Why else 'mary' bleed, but no die?"

Accordingly, men and women live in separate quarters. When a boy is thirteen, he leaves his mother to reside in the dwelling of warriors. So as not to be tainted by the hand of a menstruating female, the men harvest their own crops and do all their own cooking. Both sexes, however, participate in the planting and maintenance of sweet-potato plots, the burden falling principally upon the women, who also handle the bulk of the marketing.

Exposure to Western notions of sex roles may greatly alter traditional attitudes of Huli women. Adolescent girls at one mission, bitterly chiding their male classmates for refusing to do an equitable amount of work in the school's garden, caused a near riot by passing harvested sweet potatoes between their legs. The teaching staff had to interpose their own bodies to keep the outraged boys from thrashing those who broke the menstrual taboo. A first step, perhaps—Women's Liberation penetrating the valley of the wigmen!

Clan warfare is sparked largely by disputes over land, pigs, or women (usually in that order). Out of curiosity, we approached a young American volunteer, teaching at a mission school, to inquire how his students perceived various international events. When asked what they thought had instigated the Vietnam war, the students' unanimous reply was most telling: "Land!"

For defensive purposes, sharp wooden stakes frame the entrance to each Huli clan's residence. Through gaps between these stakes, warriors can shoot deadly bone-tipped arrows at invaders. Among the wigmen, payback is a constant threat: they are renowned for their hair-trigger temperament and disputes flare quickly into combat. Any casualty, if not reconciled by an exchange of pigs, produces a standing obligation for vengeance. Payback is not a rare occurrence here; the doctor running the local clinic told us that he removes arrowheads from a goodly number of patients.

We questioned Tari's Australian administrator about the prevalence of revenge raids. "Payback has been very difficult for us to halt, not only among the Huli but even around towns like Mount Hagen. The government has rightfully concluded that stiff terms of imprisonment serve as little deterrent because these blokes simply don't understand why they are being put away. Their whole lives are wrapped around being warriors.

"To tell you the truth, most of the offenders welcome a stay in the pokey. First of all, we have to fly the murderer to Mount Hagen's prison. When he takes off, his 'one-talks' see him as a hero for riding that 'big bird.' Secondly, he eats better in jail than he ever has before; all he gets at home is 'kow-kow.' Lastly, locked behind bars, he's safe from the payback raid certain to come in retaliation for his murderous deed. Payback in these parts means an eye for anybody's eye, so one of his kinsmen will get it in his place."

It is not so ironic to see a fierce Huli tranquilly playing on bamboo "pipes of Pan" when one surveys his environment, a valley of unsurpassed natural beauty. Clear, gurgling streams rush through emerald forests. Fragrant alpine flowers blossom everywhere. The air is brisk and clean at this altitude, the sunshine plentiful. The towering mountains which enclose the valley, coupled with the Stone Age inhabitants, reinforce the feeling that one has truly entered a world apart.

If at times we felt a trifle disoriented, imagine an eleven-year-old Huli boy confronting the specter of Western civilization. Budger, an orphan "adopted" by our host, tore through our *Time* magazine, pointing out photos of gleaming jetliners, skyscrapers, all-electric kitchens, asking incredulously, "Is that real?! Is that real?!" He refused to believe that astronauts had walked upon the moon, for surely he would have seen them.

Budger had never ridden in an auto, nor ventured on foot out of the valley. One day soon, highlanders like Budger will be trained as doctors, engineers, pilots, and scientists—light-years removed from the warrior existence of their fathers.

Before leaving this region, we were invited to a "sing-sing" celebrating the opening of a new church. The missionaries shrewdly allowed the inaugural festivities to be staged traditionally, and as a result, clansmen trekked great distances to attend the event. Warriors daubed on their best paint, anointed their bodies in lustrous festival oils, brought ceremonial kundu drums, and danced all afternoon.

The event was climaxed by a huge pig feast—more than a hundred pigs purchased by the church were slaughtered (a primary motivating factor for the attendance of so many clans—these missionaries really knew their business). Butchered pork, sweet potato, pumpkin, ferns, and edible weeds were laid over stones heated until white hot. Wrapped in banana leaves, the food was covered over with soil and cooked until ready. The earthen oven steamed in all the juices. Delicious!

The Huli, ignoring the concurrent religious service, ate until bursting, and then slept contentedly to the drone of the priest's sermon.

Missions have had a mixed impact upon the highlanders' well-being. They frequently provide badly needed vocational training and medical care; indeed, some missionaries have shown remarkable cultural sensitivity and dedication to their parishioners.

Unfortunately, there have been others who have calculatingly undermined tribal cultures. Along the Sepik River, magnificent artifacts have been ordered destroyed by missionaries who link these artistic treasures to "heathen practices." At times, conversion has been the product of deceit. We were told of one instance in which a mission plane dropped eye-catching fabric and trinkets on the home grounds of a newly contacted tribe and then waltzed in as miracle makers. The overawed tribespeople needed little further persuasion.

Papua New Guinea, lacking its own teachers and physicians, must remain dependent upon mission personnel for some time. Although there is considerable speculation concerning the island's untapped mineral resources, today's independent P.N.G. has few funds for development. The copper mines of the off-island, Bougainville, provide most of P.N.G.'s revenue. But there are strong separatist feelings, for that island is reluctant to share its wealth with the rest of the country. In a land of seven hundred language groupings, regional schism is a constant danger that must be tactfully confronted.

Some of the newly educated highlanders we met feared P.N.G.'s independence, asserting that continued unity will be impossible under home rule, given tribal loyalties and indigenous authorities. The pistol-packing white patrol officer, seen as impartial in handling disputes, was respected as a competent (albeit heavy-handed) law enforcer. Will native policemen from rival tribes be accorded the same sense of authority necessary to keep the peace?

Most importantly, will the Huli and other Stone Age cultures be able to make that quantum leap into the twentieth century? If so, at what cost of cultural identity? The title of an autobiography by a prominent New Guinean politician perhaps best sums up the plight and challenge of the world's youngest nation: *10,000 Years in a Lifetime.*

SOUTH PACIFIC: FIJI, SAMOA, TAHITI

Too long a place in the Sun

Our ticket permitted stops on several South Pacific islands en route to the States. Nevertheless, I held no great expectations. With the onset of jet service, we assumed, these islands had lost whatever was left of their exotic allure; indeed, we expected to find intensive tourism, the disintegration of traditional life styles—and a lack of budget accommodations and restaurants. All these apprehensions would prove true, at least in part. But on these isles of uneclipsed natural beauty, we discovered some surprisingly resilient cultures.

During a brief stopover on Guadalcanal, scene of the Pacific campaign's bloodiest hand-to-hand combat, one of the more poignant encounters of our journey unfolded. It occurred at a memorial to the dead in a sleepy grove outside the town of Honiara. There, we observed a contingent of former GI's in American Legion caps paying homage. As they were about to reenter their bus, a group of Japanese veterans drove up. Disembarking from their van, they gazed wide-eyed at former adversaries, who returned their stare. For what seemed an infinity, no one said a word. Finally, the heavy silence was shattered by the scream of a gull. It was over. The Americans boarded their bus; the Japanese unsheathed their cameras.

From what little I knew of Fiji, I wanted to bypass it. We had heard that the main island, Viti Levu, had become an Aussie Caribbean, inundated with a loud and insensitive breed of tourists. Furthermore, a majority of the locals were of East Indian descent and I just didn't want to deal with such a high-pressure culture so close to journey's end. Fortunately, Marzi convinced me that we should at least have a look.

Fiji was known to many a sea captain as the "Cannibal Isles." William Endicott, a sailor shipwrecked here in 1831, reported: "One chief was so fond of human flesh that he never passed a person without wondering how he would taste." I wondered if that famous Will Rogers quote, "I never met a man I didn't like," had been plagiarized from the Fijians.

Cannibalism was not entirely eliminated until the 1890s. Some early observers attributed the natives' predilection for human flesh to the absence of alternative sources of meat (their only domestic animals were pigs). But the Fijian's explanation for consuming his fellow man was to both "humiliate" the victim and acquire his prowess.

Six-foot Fijians in sarong "sulus" look every bit the caricature of the cannibal. A sturdy mixture of mocha Melanesian and lighter-skinned Polynesian, the islanders' woolly Afros lend prominence to their towering height. By physical characteristics alone, Fijians are the quintessential wild men. But by temperament, few peoples on earth are as infectiously friendly.

After snorkeling the touristy, though gloriously transparent, waters of the Coral Coast, Marzi and I hitched into the island's central mountains where few travelers venture. Native custom prescribes that any visitor bearing a gift of "kava" be housed and fed. To get a closer look at the islanders' life, we decided to take advantage of such traditional hospitality. I presented a village chief with a pound of "yaquona." Beaming broadly, he called his wife to prepare the brew.

Kava is derived from a shrub related to a black pepper plant. The extract is ground into a powder, mixed with water, and served in a nipple-ended ceremonial cup. In accordance with tradition, I chugged the café-au-lait liquid, draining the cup. The beverage tasted rather bland, though not unpleasant. Its effects were exceedingly subtle: not the woozy stupor induced by alcohol, merely a numbing of tongue and lips coupled with a languid feeling perfectly attuned to the islanders' leisurely life style.

Fijians remain predominantly rural. Viti Levu's fertile volcanic soils and abundant seas supply all their needs. Gardens produce taros, yams, and a wide variety of delectable tropical fruits. The ocean teems with fish. Coconut trees hugging the shore provide not merely food and drink, but also shelter. Traditional "bure" huts are constructed of latticed bark walls designed to admit welcome sea breezes, and crowned by thatch roofs.

Our host exclaimed, "My family has plenty food, kava, a bure, what more I need?" He, like other Fijians, was satisfied with subsistence and saw little reason in toiling to acquire material possessions.

It was for this reason that the British colonists imported indentured Indian labor in the 1870s to cut sugar cane, the island's chief export. In 1884 there were but three thousand of these industrious Asians on Viti Levu. Fifty years later they numbered eighty-three thousand. And now the Fijians are a minority in their own land. (The islands' quarter-million Indians presently outnumber the natives by a ratio of five to four.)

The Asians, along with a few affluent whites, reap most of the profits from the lucrative tourist influx. Living largely in cities, Indians dominate commerce and transport. Fijians, on the other hand, are employed as bus boys, chambermaids, and waiters.

In contrast to the easygoing Fijians, the Indians are hardworking and aggressive. The roots of these characteristics may be traced back to a survival society in which to act otherwise could be fatal. So by temperament, the dour, perenially unsmiling Indian is the polar opposite of the exuberant, good-humored Fijian. Many an unwitting traveler, conned by Indians in Nadi and Suva, is taken aback by the disarming Fijian friendliness he encounters in the countryside. From how many visitors did we hear minor variants on the refrain, "Lovable Fijians, despicable Indians"?

Both the Indians and Fijians have sects which tread barefoot over hot coals—an appropriate metaphor for the country's racial straits. Although the Asians have unquestionably contributed some measure of economic solvency, I could not help but sympathize with the Fijians. Due to the Asians' prodigious birth rate, they may soon assume full elected political power. Consequently, many Fijians we spoke with felt it would be only a matter of time until laws are changed and their properties usurped by the Indians.

Given the extreme cultural clash, full-fledged ethnic strife may be difficult to avert. Indians see Fijians as incorrigibly "lazy and stupid" for not pushing to get ahead, an economic liability for not developing their land to the fullest. In response to such derisive attitudes, only the Fijians' remarkable tolerance has kept the situation from exploding to date. But if their land holdings are ever threatened . . .

It was in little known Western Samoa, rather than ballyhooed Tahiti, that we were exposed to the real Polynesia. Neither the rigidity of early German colonialism, nor the puritanical conservatism of later New Zealand rule could undermine the Samoans' "joie de vivre." These enchanting isles were as close to the Hollywood ideal as any we visited in the South Pacific.

In the tiny capital, Apia (twenty-five thousand residents), Marzi and I met Peace Corps volunteers who suggested that we buy tobacco for gifts and visit villages along the southern shore. Taking their advice, we bused to a sleepy hamlet situated along "Paradise Beach" (so named because a Gary Cooper movie, Return to Paradise, was filmed there a quarter-century ago).

The vintage bus—ramshackle wooden seats mounted on the rickety trestle of a truck—was suspensionless and took six hours to rumble forty miles. But we didn't really mind. What scenery! Tropical foliage bursting with the flame and fragrance of bougainvillaea blossoms, charming open-air "fales" (huts), and sunlit waterfalls under which young Polynesian women bathed. Every so often, the curtain of giant palms and ferns would part, revealing on one side, the tree-sloped central mountains where Robert Louis Stevenson requested to be buried and, on the other, the aquamarine of the sea.

The bus waited patiently at fale after fale for commuters to load up their copra (dried coconuts pressed for cooking oil) and produce for larger markets. It ran on no timetable. In Western Samoa watches become obsolete.

Arriving at palm-fringed Paradise Beach, which is true to its name, we introduced ourselves to the village "maitai." Samoan men run from immense to gargantuan and this chief was no exception, weighing well over three hundred pounds. He was an imposing sight, blue-black patterns of coconut-soot tattoos leading from the small of his back to his ankles. When in motion, the surprisingly agile chief reminded me of a holiday parade float.

Thanking us for the tobacco, the maitai graciously welcomed us to stay in his fale, which reflected the genius of Samoan simplicity. Lying just south of the equator, these islands are quite muggy, humidity averaging about eighty per cent. To catch the breeze, a fale is little more than a roof overhead—a beam-supported canopy of thatch. Even though it rains several times each day in brief bursts and a fale lacks permanent walls, no worries. Sheltering bamboo screens may be easily erected in minutes. Just outside the huts grow coconuts, yams, mangoes, papayas, and breadfruit. Because most villages are picturesquely situated on the shore, one need only walk a few paces from his home to fish or bathe.

One facet of Samoan culture particularly impressed us, especially since we were headed back to the States. The islanders leave all their valuables visible within their fales. They are free of anxiety, for stealing is unheard of here.

The inhabitants of Paradise Beach, avid churchgoers like most of their countrymen, pointed with pride to their temple with its lofty whitewashed steeple. The bigger a community's house of worship, the more prestigious, we were told. It appeared that nineteenth-century missionaries had made a tremendous impact. Yet the puritanical evangelists were only able to modify, not repress, the Polynesians' once unabashed erotic behavior. Today the exuberant consummation of premarital passions remains unchecked on these sultry islands, albeit in a more discreet form.

A former director of the Samoan Peace Corps remarked, "In

response to the missionaries' fire-and-brimstone preaching, what I would call a 'shame culture' evolved. The Samoan ethos consists in doing whatever you like, so long as you're not found out. This is how they have accommodated Christianity to custom. When it comes to sex, everyone looks the other way."

Indeed, I noticed Paradise Beach men averting their eyes while local beauties undraped their "lavalavas" to wash at the village water tap. This was one taboo I had no compunction to share.

Eligible Polynesian women signify they are available by wearing a hibiscus blossom over the left ear. Eye, rather than verbal, contact leads to liaisons in the bush. Small wonder so many Peace Corps men extend their tour for a third year. Young Samoan women in their form-fitting lavalavas are most fetching, though a steady diet of starches makes them prone to obesity later in life.

On the evening prior to our departure, our host announced, "Tonight we have prepared a special meal for you. 'Peasoupo.' "

"Peasoupo?" Looking at my plate, I was able to recognize taro, breadfruit, a mango, and something that looked suspiciously like bully beef.

"This is 'peasoupo'?" I asked, pointing at the meat.

The maitai laughed. "When the League of Nations took our islands away from Germany and placed them in the hands of New Zealand, Kiwi administrators began importing Australian corned beef. People here really developed a taste for it. We had previously become familiar with tinned pea soup, and because bully beef also came in a can, the name 'peasoupo' stuck."

Although independent Western Samoa had been an unexpected delight, our brief stopover in neighboring American Samoa imparted a disturbing image of U.S. colonial influence. From 1900 when the States took control, designating Tutuila Island a territory, its inhabitants endured fifty-one years of maladministration by a governing body of U.S. Naval officers. The Polynesians' culture was drained of its pride and vitality; the island's economic and health conditions were abominable, the neglect far from benign.

Under civilian governors since 1951, the situation improved somewhat and the standard of living is now higher than on Western

Samoa. But native traditions hover near death. Children are named after American television characters, Polynesian women set their hair in plastic rollers, snack shops next to the Pago Pago market dispense hot dogs and Kool Aid, and the ideal has become saving enough money for the expensive flight to that land of milk and honey. Western Samoans may not have benefited much economically under the auspices of first New Zealand, and now their own administrators, but at least they know who they are.

Scene of Somerset Maugham's "Rain," the Pago Pago harbor is truly alluring and the isle boasts several attractive beaches. But we quickly moved on, for the immigration officials posted here from the States allow neither lodging in fales nor camping. They "discourage" young budget travelers from visiting Tutuila unless they register at one of the island's two luxury hotels.

As one officer, in his best Merle Haggard country drawl, put it, "We don't want any damn hippy troublemakers stirring up the natives."

And to think that I complained about Singapore! Ah well, we would have plenty of opportunity to sun and swim in Tahiti.

The 1960 opening of Papeete's jet airport and the subsequent construction of landing strips on the out-islands spelled doom for Tahiti's fabled way of life. Nonetheless, tourist brochures continue to promise naive travelers an unspoiled Rodgers and Hammerstein wonderworld where they might also enjoy all the amenities of Miami. James A. Michener's evocative short stories also linger in the minds of those contemplating the South Pacific. But Michener's works are nearly thirty years old. Regrettably, no one has written an updated popular account, for in the last two decades, "paradise" has ceased to be.

Gauguin would find little inspiration to paint a people whose culture has so thoroughly disintegrated and whose gods have been replaced by the franc. No longer a sensuous Shangri-La of contented island life, Tahiti has mutated into a mass-consumer society. Papeete is an appalling disarray of tacky newer structures fighting for space amid decrepit Chinese shops. Through its streets roar hundreds of

271

motorcycles and cars, fouling the once-fragrant tropical air. The invasion of ten thousand French troops and nuclear technicians has irrevocably Gallicized the city.

Because most Tahitians now work primarily in the tourist or military-service industries, agriculture and fishing have been neglected and nearly everything must be imported. Tahiti being a long way to ship goods, the cost of living is astronomical. We could not believe food prices—even the simplest meals were a minimum of five dollars. Hotels (by our standards) were also expensive—ten dollars a night for the cheapest sailors' dive-cum-brothel. Finding little reason to remain on the budget-breaking main island, we flew to Bora Bora, where at least we could camp and cook our own food.

The name Bora Bora is legendary—synonymous with all the romance of the South Seas. The isle's fame was spawned by American military personnel, who erected a base here during the war and succeeded in bastardizing the culture. The establishment of plush Hotel Bora Bora and Club Med dealt the coup de grâce.

As most of the locals were irredeemably money-hungry and soured by tourist saturation, we reconciled ourselves with the atoll's manifest natural charms. There can be little question but that Bora Bora is one of the most attractive isles on earth. Beyond the reef that rings its shores is a luminous diamond-blue sea that breaks frothy white upon the coral. Within, the barrier reef has created a placid lagoon of turquoise glass which laps finely textured, silvery beaches. At the fringe of these soft sands stands an emerald rain forest bedecked with elephant-ear ferns and crimson flamboyants. And from the island's heart soar jagged volcanic peaks, thrust from the sea during the explosive dawn of its creation.

Leaving the port, we hiked five miles along the shoreline to a promontory jutting into the bay. There we found a picnic table, water tap, and toilet. From the point, we could enjoy both the spectacular Tahitian sunrise and sunset, swimming in tranquil waters and basking under tropical rays. Who could ask for a lovelier campsite?

Otherwise undisturbed, once daily we confronted the intrusion of the Club Med tour bus. Its driver would announce over the loudspeaker, "You are now standing upon the world's most beautiful beach." The entourage of Americans were given all of five minutes to snap photos, then hustled back to their fifty-dollar-a-night accommodations.

So we stayed free on "the world's most beautiful beach" (who am I to dispute Club Med?). Only eating posed a problem. The restaurant at Hotel Bora Bora two miles down the road was ridiculously expensive; shops were distant, prices out-of-sight. Fortunately, the enterprising proprietress of a Chinese grocery drove by twice a day, and we bought baguettes and tinned goods from her mobile store. Tuna, the cheapest food at a dollar per tin, became our staple. We supplemented it with rice and the coconuts knocked from statuesque trees gracing the point.

We shared the beach with two disillusioned American medical students, Rob and Steve. These robust fellows, on their way home from touring New Zealand, had been enticed here by Tahiti's vaunted sexuality. Ever since the first seafaring Europeans set foot on these islands, Tahiti has been identified with the ultimate in erotic abandon.

A naturalist accompanying explorer Bougainville wrote that Tahitians were a people who "ne connaissent d'autre Dieu que l'amour." An amusing vignette in Captain Cook's diary revealed why the famed navigator had to pull out of these islands earlier than planned in order to salvage his vessel. Since "wahines" traded sexual favors for metal filings, the crew soon began dismantling the ship in a feverish hunt for nails. In bravely giving the orders to set sail, Cook risked a full-scale mutiny.

Though cognizant of the islands' historic reputation, Rob and Steve were better acquainted with Michener's more modern tales of the carnal blessings showered upon visitors. Indeed, the young Americans were not disappointed in the least by the beauty of young Tahitian women, especially those of mixed Chinese ancestry. But from the storied Quinn's Bar in Papeete, to Moorea, to Bora Bora, Rob and Steve discovered that wahines now were interested only in those foreigners affluent enough to "show them a good time." The boys, despite numerous snubs, could not shake the mystique, and we watched in amusement as they relentlessly pursued Tahitiennes indifferent to beachcombers.

During our stay in Bora Bora, we were blessed with the finest weather—not a cloud in the heavens and nights so pleasant that we slept outside our tent under a chandelier of twinkling stars.

The days went so fast. Watching the sun supplant the moon, we would roll directly from our bed of sand into the sea. Then eat a little, read a bit. Swim the languorous lagoon. Borrow snorkels and fins and explore the teeming reef, so vibrantly brimming with flashing color and life that at times I thought I was hallucinating.

Snorkeling near Hotel Bora Bora one afternoon, we heard a throbbing of slit drums. Curious, we wandered over and watched the hotel's version of "traditional Tahitian entertainment." Grass-skirted wahines performed the pelvis-thrusting "tamara," which can be the most suggestive of dances. But the look of boredom on the wahines' faces negated any erotic communication as far as I was concerned. Then, to our utter disbelief, the climax of the show starred a nine-year-old Tahitian boy, demonstrating how to climb a coconut tree, husk the nut, and drink the milk.

After that, Marzi and I stayed well away from the hotel.

Except for a brief panic with the sighting of a shark, life on the point was idyllic. "I can think of only one reason for leaving," Marzi remarked. "I'm tired of tuna."

We finally broke away and booked a flight Stateside. Standing in the translucent lagoon at sunset, I watched still-glowing waters reflect a kaleidoscope of imagery culled from our journeys. Two years packed with adventure, challenge, and the unpredictable. To-morrow, home.

HOME?

"So you've been in the Orient?" the stern-faced U.S. customs inspector said, staring at my beard.

He commenced the most rigorous search to which I had yet been exposed. Ransacking my backpack, he shook each article of clothing and dismembered all toiletries. At length, he spied my can of odoriferous bedbug powder.

"What's this?" he snapped.

"Assuming you can read, the contents are clearly marked in English," I replied, angry at the ardor he displayed in tearing through my gear.

Suspicious, the official nearly strained himself trying to open the tin. Not realizing it was a sprinkle can, he gave the lid one final determined twist. Whoosh! The vile, floury powder exploded, enveloping him in a cloud of pasty-white. The search was over.

Los Angeles. We might have chosen a better place to reintegrate ourselves. The shock was total. Smog, blinding lights, unending freeways. We stayed with relatives for a few days, then took off for

Boston, only to be assaulted for the first time by the commercial inanities of the "Buy-Centennial."

A friend visited us in Cambridge's Central Square. "I envy you," Sandra said. "I've always dreamt of that sort of travel. But I could never just up and tear away like you people."

"I don't understand," Marzi replied. "You're not tied down with young kids and at three thousand dollars for a full year's expenses, it's hardly a question of funds."

"I've put a lot of effort into fighting my way up the hierarchy. To leave would mean a loss of what I've struggled for. Yet, I must confess, for all the money and prestige of my professional standing, it often seems as if I'm 'unemployed at my work.' Know what I mean? It's when I contemplate my two-week annual vacation and otherwise vicarious living that I think of you.

"Out of curiosity, venturing through such 'uncivilized lands,' weren't you ever afraid?"

"Frankly, those occasions were rare," Marzi and I concurred.

Before leaving, Sandra asked for safety's sake that we escort her to her car. I had long forgotten that aura of urban fear. Welcome home.

The utter familiarity of it all proved to be our most vexing adjustment: to arise and know pretty much how the day would unfold. Falling back almost unconsciously into a routine dictated by the clock after the euphoric spontaneity of life on the road, I began to feel like the proverbial "ship in the bottle."

But there was no reason for despair. Our odyssey had not ended. It was merely time to digest our experiences and put them in perspective, as well as to come to grips with what was happening within our own society. Looking enthusiastically to the future, I realized that exploration of far-off lands need not be limited to movies or magazines. After all, I reminded myself, the most difficult part of overlanding the globe rested simply in making that decision to go.

And it would not be long. For the pangs of wanderlust refused to subside ...